Book of

The Wordsworth
Book of Spells

—

Arthur Edward Waite

Wordsworth Reference

Originally published 1992 as *Chambers Dictionary of Beliefs and Religions* by W&R Chambers Ltd, Edinburgh.

This edition published 1995 by Wordsworth Editions Ltd, Cumberland House, Crib Street, Ware, Hertfordshire SG12 9ET.

ISBN 1-85326-354-0

Printed and bound in Denmark by Nørhaven.

The paper in this book is produced from pure wood pulp, without the use of chlorine or any other substance harmful to the environment. The energy used in its production consists almost entirely of hydroelectricity and heat generated from waste materials, thereby conserving fossil fuels and contributing little to the greenhouse effect.

Book of Spells

PLATE I

EDWARD KELLEY, A MAGICIAN
In the act of invoking the spirit of a deceased person

PREFACE

THE art which is called Goëtic, being that of incantation, of sorcery, fascination and of the illusions and impostures connected therewith, has come somewhat arbitrarily to signify the last issue in diabolism of the more catholic and general art which is termed Practical Magic. The latter designation implies that there is a Magic on the theoretical side, or, as it may be, a philosophy of the subject, and this again is of two kinds : in modern days it has embodied various attempts to provide an explanation, a working hypothesis, for alleged phenomena of the past ; of old it came forward with the accent of authority and carrying the warrants of a peculiar and secret knowledge ; it taught rather than explained. Behind this, in virtue of a specific assumption, there stood the source of such authority, the school or schools that issued, so to speak, the certificates of title which the records of the expounding master are supposed to shew that he possessed. Herein resided presumably that Higher Magic which justified the original meaning of the term Magic ; this was the science of wisdom, and of that wisdom which was the issue of experience and knowledge particular to sacred sanctuaries in the years of the Magi. In this manner a remote and abstract magnificence has been allocated to the practical work ; but between this aspect as we know it otherwise and that dream as it has been dilated in the forms of its expression there is the kind of relation which subsists between renown and its non-fulfilment. If Magic in its proper and original meaning

Preface

be synonymous with wisdom ; if that wisdom, by virtue of this assumption which I have mentioned, were something inconceivably great, it is of certitude that it had no causal connection with the congeries of arts and processes which are understood by Practical Magic. That there was, as there still is, a science of the old sanctuaries, I am certain as a mystic ; that this science issued in that experience which imparts wisdom I am also certain ; but it did not correspond to any of the arts and processes to which I refer here, nor to anything which can be received by the mind as the result of their exaltation. The consideration of a possibility thus already condemned is therefore ruled out of the inquiry which I have attempted in the present work. I have also ruled out, as it will be seen, the distinctions which have subsisted between the good and evil side of the arts and processes, not that it does not exist on the bare surface, but because the two aspects dissolve into one another and belong one to another in the root that is common to both. The actual question before us is after what manner, if any, magical procedure draws anything from secret tradition in the past, and so enters into the general subject of such tradition, whether in Christian or anterior times. It would and could only be of tradition on its worthless side, and it will not exalt a subject which the records of centuries have shewn to be incapable of being raised ; it will, however, let us know where we are. On the face of the question a tradition of all kinds of rubbish is very likely to have been handed down from antiquity, and in respect of occultism, the last drift and scattermeal has passed into the *Grimoires, Keys of Solomon* and other rituals innumerable by which Art Magic has passed into written record.

As this book represents, under a new title and with many additions, a work which was issued originally in 1898, I have

Preface

accepted the opportunity to indicate its position in respect of far more important works embodying my construction of the Secret Tradition in Christian Times. I have secured this object —which after all is clear and simple—not by a regrettable comparison of what I have written there with that which appears in the present place, but by shewing in a brief introduction the proper sense in which phenomenal occultism and all its arts indifferently connect with the tradition of the mystics: they are the path of illusion by which the psychic nature of man enters that other path which goes down into the abyss. The book in its present revision remains of necessity a presentation of old texts by the way of digest; I have added some new sections that in this department it may be rendered more representative, and if a touch of fantasy, which is not wholly apart from seriousness, will be pardoned here at the inception, the work itself is now an appendix to the introductory thesis—the textual, historical and other evidence by which it is supported.

In the year 1889 an expositor of the more arid and unprofitable side of Kabalistic doctrine edited in English a text of Ceremonial Magic, entitled *Clavicula Salomonis*, or, the *Key of Solomon the King*. In an introduction prefixed to the work he stated that he saw no reason to doubt, and therefore presumably accepted, the tradition of its authorship,[1] which in respect of the critical sense may be taken to summarise his qualifications for a *mentor stultorum*. It should be added, as an additional light, that he undertook his translation more especially for the use of occult students, that is to say, for those persons who believe in the efficacy of magical rites and may, as an illustration of their faith, desire to put them in practice. With this

[1] The work as it now stands quotes Ezekiel, Daniel, the fourth Gospel, and mentions SS. Peter and Paul. Many of these anachronisms are to be found in the pentacles accompanying the text.

Preface

exception, the large body of literature which treats of Theurgic Ceremonial in its various branches has remained inaccessible to the generality of readers, in rare printed books and rarer manuscripts, in both cases mostly in foreign languages. There is probably a considerable class outside occult students to whom a systematic account of magical procedure may be not unwelcome, perhaps mainly as a curiosity of old-world credulity, but also as a contribution of some value to certain side issues of historical research ; these, however, an edition for occult students would deter rather than attract. In the present work several interests have been as far as possible considered. The subject is approached from the bibliographical and critical standpoints, and all sources of information which many years of inquiry have made known to the writer have been consulted to render it complete. At the same time, seeing that there is a section of readers who will not disdain to be classed as professed occultists, whatever my view of their dedications, I am dealing with texts over which their interest may be held to exercise a certain primary jurisdiction, and I have therefore studied their requirements in two important respects, which will not, as I believe, be a source of offence to merely historical students. They have been studied, firstly, by the observance of strict technical exactitude ; the ceremonial produced in this book is absolutely faithful to the originals, and removes all necessity of having recourse to the originals before determining any doubtful point of magical procedure in the past. For convenience of reference —if I may venture to make the modest bid for recognition on the part of such a circle—it is indeed superior to the originals, because it has been put systematically, whereas they often exceed understanding owing to the errors of transcribers, the misreadings of printers, the loose methods of early translators, and seemingly, it must be added, the confused minds of the

Preface

first compilers, "Solomon" himself not excepted. The innumerable offices of vain observance which constitute Ceremonial Magic, as it is presented in books, will therefore be found substantially intact by those who concern themselves with such observance.

The second respect in which the interests of the occult student have been considered is, however, of much more importance, though he may not be as ready to admit the suggestion, having regard to all that it implies. Robert Turner, the English translator of the *Magical Elements*, written, or—more correctly —supposed to be written, by the unfortunate Peter of Abano, describes that treatise as an introduction to "magical vanity," a term which was possibly used in a symbolical or exotic manner, to intimate that most things which concern the phenomenal world are indifferently trivial. Now, the more inward purpose of the present investigation is to place within reach of those persons who are inclined to such a subject the fullest evidence of the futility of Ceremonial Magic as it is found in books, and the fantastic nature of the distinction between White and Black Magic—so far also as the literature of either is concerned. As to the things which are implied within and may lie behind the literature, they are another consideration, about which I will say only at the moment that, judged by the fruits which they have produced, they are not incomparable to the second death beyond the gates of perdition. It would be unbecoming in a writer of my known dedications to deny that there is a Magic which is behind Magic, or that even the occult sanctuaries possess their secrets and mysteries; of these the written ceremonial is held by their self-imputed exponents to be either a debased and scandalous travesty, a trivial and misconstrued application, or, in respect of diluted views, it may be alternatively "as moonlight unto sunlight and as water unto wine." The exponents withhold their warrants; but in the presence or absence of these, it may be as well to say at the beginning that if the secrets and mysteries belong to the powers and wonders of the psychic side, and not to the graces of the spirit, then God is not present in those sanctuaries. Let a mystic assure the occult student that as he, or any one, is dealing herein simply with nauseating follies of the inside world of distraction, so he would be concerned in the alleged schools behind them—supposing that he had the right of entrance—with the same follies carried to the *ne plus ultra* degree. The texts, for this reason, may be more innocent because they are more ridiculous and have the advantage—for the most part—of being impossible to follow. The statement just made will explain why it is permissible to bring forth from the obscurity of centuries a variety of processes which would be abominable if it could be supposed that they were to be seriously understood. The criticism applies to all the extant Rituals, whatever their pretended claims, whatever their surface distinction. Some are more absurd than others, some are perhaps more iniquitous, but they are all tainted with Black Magic in the same way that every idle word is tainted with the nature of sin. The distinction between White and Black Magic is the distinction between the idle and the evil word.

It would, naturally, be unsafe to affirm that all persons making use of the ceremonies in the Rituals up to the point of possibility would fail to obtain results. Perhaps in the majority of cases most of such experiments made in the past were attended with results of a kind. To enter the path of hallucination is likely to insure hallucination, and in the presence of hypnotic, clairvoyant and a thousand kindred facts it would be absurd to suppose that the seering processes of Ancient Magic—which are many—did not produce seership, or that the auto-hypnotic state which much magical ritual would obviously tend to occa-

Preface

sion in predisposed persons did not frequently induce it, and not always only in the predisposed. To this extent some of the processes are practical, and to this extent they are dangerous.

For convenience of treatment the present work is divided into two parts. The first contains an analytical and critical account of the chief magical rituals known to the writer; the second forms a complete Grimoire of Black Magic. It must be remembered that these are the operations which gave arms to the Inquisitors of the past, and justified Civil Tribunals in the opinion of their century for the sanguinary edicts pronounced against witch, warlock and magician. It is, in truth, a very strange and not reassuring page in the history of human aberration; nor has it been a pleasing exercise which has thus sought to make it plain, once and for all.

A SERPENT BEFORE THE CURSE.

From the " Speculum Salvationis."

THE TEMPTATION OF EVE.

From Cædmon.

INTRODUCTION

THE mystic tradition in Christian Times is preserved, apart from all questions and traces of Instituted Mysteries, in the literature of Christian Mystical Theology; it is a large and exceedingly scattered literature; some of its most important texts are available in no modern language; they stand very seriously in need of codification, and—if I may be so frank—even of re-expression. But if, for other reasons, they are in their entirety a study which must be left to the expert, there is no person now living in Europe who has not close at his hands the specific, simple, isolated texts—much too numerous to name—which are sufficient to give some general idea of the scope and aims of the tradition. If I were asked to define the literature shortly and comprehensively as a whole, I should call it the texts of the way, the truth and the life in respect of the mystic term. It is not only full but exhaustive as to the way—which is that of the inward world, recollection, meditation, contemplation, the renunciation of all that is lower in the quest of all that is higher—but perhaps the most catholic word of all would be centralisation. It is very full also on the fundamental truth, out of which it arises, that a way does exist and that the way is open. The truth is formulated in all simplicity by the *Epistle to the Hebrews*—that God is and that He recompenses those who seek Him out. I have cited this testimony on several occasions in the same connection, and I do so here and now without a word of apology and with no sense of repetition, since it can never be a matter of redundancy to remember after what manner the Divine ways are justified to humanity, when humanity is seeking the Divine. The litera-

ture, in fine, is full as to that which it understands in respect of
the life, but this is the Divine Life; it is grace which fills the
heart; it is the Holy Spirit of God which makes holy the spirit
of man; it is life in God. There is no doubt that in its formula-
tion it was presented to the mind of Christian Mysticism as the
life which was hidden with Christ in God, and this ineffable
concealment was equivalent to the presentation in open teaching of that mystery of emblematic death which lies behind all
the pageants of initiation. This was the state, and the dogma
from which the state depended is defined by that Johannine
Epistle which affirms: (1) That God hath given to us eternal
life; (2) That this life is His Son; (3) That whosoever hath
the Son hath life; (4) That whosoever is without the Son is
without life also. These points follow naturally enough from
the testimony of the Fourth Gospel: (1) In the person of the
Divine Voice, saying—I am the Way, the Truth and the Life:
I am the Resurrection and the Life: I am the Bread of
Life; (2) In the person of the witness, saying: In Him was
life and the life was the light of men.

There is no doubt, in the second place, that the Divine Voice
was incarnate for Christian Mysticism in Jesus of Nazareth, and
we must cast out from us the images of those false witnesses
who from time to time have pretended that the masters of the
hidden life in the Christian centuries had become far too enlightened spiritually to tolerate the external cortex of their
faith and creed. This point is of much greater importance than
it may appear in the present connection, for I am not doing less
than establish a canon of criticism. I will take two typical
examples, one of which is moderately early and the other
sufficiently late to serve as a distinction in time. The anonymous *Cloud of Unknowing* belongs, I believe, to the early part
of the fifteenth century, and it is to be classed among the most
signal presentations of the conditions and mode of the Union
which I have met with in Christian literature. It offers an

Introduction

experiment in integration which seems to me more practical because it is more express than the great intimations of Dionysius. The integration is grounded on the identity of our essential nature with the Divine Nature and our eternal being therein: "That which thou art thou hast from Him, and He it is"; and again: "Yet hath thy being been ever in Him, without all beginning, from all beginning, from all eternity, and ever shall be, without end, as Himself is." There is sufficient kinship on the surface of these statements for the casually literate and not too careful reader to speak of them as a simple presentation of the pantheistic doctrine of identity; but they are saved herefrom by the important qualification that—this state of eternal Divine indwelling notwithstanding—man had "a beginning in the substantial creation, the which was sometime nothing." This beginning signifies the coming forth of man's spirit into the state of self-knowing in separateness, or some more withdrawn condition to which we cannot approximate in language—I mean in language that will offer a satisfactory consideration to the higher part of our understanding. If it is conceivable that there is a possible state of distinction in Divine Consciousness by which the true self of our spirit became self-knowing, but not in separateness, then it is this state which is called in *The Cloud of Unknowing* "a beginning in the substantial creation." It will be seen that I set aside implicitly the suggestion that the passage is a simple reference to the soul in physical birth. I do not think that the mystic whose chief flowers are of all things exotic would offer a distinction like this as a qualification of the soul's eternity by integration in the Godhead, or, more correctly, by substantial unity. That which I take, therefore, to have been present to the writer's mind was the implicit pre-existence of all souls in the Divine Being for ever, and secondly their explication—as if the living thought became the living word; but there are no commensurate analogies. In this manner there arose "the substantial creation, the which was sometime nothing," and we know of all that has followed in the past and continued ages of our separateness. This state is our sickness, and the way of return is our healing. That return, according to *The Cloud* and its connections and identities in the great literature, is "the high wisdom of the Godhead . . . descending into man's soul . . . and uniting it to God Himself." The path is a path of undoing, though it is at this point that so many mystics stand in fear of the irresistible consequences which follow from their own teachings : it is the returning of the substantial creation into nothing ; it is an entrance into the darkness ; an act of unknowing wherein the soul is wholly stripped and unclothed of all sensible realisation of itself, that it may be reclothed in the realisation of God.

It may well seem that in this House Mystic of ineffable typology all the old order has passed away. The secret of attainment does not lie in meditation or in thinking, in the realisation of Divine qualities, in the invocation of saints or angels ; it is a work between the naked soul and God in His uttermost essence, in an essence so uttermost that "it profiteth little, or nothing at all, to think upon the loving kindness of God, or upon the holy angels and saints, or else upon the glory and joys of heaven." That, and all that, is fair work and square work, good and true work, but it is not materials for building the Most Secret, Most Holy Temple, into which God and the soul go in and one only comes out. Yet is the old doctrine the true doctrine still ; there is nothing abrogated and there is nothing reduced. In all but the deepest paths, it is meet and right and salutary to seek the interceding angels and the communion of saints, to dwell upon the Passion of Christ, and so forth. The old histories also are truly understood in the old way ; the Passion was no shadowy pageant ; Christ died and rose in the body ; in the body He ascended into Heaven, and no less and no differently in that body He sitteth at the right hand of the Father Almighty.

Introduction

And yet these references to doctrine and practice, to symbol, rite and ceremony, are only like the hills standing about Jerusalem, and into the city mystic, into the central place of debate, they do not enter anywise. They have not been expelled—they are simply not there, and the reason is that there they do not belong. Once more, it is between God and the soul. It is as if the ways were filled with the pageants of the Heavenly and Ecclesiastical Hierarchies; as if the Masses and the Matins and the Vespers celebrated in marvellous and stately measures the Holy Trinity, the dilucid contemplation of the Persons, the ineffable secrets of the hypostatic state and the super-incession of Divine natures. But after all these wonders, rank after rank of the Blessed Angels, after all visions of the Great White Throne, it is as if a quiet centre opened unawares and through an immeasurable silence drew down the soul—from the many splendours into the one splendour, from the populous cities of the blest, from the things that are without in the transcendence into the thing that is of all within—as if the soul saw there the one God and itself as the one worshipper. But after a little while the worshipper itself has dissolved, and from henceforth and for ever it has the consciousness of God only. This is the knowledge of self, no longer attained by a reflex act of the consciousness, but by a direct act in the unity of the infinite consciousness; in this mode of knowledge there is that which knows even as it is known, but such mode is in virtue of such an union that the self does not remain, because there is no separateness henceforth. It follows that the Divine Union, as I have sought to give it expression apart from all antecedents and warrants of precursors—I think indeed that there are none—is something much deeper and higher than is understood by the Beatific Vision, which shines with all the lights of noon and sunrise and sunset at the summit of the mountain of theology. That Vision is more especially of St. Thomas, the Angelic Doctor, the mighty Angel of the

Introduction

Schools, expounding the Transcendence to himself in the most resplendent and spiritual terms of the logical understanding. The intervening distinction between it and the term of all is that the one is the state of beholding and the other is the state of being; the one is seeing the Vision and the other is becoming it. Blessed and Holy are those who receive the experience of God in the dilucid contemplation, but sanctity and benediction and all in all is that state wherein contemplation is ineffably unified, by a super-eminent leap over of love, with that which is its object; and in that love and in that joining together there is no passage longer from subject to object. But this is the Godhead.

These considerations have got so far beyond even *The Cloud of Unknowing* that it seems almost a fall into matter to speak, as I had intended, of Molinos and his *Spiritual Guide*, which is in no sense really comparable to the older work. It is a more ascetic treatise, and by its asceticism is a little hindered; it is a less catholic treatise, and it suffers here and there from the particular sense. Yet it bears the same testimony of a full and complete intention—much too complete and too full to carry anything of the concerted air—to maintain the veils of doctrine, to speak the high and orthodox language of the official Church; but again it is like a moving, yet all remote, echo from a world which has almost passed out of knowledge. What is there left to the soul that it should say of the Holy Humanity, of the Precious Blood, of the five wounds, of the dolorous death and passion? It is not that all this has been swallowed up in the glories of resurrection, but that those who have entered "where God keeps His Throne and communicates Himself with incredible intensity"—and those who have obeyed the last precept "to be lost in God"—have entered into a new order; the ships that carried them have dropped out of sight with the tide, with the breeze, in the sunshine.

Introduction

Now, the secret of this is—not that Dionysius and Ruysbroeck, with all their *cohæredes et sodales*, had become unitarians, but that the term of the Christian dispensation, to each of them personally, had been fulfilled in each. Christ had been born and lived, had taught and suffered and died, had risen and ascended and reigned in them. So that Divine life, in fine, carried them to its last stage. It was not Dionysius or Ruysbroeck, the author of *The Cloud of Unknowing*, or the soul of the poor imprisoned Jesuit Molinos, but the Christ nature within each and all of these, within ten thousand times ten thousand of their peers, in all ages and nations and faiths and climes, which entered into the incredible intensity ; and that which is termed the act or state of being lost in God is that which I have elsewhere described in a perfection of all similitudes—which is of my adaptation but not of my making—when Christ delivers up the Kingdom of each soul to His Father, and God is all in all.

This is the state which is beyond the state when it is said that "they shall see His face."

Hereof is the mystic tradition in Christian Time ; it has been perpetuated in an unbroken line from the beginnings of the new dispensation until this now. It is of course in itself the most secret, exotic and incomprehensible of all languages, though at the same time it is the most open, universal and simple. The understanding of it is a question of experience, and the experience is attained in sanctity, though—as I have said, but also elsewhere—the intellectual light concerning it belongs rather to the dedication out of which sanctity may at length issue than to the state of saintship itself. The technicalities of the occult sciences may seem hard to the beginner, and they are actually hard like the wilderness, because they are barren wastes, but they are in words of one syllable if compared with the little catechisms of eternal life, which are exclusive to the children of God.

Introduction

Behind this Open Entrance to the Closed Palace of the King—which is so like the eye of the needle—there is the concealed tradition in and behind the mysticism of Christian Times. About this it is scarcely possible to speak here, and it will require some care not to confuse the image with which I have opened my statement. The Open Entrance of course leads to the Palace, but at a certain point there is found an exceedingly hidden postern and a path beyond, which is absolutely unattainable except through the lawful entrance, because, although the Kingdom of Heaven tolerates a certain quality of enlightened and loving violence, the sanctuary of all its sanctuaries responds only to the violence of that man who knows how to lay hands on himself, so that he may carry none of his extrinsics to the most *intrinsecus* place in all the world of God. This postern is hidden deeply on the deepest side of tradition, but by what can be traced concerning it, I think that there has been such a going to and fro upon the Ladder of Jacob that something more of the states which are not the term, but are perhaps penultimate thereto, has been brought back by those who have accomplished the next but one to all of the Great Work. I think further that they have gone so far that they have seen with their own eyes some intimacies of the term itself—being the state of those who go in and do not evermore come back.

These are aspects of the Secret Tradition in so far as it has declared itself on the side of God. It remains now to be said that there is a tradition *à rebours*, and though it may seem very hard to put it so roughly and frankly, I have not taken all the consciousness of the inward man for my province to smooth or reduce any of the distinctions between the loss and gain of the soul. The tradition *à rebours* is definitely and clearly that of miraculous power in the quest and attainment thereof. It is summarised by the ambition of the Magus in its contrast with the desire of the eyes and the hope which

Introduction

fills the heart of the true mystic. I am not intending to suggest that the Magus as such is of necessity at issue with the decalogue, or that he is under judgment by this sole standard, whether for vengeance or reward. As the position is capable of dogmatic statement, and as such is without any subjection to vicissitude, I will express it in dogma as follows : Whosoever goes inward to find anything but the Divine in his centre is working on the side of his own loss. As there is the height of *Kether* in Kabalism, so there is the abyss which is below *Malkuth*, and those who are seeking to exercise the powers of the soul apart from its graces are treading the downward path. The operation of grace is so utterly catholic, and there is correspondingly so much of the Divine prevention operating everywhere, that in most instances the experiments come to little and the frittering does not continue from the mere weariness of its business ; but the quest of miraculous power—and I use an unscientific phrase of set purpose, because I am dealing now with the most inexact of all subjects—is that which is usually comprehended by the term occult science, and the occult sciences, speaking generally, are the sciences of the abyss. I except astrology, which —only through the accident of many associations—has been taken by force into the category : it is not an occult science, and notwithstanding a few negligible claims on the part of a few sanctuaries, it has no secret mode of working whatsoever. It is the calculus of probabilities on the basis of experience in respect of empirical things. Putting it aside, on the fringe of the whole circle there are further a few score of follies which one would not term the grades of preparation for the abyss unless there were a solid reason for being preternaturally serious. I have characterised these sufficiently in the text, and here I will say only that all paths of folly lead to the Houses of Sin.

There remains the question of Magic. As to this, I am aware that the professors, who are many, and the

Introduction

amateurs, who are many more, may be disposed to intervene at this point and call attention to the ancient and honourable distinction between White and Black Magic. But with this also I have dealt so fully in the text that I question whether the entire work is not an illustration of my thesis that, except in a very slight, verbal and fluidic sense, no such distinction exists—I mean to say that it is unrooted in the subsoil of the subject. Lest I should appear, however, uncritical over things of sufficient importance to be regarded in their several phases, it is necessary to make two further distinctions on my own part. One of the secret sciences is of course Alchemy, and so far as this was the mode, mystery, or art of transmuting metals, of healing material human disease, of prolonging human life by certain physical methods—to this extent it is, as it was always, a matter of learned research; and though I should not say that the students of the old literature are in the least likely to discover the secrets from the books, there is such an excusable and pleasant air about the quest and its enthusiasm, that it is rather a consolation to know that it is of more danger to the purse than it will ever be to the soul of man.

Alchemy has, however, another and if possible a more secret side, from which it enters the science of the soul. I distinguish it at once and entirely from occultism and all its ways; it is approximately and almost literally identical with that postern within the first entrance of the Closed Palace which I have already mentioned. The postern, however, stands for several manners of research which are not in competition with and are without prejudice to each other.

We shall come presently to a third distinction which is much nearer to our hands and feet than are the two others, and will call for some courage on my part in consequence. I will leave it for this reason to such spur of necessity as may arise at the end—to which indeed it belongs otherwise.

Introduction

As there is a door in the soul which opens on God, so there is another door which opens on the recremental deeps, and there is no doubt that the deeps come in when it is opened effectually. There are also the powers of the abyss, and this is why it has been worth while to look at the subject seriously. Being thankful to say that I am, and hoping under God to continue, without first-hand experience in these departments, it must be understood that I speak here under the reserves of derived knowledge. It should, I think, be understood that there is no sublimity in those deeps; they are the cesspools of spiritual life and the pit of the second death; their powers are those of the pesthouse, and they are as remote from the sombre terrors and splendours of Dante's *Inferno* as are the gold bars of heaven and the stars and lilies of the Blessed Damozel far—and how far—away from the Vision and the Union.

There is no especial reason to suppose that there is a Black Sanctuary, a Hidden Church of Hell opened to Christians; but it may be, and in the analogy it would seem that there must be, a communion of self-lost souls, as there is a communion of saints. I should imagine that the Lords of its Convention are to be feared in a certain manner, like the Red and the Black Death. But the versicles and aspirations and formulæ which must be strong enough at any moment to undo all the gates of hell and to cast down all its citadels have been taught us almost at our mothers' knees. I should think that the *Noctem quietam et finem perfectum concedat nobis Dominus omnipotens* would be sufficient to disperse cohorts and not only the isolated *negotium perambulans in tenebris*. The *Pater noster*, moreover, is worth all the Golden Verses of Pythagoras, all the Commentary of Hierocles, and every oracle of Zoroaster, including the forged citations. And, in fine, I do not think that there is any power of the abyss, or any thrice-great Magus, or any sorcerer in final impenitence who has charm, talisman, or conjuration which could look in the face without perishing that one loving supplication:

Introduction

Custodi nos, Domine, ut pupillam oculi; sub umbra alarum tuarum, protege nos.

It is improbable that there is any hidden science in respect of Magic, whether Black or White, but it should be noticed that the occult sciences with which I am concerned here are reducible under this especial head, as it is the greater which includes the lesser. Its processes lie on the surface, and the so-called sanctuaries of occultism may extend the codices but are unlikely to increase the efficacy. In respect of Black Magic, so far as there is a textual excuse for separating it from that uterine sister which was reared on the same milk, I have indicated that there is nothing to suggest one touch of sublimity in diabolism. In its, so to speak, pure state, but *absit verbum*—I should rather have said undiluted—it is the simple ambition and attempt to compel demons, and observe here that it is Satanism to deal, *ex hypothesi*, with the abyss, for whatever purpose. In its worst state it is the Grimoires and the little books of wicked and ultra-foolish secrets. The difference between the *Grimorium Verum* and the *Key of Solomon* is that the one deals openly with the devil and his emissaries, and the other with spirits that are obviously of the same category but are saluted by more kindly names. If it were possible to formulate the motive of Black Magic in the terms of an imputed transcendence, it is the hunger and thirst of the soul seeking to satisfy its craving in the ashpits of uncleanness, greed, hatred and malice. It is exactly comparable to the life of that *Chourineur* in *The Mysteries of Paris* who lived upon diseased offal and grew to be satisfied therewith. But this unfortunate could not help himself exactly, while the soul of the black magician has usually sought evil for its own sake.

I recur therefore for a moment to that door of the soul which, as I have said, opens on God, and it is that which by a necessary but somewhat arbitrary distinction must be called the door to the heights. In their proper understanding, the deeps are holy

Introduction

as the heights, and of course in any true philosophical sense there is neither height nor deep, for these are not journeys made in space and time. However, that symbolic door is the golden way of satisfaction; but it is not of magic, of divination, of clairvoyance, of the communication with spirits, of what order soever; it does not offer the fabled power over Nature of which the Magus is said to be in search and to which lying rituals have from all time pretended that he can attain. It is the hunger and thirst after sanctity and the overfilling of the soul therewith.

The word clairvoyance brings me to the last point and to the third distinction which I have promised to mention.

The office of occultism is of course comparable to the empirical science of the psychic side of things which is being followed at the present day with circumspection and keenness all over Europe and America. It is a poor compliment in one way to institute the comparison, because that which has passed through the alembics of occultism is the dregs and lees of thought, intelligence, motive, and of all that goes to make up the side of action in man. Psychical research, on the other hand, has throughout been actuated by an honourable—often by a pious—motive; it has adopted a scientific method, so far as the subject would permit; it has put forth no claims and abides judgment by results. It is of course, from my point of view, very far from the term. I do not believe for one moment that anything responds to its methods from the unseen side of things which can bring good to man by the intercourse. But it has to be remembered that every supramundane or abnormal fact which is registered by this kind of research is so much evidence added to the *dossier* of occult science. If the phenomena of psychism are as psychical research has registered, the old processes of Magic may be unquestionably veridic processes within their own lines. They did not put the operator in communion, on the highest supposition, with Raphael, Gabriel and Uriel, or with Astaroth and Belial and Lucifer, on the lowest, any more than

Introduction

psychical research and spiritism have ever established inter-course with the souls of the faithful departed.   But both have produced the extraordinary pathological condition and the phe-nomena of the soul manifesting.   The distinction between the two methods is that one was usually the result of personally induced hallucinations, complicated by the frequent intervention of abnormal psychic facts—the whole following a more or less maniac ceremonial—while the other is the scientific investigation of similar and analogical states in predisposed subjects whom the operator may seek to control.   I have no reason to suppose that the sober, ordered and well-judged methods of such ex-perimental research will succeed in taking the subject into any grade of certitude which will be of permanent value to man, and the question closes here so far as I am concerned.   The indications—such as they are—gather rather on the other side.   The path of certitude is in the inward man, as it stands to all reason that it must be, if God and His Kingdom are within.   There is thus, on the best and most temperate hypo-thesis, no object in going towards any other direction than thither wherein is contained the All.

Two things only now remain to be said: It will be seen, in the first place, that from that part of the Secret Tradition in Christian Times, with the summary details of which I opened the present conference, there could have never been any deriva-tion to occult tradition and so-called occult science.   In the second place, the work which hereafter and now follows shall permit the Rituals of White and Black Magic to speak for themselves as to the tradition therein and its value.

CONTENTS

PART I

The Literature of Ceremonial Magic

CHAPTER I

THE ANTIQUITY OF MAGICAL RITUALS

CHAPTER II

THE RITUALS OF TRANSCENDENTAL MAGIC

CHAPTER III

COMPOSITE RITUALS

Contents

CHAPTER IV

THE RITUALS OF BLACK MAGIC

PART II

The Complete Grimoire

CHAPTER I

THE PREPARATION OF THE OPERATOR

Contents

CHAPTER II

THE INITIAL RITES AND CEREMONIES

CHAPTER III

CONCERNING THE DESCENDING HIERARCHY

CHAPTER IV

THE MYSTERIES OF GOËTIC THEURGY ACCORDING TO THE LESSER KEY OF SOLOMON THE KING

CHAPTER V

Contents

EXPLANATION OF FULL-PAGE PLATES

PLATE I

FRONTISPIECE.—Edward Kelley, the Alchemist and alleged Magician, in the act of invoking the Spirit of a Deceased Person.

The plate is reproduced from the second edition of Ebenezer Sibley's *Illustration of the Occult Sciences.* The companion of Kelley within the circle is presumably Paul Waring, who, according to Weaver (*Funereal Monuments*, 1631, pp. 45, 46), was associated with him in all his conjurations. The scene is intended to represent the churchyard of Walton Ledale, "in the county of Lancaster." The information of Sibley is derived from Weaver, whose authority is said to have been Waring. On this point and the general question of Kelley's necromantic pursuits, see my *Alchemical Writings of Edward Kelley*, Biographical Preface, pp. xxvii.–xxx.

PLATE II

The Angels of the Seven Planets, their Sigils, the Signs and Houses of the Planets, the names of the Seven Heavens, according to the *Magical Elements* of Peter de Abano, with the names of the Olympic Spirits of the Planets according to the *Arbatel of Magic*, and the Infernal Sigils of the Evil Planetary Spirits according to the *Red Dragon.*

The name of Michael, the Angel of the Lord's Day, appears over his Sigil, together with the Astrological Symbol of Sol, the Zodiacal Sign of Leo, which is the House of the Sun, and the name of the Fourth Heaven, Machen. The name of Gabriel, the Angel of Monday, appears over his Sigil, together with the Astrological Symbol of Luna, the Zodiacal Sign of Cancer, which is the House of the Moon, and the name of the First Heaven, Shamain. The name of Samael, the Angel of Tuesday, appears over his Sigil, together with the Astrological Symbol of Mars, the Zodiacal Signs of Aries and Scorpio, which are the Houses of the Planet, and the name of the Fifth Heaven, Machon. The name of Raphael, the Angel of Wednesday, appears over his Sigil, together with the Astrological Symbol of Mercury, the Zodiacal Signs of Gemini and Virgo, which are the Houses of the Planet, and the name of the Second Heaven, Raquie. The name of Sachiel, the Angel of Thursday, appears over his Sigil, together with the Astrological Symbol of Jupiter, the Zodiacal Signs of Sagittarius and Pisces, which are the Houses of the Planet, and the name of the Sixth Heaven, Zebul. The name of Anael, the Angel of Friday, appears over

Explanation of Full-Page Plates

his Sigil, together with the Astrological Symbol of Venus, the Zodiacal Signs of Taurus and Libra, which are the Houses of the Planet, and the name of the Third Heaven, Sagun. The name of Cassiel, the Angel of Saturday, appears over his Sigil, together with the Astrological Symbol of Saturn, and the Zodiacal Signs of Capricornus and Aquarius, which are the Houses of the Planet.

PLATE III

Mystic Figures of the Enchiridion.

Figure I., the mystic symbol of the Tau, converted into a monogram which has been supposed to signify the word Taro or Tora. Figure II., the triple Tau. Figure III., an arbitrary figure supposed to represent the fortieth part of the stature of Jesus Christ. Figure IV., the Labarum of Constantine, with the usual inscription, "In this sign thou shalt conquer," and the emblems of the Passion of Christ. Figure V., a double door, connected by a bar, and inscribed with the first seven letters of the Latin alphabet. Figure VI., a composite symbol of unknown meaning. The second circle contains twenty-two letters, which recall the Keys of the Tarot. Figure VII. represents the dimensions of the wound produced by the lance of the Centurion in the side of Jesus Christ. Figure VIII., a two-edged sword, for which various simple meanings may be conjectured. Its inscription has been adopted by alchemists.

PLATE IV

Mystic Figures of the Enchiridion.

Figure I., the reversed form of a well-known occult symbol. The Hebrew words signify *Jehovah Elohim, Agla, Elohim Tsabaoth.* Figure II., the Labarum of Constantine, another form. Figure III., the inscription on this talisman is unintelligible. Figure IV., the occult symbol of the pentagram, reversed, and therefore the sign of the Demon, according to Éliphas Lévi. Possibly misplaced by the ignorance of the printer, but it occurs in this manner in many books which do not apparently connect with Black Magic. Figure V., a talisman with the monogram of Michael. Figure VI., undescribed, but belonging to a prayer of St. Augustine addressed to the Holy Spirit to receive a revelation. Figure VII., the characters of this talisman would seem to be Hebrew, but are so corrupt that they are unintelligible. Figure VIII., a talisman with the monogram of Gabriel. Figure IX., the talisman and monogram of Michael.

PLATE V

The Characters of Evil Spirits, from the so-called "Fourth Book" of Cornelius Agrippa, and described as follows in the original.

1. A right line; 2. a crooked line; 3. a reflexed line; 4. a simple figure; 5. penetrate; 6. broken; 7. a right letter; 8. a retrograde letter; 9. an inverted letter; 10. flame; 11. wind; 12. water; 13. a mass; 14. rain;

Explanation of Full-Page Plates

15. clay; 16. a flying creature; 17. a creeping thing; 18. a serpent; 19. an eye; 20. a hand; 21. a foot; 22. a crown; 23. a crest; 24. horns; 25. a sceptre; 26. a sword; 27. a scourge.

PLATE VI

The Sabbatic Goat, from the *Ritual of Transcendental Magic*, by Éliphas Lévi, who identifies it with the Baphomet of Mendes, and does not regard it as connected with Black Magic, but as "a pantheistic and magical figure of the absolute."

PLATE VII

The instruments of Black Magic, from the Grimoire entitled *True Black Magic*.

Figure I., the knife with the white handle. Figure II., the knife with the black handle. Figure III., the arctrave, or hook. Figure IV., the bolline or sickle. Figure V., the stylet. Figure VI., the needle. Figure VII., the wand. Figure VIII., the lancet. Figure IX., the staff. Figure X., the sword of the master. Figures XI., XII., XIII., the swords of the assistants.

PLATE VIII

The Magical circle used in Goëtic Theurgy, according to the *Lesser Key of Solomon the King*, showing the position of the operator, the divine names and symbols to be inscribed within and about the double circle, and the situation of the lights.

The figure and place of the triangle into which the spirit is commanded will be found, with description, in the text, pp. 220–223. The Divine Names differ in some of the manuscripts.

PLATE IX

The Goetic Circle of Black Evocations and Pacts, according to Éliphas Lévi.

The circle is formed from the skin of the victim, fastened to the ground by four nails taken from the coffin of an executed criminal. The skull is that of a parricide; the horns those of a goat; the male bat opposite the skull must have been drowned in blood; and the black cat, whose head forms the fourth object on the circumference of the circle, must have been fed on human flesh. There is no authority for any of these stipulations. The small circles within the triangle show the place of the operator and his assistants.

FROM BOTTICELLI'S "TEMPTATION."
SISTINE CHAPEL, ROME.

PART I

THE LITERATURE OF CEREMONIAL MAGIC

THE SERPENT OF THE GARDEN
OF THE HESPERIDES.

From a Greek Vase Painting.

CHAPTER I

Ⲧ⳧e Antiquity of Ⲙagical Rituals

§ 1. *The Importance of Ceremonial Magic*

THE ordinary fields of psychological inquiry, largely in possession of the pathologist, are fringed by a borderland of occult and dubious experiment into which pathologists may occasionally venture, but it is left for the most part to unchartered explorers. Beyond these fields and this borderland there lies the legendary wonder-world of Theurgy, so called, of Magic and Sorcery, a world of fascination or terror, as the mind which regards it is tempered, but in either case the antithesis of admitted possibility. There all paradoxes seem to obtain actually, contradictions coexist logically, the effect is greater than the cause and the shadow more than the substance. Therein the visible melts into the unseen, the invisible is manifested openly, motion from place to place is accomplished without traversing the intervening distance, matter passes through matter. There two straight lines may enclose a space ; space has a fourth dimension, and untrodden fields beyond it ; without metaphor and without evasion, the circle is mathematically squared. There life is prolonged, youth renewed, physical immortality secured. There earth becomes gold, and gold earth. There words and wishes possess creative power, thoughts are things, desire realises its object. There, also, the dead live and the hierarchies of extra-mundane intelligence are within easy communication, and become ministers or tormentors, guides or destroyers, of man. There the Law of Continuity is suspended by the interference of the higher Law of Fantasia.

But, unhappily, this domain of enchantment is in all respects comparable to the gold of Faerie, which is presumably its medium of exchange. It cannot withstand daylight, the test of the human eye, or the scale of reason. When these are applied, its paradox becomes an anticlimax, its antithesis ludicrous; its contradictions are without genius; its mathematical marvels end in a verbal quibble; its elixirs fail even as purges; its transmutations do not need exposure at the assayer's hands; its marvel-working words prove barbarous mutilations of dead languages, and are impotent from the moment that they are understood; departed friends, and even planetary intelligences, must not be seized by the skirts, for they are apt to desert their draperies, and these are not like the mantle of Elijah.

The little contrast here instituted will serve to exhibit that there are at least two points of view regarding Magic and its mysteries—the simple and homogeneous view, prevailing within a charmed circle among the few survivals whom reason has not hindered from entering, and that of the world without, which is more complex, more composite, but sometimes more reasonable only by imputation. There is also a third view, in which legend is checked by legend and wonder substituted for wonder. Here it is not the Law of Continuity persisting in its formulæ despite the Law of Fantasia; it is Croquemetaine explained by Diabolus, the runes of Elf-land read with the interpretation of Infernus; it is the Law of Bell and Candle, the Law of Exorcism, and its final expression is in the terms of the *auto-da-fé*. For this view the wonder-world exists without any question, except that of the Holy Tribunal; it is not what it seems, but is adjustable to the eye of faith in the light from the Lamp of the Sanctuaries; in a word, its angels are demons, its Melusines stryges, its phantoms vampires, its spells and mysteries the Black Science. Here Magic itself rises up and responds that there is a Black and a White Art, an Art of Hermes and an Art of Canidia, a Science of the Height and a Science of the Abyss, of Metatron and Belial. In this manner a fourth point of view emerges; they are all, however, illusive; there is the positive illusion of the legend, affirmed by the remaining adherents of its literal sense, and the negative illusion which denies the legend crassly without considering that there is a possibility behind it; there is the illusion which accounts for the legend by an opposite hypothesis, and the illusion of the legend which reaffirms itself with a distinction. When these have been disposed of, there remain two really important questions—the question of the Mystics and the question of history and literature. To a very large extent the first is closed to discussion, because the considerations which it involves cannot be presented with profit on either side in the public assemblies of the reading world. So far as may be held possible, it has been dealt with already. As regards the second, it is the large concern and purpose of this inquiry, and the limits of its importance may therefore be stated shortly.

There can be no extensive literatures without motives proportionate to account for them. If we take the magical literature of Western Europe from the Middle Ages and onward, we shall find that it is moderately large. Now, the acting principles in the creation of that literature will prove to rule also in its history; what is obscure in the one may be understood by help of the other; each reacted upon each; as the literature grew, it helped to make the history, and the new history was so much additional material for further literature.

There were, of course, many motive principles at work, for the literature and history of Magic are alike exceedingly intricate, and there are many interpretations of principles which are apt to be confused with the principles, as, for example, the influence of what is loosely called superstition upon ignorance ; these and any interpretations must be ruled out of an inquiry like the present. The main principles are summed in the conception of a number of assumed mysterious forces in the universe which could be put in operation by man, or at least followed in their secret processes. In the ultimate, however, they could all be rendered secondary, if not passive, to the will of man ; for even in astrology, which was the discernment of forces regarded as peculiarly fatal, there was an art of ruling, and *sapiens dominabitur astris* became an axiom of the science. This conception culminated or centred in the doctrine of unseen, intelligent powers, with whom it was possible for prepared persons to communicate ; the methods by which this communication was attempted are the most important processes of Magic, and the books which embody these methods, called Ceremonial Magic, are the most important part of the literature. Here, that is to say, is the only branch of the subject which it is necessary to understand in order to understand the history. Had Magic been focussed in the reading of the stars, it would have possessed no history to speak of, for astrology involved intellectual equipments which, comparatively speaking, were possible only to the few. Had Magic centred in the transmutation of metals, it would never have moved multitudes, but would have remained what that still is, the quixotic hope which emerges at a far distance from the science of chemistry. We may take the remaining occult sciences collectively, but there is nothing in them of themselves which would make history. In virtue of the synthetic doctrine which has been already formulated, they were all magically possible, but they were all subsidiary to that which was head and crown of all—the art of dealing with spirits. The presumed possession of the secret of this art made Magic formidable, and made therefore its history. There was a time indeed when Ceremonial Magic threatened to absorb the whole circle of the occult sciences; it was the superior method, the royal road; it effected immediately what the others accomplished laboriously, after a long time.[1] It had, moreover, the palmary recommendation that it was a conventional art, working by definite formulæ; above all, it was a process in words.

It was the fascination of this process which brought men and women—all sorts and conditions of both—to the Black Sabbath and to the White Sabbath,[2] and blinded

[1] Thus, the abstruse processes of astrology might, on the hypothesis, be dispensed with altogether in favour of the evocation of one of those numerous spirits whose office it was to give instruction in astrology and an instantaneous knowledge thereof. It is otherwise obvious that the least occult of the esoteric sciences was exploded by an art which provided familiar spirits who could discern the past, present and future. In like manner, Alchemy was superfluous for a magician who could cause treasures to be transported from the depths of the sea or the bowels of the earth, and even from the royal exchequer, in the more convenient shape of current coin.

[2] There is much the same ground for this distinction as for that made between the Black and White Magic of the Rituals. Such meetings were abominable or fantastic according to the disposition of those who frequented them. As a whole, they have probably been much exaggerated. Jules Garinet, in his *Histoire de la Magie en France, depuis le commencement de la Monarchie jusqu'à nos jours* (1818), speculates that the monks, who abused public credulity for the sake of diversion amidst their idleness, may have assumed ridiculous disguises, and may themselves have committed the extravagances which they attributed to devils. The same author affirms, as certain and incontestable, that in all the criminal trials of sorcerers and sorceresses the scene of the Sabbath was invariably in the neighbourhood of a monastery. "Since the destruction of the monastic orders," he concludes triumphantly, "no more is heard of such assemblies, even in places where the fear of the devil still exists." Add to this that seventy-five years later, Papus, the French occultist, would persuade his readers that all the Grimoires of Black Magic were the work of priests, and the case is almost as complete as French reasoning can make it. It is cited here to show that, outside the demonologists, the Sabbath has been viewed rather as a moonlight mummery, where the presiding genius was not the fallen star Wormwood, but Venus, and, even on the monkish hypothesis, the mysteries were those of Priapus rather than Pluto. The records of trials for sorcery rest under the gravest suspicion, firstly, because there is no guarantee that they have not been garbled, and, secondly, because information extracted by torture is, in the ultimate, always of the nature which it was intended to extract; but they are also, or at least largely, records of sexual mania.

them to the danger of the stake. It was the full and clear acceptation of this process as effectual by Church and State which kindled the faggots for the magician in every Christian land. Astrology was scarcely discouraged, and if the alchemist were occasionally tortured, it was only to extract his secret. There was no danger in these things, and hence there was no judgment against them, except by imputation from their company ; but Magic, but dealing with spirits, was that which made even the peasant tremble, and when the peasant shakes at his hearth, the king is not secure in his palace nor the Pope at St. Peter's, unless both can protect their own. Moreover, in the very claim of Ceremonial Magic there was an implied competition with the essential claim of the Church.[1]

The importance of Ceremonial Magic, and of the literature which embodies it, to the history of the occult sciences being admitted, there is no need to argue that this history is a legitimate and reasonable study ; in such a case, knowledge is its own end, and there can be certainly no question as to the distinguished influence which has been exercised by the belief in Magic throughout the ages. In order, however, to understand the literature of Magic, it is necessary to obtain first of all a clear principle of regarding it. It will be superfluous to say that we must surrender the legends, as such, to those who work in legends, and dispute about their essential value. We need not debate whether Magic, for example, can really square the

---

[1] That is to say, the Church communicates the supernatural world by a sacramental system, and the direct communication which Magic pretends to establish must, if established, tend to supersede the Church, in the mind of occultism at least. It is not surprising that a sacerdotalism so acute, especially along the lines of its own interests, as that of the Roman Church should discern that the rival claim assailed its fundamental position, but it is regrettable that an institution possessing the sacramental system should have disturbed itself about a direct communication of the kind attempted by Ceremonial Magic. If it be said that the Church recognised the possibilities which, on certain sides, lie behind the veil of vain observance, then it was not so acute as would seem, for behind that veil there is no danger to the sacramental system. Those possibilities belong to the life within, and the Church has its heritage therein.

circle, as magicians testify, or whether such an operation is impossible even to Magic, as commonly would be objected by those who deny the art. We need not seriously discuss the proposition that the devil assists the magicians to perform a mathematical impossibility, or its qualified form, that the circle can be squared indifferently by those who invoke the angel Cassiel of the hierarchy of Uriel and those who invoke Astaroth. We shall see very shortly, as already indicated in the preface, that we are dealing with a bizarre literature, which passes, by various fantastic phases, through all folly into crime. We have to account for these characteristics.

The desire to communicate with spirits is older than history ; it connects with ineradicable principles in human nature, which have been discussed too often for it to be necessary to recite them here ; and the attempts to satisfy that desire have usually taken a shape which does gross outrage to reason. Between the most ancient processes, such as those of Chaldean Magic, and the rites of the Middle Ages, there are marked correspondences, and there is something of common doctrine, as distinct from intention, in which identity would more or less obtain, underlying them both. The doctrine of compulsion, or the power which both forms pretended to exercise even upon superior spirits by the use of certain words, is a case in point. In approaching the Ceremonial Magic of the Middle Ages, we must therefore bear in mind that we are dealing with a literature which, though modern in its actual presentation, embodies some elements of great antiquity.[1] It is doubtful whether the presence of these elements can be accounted for on the principle that mankind in all ages works unconsciously for the accomplishment

---

[1] The Ceremonial Magic of certain Græco-Egyptian papyri offers the closest analogies with the processes of the Kabalistic school, but they are the channel and not the source. We must look beyond history, certainly far beyond the documents of Leyden, for the origin of Ceremonial Magic.

of similar intentions in an analogous way; a bizarre intention, of course, tends independently to be fulfilled in a bizarre manner, but in this case the similarity is so close that it is more easily explained by the perpetuation—sporadic and natural or concerted and artificial—of an antique tradition, for which channels could be readily assigned. There is one upon the face of the literature, and that is the vehicle of Kabalistic symbolism, though it cannot be held to cover the entire distance in time.

There have been two ways of regarding the large and imperfectly explored literature which embodies the Kabalah of the Jews, and these in turn will give two methods of accounting for the spurious and grotesque processes which enter so extensively into Ceremonial Magic. It is treated either as a barren mystification, a collection of supremely absurd treatises, in which obscure nonsense is enunciated with preternatural solemnity, or it is regarded as a body of theosophy, written chiefly in the form of symbolism. The first view is that which is formed, I suppose, almost irresistibly upon a superficial acquaintance, and there is not any need to add that it is the one which obtains generally in derived judgments, for here, as in other cases, the second-hand opinion issues from the most available source. It is just to add that it does not differ very seriously from the opinions expressed in the past by a certain section of scholarship. The alternative judgment is that which prevails among those students of the literature who have approached it with a certain preparation through acquaintance with other channels of the Secret Tradition. From the one it would follow that the Ceremonial Magic which at a long distance draws from the Kabalah, reproduces its absurdities, possibly with further exaggerations, or it is the subject-matter of the literature carried to its final results. Two erroneous views have issued from the other—an exaggerated importance attributed to the processes in question on the ground of their exalted connections, and—this, however, is rarely met with—an inclination to regard them also as symbolical writing.

There is no ground for the criticism of the first inference, which has arisen legitimately enough and is that which will be most acceptable to the majority of readers. Those who value Kabalistic literature as a storehouse of symbolism, the inner sense of which is or may be of importance, but see nothing in the processes of Ceremonial Magic to make them momentous in their literal sense or susceptible to interpretation, will be tempted to dismiss them as mediæval and later impostures, which must be carefully distinguished from the true symbolical tradition. In either case the ceremonial literature is disdainfully rejected, and it follows in this manner that alternatives which exclude one another both reach the truth as their term.

There is, however, yet another point of view, and it is of some moment, as it connects with that question of the Instituted Mysteries about which it has been already observed that very little has transpired. Most students of occultism are acquainted with intimations and rumours of the existence in modern times of more than one Occult as of more than one Mystical Fraternity, deriving, or believed to derive, from other associations of the past. There are, of course, many unaffiliated occultists, as most mystics are unaffiliated, but the secret Fraternities exist, and the keys of occult symbolism are said to be in their possession. From a variety of isolated statements scattered up and down the works of professed occultists in recent years, it is possible to summarise broadly the imputed standpoint of these bodies in respect of Ceremonial Magic. I will express it in brief as follows. There is no extant Ritual, as there is no doctrine, which contains, or

The Book of Ceremonial Magic

can possibly contain, the real secret of magical procedure or the essence of occult doctrine. The reason—whatever may be said in the excess of some self-constituted exponents—is not because there is, or can be, any indicible process, but because the knowledge in question is in the custody of those who have taken effectual measures for its protection; and though, from time to time, some secrets of initiation, belonging to this order, have filtered through printed books into the world at large, the real mysteries have never escaped. The literature of Magic falls, therefore, on this hypothesis, under three heads: (*a.*) The work of putative adepts, stating as much as could be stated outside the circle of initiation, and primarily designed to attract those who might be ripe for entrance. (*b.*) The speculations of independent seekers, who, by thought, study and intuition, sometimes attained veridic results without assistance. (*c.*) Travesties of occult doctrine, travesties of occult intention, travesties of occult procedure, complicated by filtrations from the superior source.[1]

The opinions of professed occultists on any subject whatsoever are of no importance to myself, and are named only to

[1] In this connection, I may perhaps be permitted to quote a general statement on the subject which I once received from a correspondent who appeared to claim in his day some connection of an unattached kind with the sources of secret knowledge. "Practical Magic is the science of the economy of spiritual dynamics, and is concerned with those Theurgic processes whereby he who has trained himself for the purpose can, by virtue of powers inherent in man's spiritual constitution (but undeveloped in the majority of mankind), enter into relations with the unseen intelligences to whom are assigned, in due order, the control of what are called natural forces. 'Ceremonial Magic'" (presumably not that of the Ceremonial Literature) "is Official Magic, in which the Magician, in connection with one or more assistants, acts as the delegate of an occult Fraternity, who, for some very important end, wish to communicate with beings of a higher order than usual. For this purpose there is a recognised ceremonial, or rather there are two—the 'ceremonial of approach' and the 'ceremonial of the presence.' It is chiefly in the former that lights, fumigations, symbolic figures and numbers, and incantations occur, all of which have their use, either as credentials of authority or as weapons of attack and defence in the intermediate hostile region between the material and spiritual universe." It should be understood that I cite this testimony merely as an illustration of fantasy presented in the guise of exactitude. I do not consider that the least credit should be attached to the statement *per se*, as representing an actual claim made by any secret fraternity, and the claim is without consequence, should it happen that it does.

12

establish a point of view; but most Ceremonial Magic belongs to the third class, on the assumption that it still exists, like some other paths of Satanism; the first, by its nature, is not represented, and the second only slightly. In a word, Ceremonial Magic reflects mainly the egregious ambitions and incorporates the mad processes of mediæval sorcery—of the Sabbath above all. The additional elements are debased applications of various Kabalistic methods, seering processes current among country people and fantastic attempts to reduce magical legends to a formal practice.

Whichever of the above views the reader may prefer to adopt, it will be seen that the net result as regards the Rituals is not generically different, that they are of literary and historical interest, but nothing further. For the occultist they will possess, from their associations, an importance which will be of no moment to another student. It is desirable that they should not be undervalued, as records of the past, because they have exercised an influence, and they are memorable as curiosities thereof; but it is more desirable still that the weak and credulous should be warned against acting like fools, and that those who are seeking spiritual certitude should be dissuaded from the science of the abyss.

§ 2. *The Distinction between White and Black Magic* [1]

Having considered the possible standpoints from which the Rituals may be regarded, we come now to the distinctions that are made between them, and, first and foremost, to that which has been already mentioned and is artificially instituted between White and Black Magic. The history of this dis-

---

[1] It should be understood that this section contains what was said upon the subject, and seemed then sufficient to say, in the original edition. It stands now substantially as it then stood; the extensions are in the preface and in the introductory part.

tinction is exceedingly obscure, but there can be no question that in its main aspect it is modern—that is to say, in so far as it depends upon a sharp contrast between Good and Evil Spirits. In Egypt, in India and in Greece, there was no dealing with devils in the Christian sense of the expression ; Typhon, Juggernaut and Hecate were not less divine than the gods of the over-world, and the offices of Canidia were probably in their way as sacred as the peaceful mysteries of Ceres.

Each of the occult sciences was, however, liable to that species of abuse which is technically but fantastically known as Black Magic. Astrology, or the appreciation of the celestial influences in their operation upon the nature and life of man, could be perverted in the composition of malefic talismans by means of those influences. Esoteric Medicine, which consisted in the application of occult forces to the healing of disease in man, and included a traditional knowledge of the medicinal properties resident in some substances disregarded by ordinary pharmacy,[1] produced in its malpractice the secret science of poisoning and the destruction of health, reason or life by unseen forces. The transmutation of metals by Alchemy resulted in their sophistication. In like manner, Divination, or the processes by which lucidity was supposed to be induced, became debased into various forms of witchcraft and Ceremonial Magic into dealing with devils. White Ceremonial Magic is, by the terms of its definition, an attempt to communicate with Good Spirits for a good, or at least an innocent, purpose. Black Magic is the attempt to communicate with Evil Spirits for an evil, or for any, purpose.

The contrasts here established seem on the surface perfectly

---

[1] I am not suggesting that the traditional knowledge was of value, but that, as a fact, it seems to have existed.

clear. When we come, however, to compare the ceremonial literature of the two classes, we shall find that the distinction is by no means so sharp as might be inferred from the definitions. In the first place, so-called Theurgic Ceremonial, under the pretence of White Magic, usually includes the Rites for the invocation of Evil Spirits. Supposing that they are so invoked for the enforced performance of works contrary to their nature, the issue becomes complicated at once, and White Magic must then be defined as the attempt to communicate with Good or Evil Spirits for a good, or at least for an innocent, purpose. This, of course, still leaves a tolerably clear distinction, though not one that I should admit, if I admitted the practical side of the entire subject to anything but unconditional condemnation. Yet the alternative between a good and an innocent object contains all the material for a further confusion. It will be made clear as I proceed that the purposes and ambitions of Magic are commonly very childish, so that we must distinguish really between Black and White Magic, not as between the essentially good and evil, but as between that which is certainly evil and that which may only be foolish. Nor does this exhaust the difficulty. As will also be made evident in proceeding, White Ceremonial Magic seems to admit of a number of intentions which are objectionable, as well as many that are frivolous. Hence it must be inferred that there is no very sharp distinction between the two branches of the Art. It cannot be said, even, that Black Magic is invariably and White Magic occasionally evil. What is called Black Magic is by no means diabolical invariably ; it is almost as much concerned with preposterous and stupid processes as the White variety with those of an accursed kind. Thus, the most which can be stated is that the literature falls chiefly into two classes, one of which usually terms itself Black, but that they overlap one another.

In what perhaps it may be permissible to call the mind of Magic, as distinct from the effects which are proposed by the Rituals, there has been always a tolerable contrast between the two branches corresponding to Magus and Sorcerer, and the fact that the ceremonial literature tends to the confusion of the distinction may perhaps only stamp it as garbled. But this is not to say that it has been tampered with in the sense of having been perverted by editors. White Magic has not usually been written down into Black; Goëtic Rituals have not been written up in pseudo-celestial terms. They are, for the most part, naturally composite, and it would be impossible to separate their elements without modifying their structure.

Modern occultism has taken up the clear distinction and developed it. Appealing to the secret traditional knowledge behind the written word of Magic—to that unmanifested science which it believes to exist behind all science—and to the religion behind all religion, as if the two were related or identical, it affirms that the advanced occult life has been entered by two classes of adepts, who have been sometimes fantastically distinguished as the Brothers of the Right and the Brothers of the Left, transcendental good and transcendental evil being specified as their respective ends, and in each case they are something altogether different from what is understood conventionally by either White or Black Magic. As might be expected, the literature of the subject does not bear out this development, but, by the terms of the proposition, this is scarcely to be regarded as an objection. For the rest, if many rumours and a few questionable revelations must lead us to concede, within certain limits, that there may have been some recrudescence of diabolism in more than one country of Europe, some attempt at the present day to communicate formally with the Powers of Darkness, it must be said that this attempt returns in its old likeness and not invested with the sublimities and terrors of the modern view. Parisian Diabolism, for example, in so far as it may be admitted to exist, is the Black Magic of the Grimoire and not the sovereign horror of the Brothers of the Left Hand Path, wearing their iniquity like an aureole, and deathless in spiritual evil. These enigmatical personages are, however, the creation of romance, as are also their exalted, or at least purified, *confrères*. Between Rosicrucian initiates of astral processes and the *amatores diaboli* there is indubitably the bond of union which arises from one fact : *il n'y a pas des gens plus embêtants que ces gens-là.*

§ 3. *The Unprinted Literature of Ceremonial Magic*

For the purposes of the present inquiry it will be convenient to consider the Rituals under the three heads of Transcendental, Composite and Black, subject, as regards the first, to some specific qualifications which will appear in the second chapter, and subject, in respect of all, to the perfect understanding that these three are one. So far as may be possible, the antiquity of individual Rituals will be determined in the course of their examination, but as this inquiry is based, with a single exception of undeniable importance, upon the printed literature, because it is that only which has exercised a real influence, it may be well, as a conclusion to this introductory part, to give some information regarding magical processes which have remained in manuscript, and are to be found only, or can at least be consulted only, in the public libraries of Europe. Almost without exception, the source of their inspiration is the work mentioned in the preface, namely, *The Key of Solomon*, and they are consequently of later date. The Library of the Arsénal at Paris has a reputation for being especially rich in Magical MSS., but there is also a large collection in the British Museum which may be regarded as typical. There is nothing of earlier date or more importance among the French treasures, and, to determine the question of antiquity in a few words, there is nothing among our own that is much anterior to the beginning of the fourteenth century.

The numerical strength of the treatises, late and early combined, is in itself considerable, but, setting aside the codices made use of by the English editor of *The Key of Solomon*, the interest of which was exhausted long since by the appearance of that work, there are only three small classes or cycles to which an especial appeal attaches in connection with the present inquiry. The first may be termed the group of Honorius, comprising three MSS.; the second is that of the *Sepher Raziel*, of which there are two forms; the third includes the English codices of the *Lemegeton*. The chief MS. of the first group is also one of the most ancient treatises dealing with Magic in the library. This is Sloane 313, a Latin MS. on vellum, in a bad state of preservation. The close writing and abbreviations make it somewhat difficult to read. It is interesting, however, because it connects with the *Grimoire of Honorius*, one of the most historical and notable Rituals of Black Magic, being the work of some person bearing that name. It belongs to the fourteenth century and has no title or other determinate name, but it appears from the text that it was understood to be the *Sworn Book of Honorius*. The introduction or prologue to the work is obscurely worded in the initial pages, but it seems to account for the condemnation of magic by the prelates of the Church on the ground that they have been deceived by demons. The result is the convocation of all the "masters of Magic," to the number of 811, all of whom seem to have come out of Naples, Athens and a place entitled Tholetus. Among these a species of spokesman was chosen, whose name was Honorius, the son of Euclidus, Master of the Thebans. He was deputed to work for the rest, and he entered into counsel with an angel called *Hochmel* or *Hocroel*, (? *Hochmaël*), and thereafter wrote seven volumes of Magical Art, "giving the kernel to us and the shells to others." From these books he seems afterwards to have extracted ninety-three chapters, containing a summary of the whole subject, and made them into a volume which "we term the sacred or sworn book." In the meantime, the princes and prelates, having burned "certain fables or trifles," concluded that they had completely destroyed the art, and were therefore pacified. The magicians, however, took an oath among themselves to preserve the masterpiece of Honorius in the most secret and careful manner, making three copies at the most, the possessor of any example being bound over to bury it before his decease, or otherwise insure its interment in his own grave, unless there were some trusty and worthy person to whom it could be transmitted. It is interesting to note that this is the Law of Transmission in respect of Alchemy. The important point about the MS. itself is that it fixes the source of the mendacious tradition which ascribes a Grimoire of Black Magic to a Pope of the name of Honorius, as will be seen at length later on. The *Sworn Book* is not, of course, the Grimoire, but the existence and reputed authorship of the one will enable us to understand the attribution of the other. Honorius the sorcerer was identified with Honorius the Pope, firstly by the confused mind of magical legend, and secondly by conscious imposture, much after the same manner that Raymond Lully, the "illuminated doctor" of Majorca, was

identified with Lully the alchemist, by tradition at the inception, and not long afterwards by the help of forged treatises.
The *Sworn Book* is in other respects remarkable, and has
been unaccountably overlooked by writers on Ceremonial
Magic; it may be taken to indicate that an association of
magicians was most probably in corporate existence during or
before the fourteenth century. While it is clearly of Christian
origin, it derives from the supposed works of Solomon, and
would appear to indicate that the Solomonic cycle was at that
time only in course of formation, as also that the earliest
elements approximate not to the Grand Clavicle, but to the
Little Key, otherwise, the *Lemegeton*. As to the operations contained in the *Sworn Book*, they are those of White and Black
Magic, undiscriminated, without, however, any trace of the
conventional " dealing with the devil." The MS. under notice
need not, of course, be regarded as the original; as to this
there is no means of knowing. The British Museum possesses
also a later transcript, belonging to the sixteenth century, and
a most valuable English translation, written on vellum in beautiful Gothic characters. It is referred to the fifteenth century.

The second group comprises two MSS., both in the Sloane
collection, and both containing, among other treatises, the important and curious work attributed to Solomon under the title
of *Sepher Raziel*. That numbered 3826 belongs to the sixteenth
century. It is an English translation of a Latin original which
in this form is unknown to myself; the first line of the original
is usually given at the beginning of each section. It is divided
into seven books, and purports to have been sent to Solomon
by a prince of Babylon who was greater and more worshipful
than all men of his time, his name being Sameton, while
the two wise men who brought it were called Kamazan and
Zazant. The Latin title of the treatise is said to be *Angelus*

20

The Antiquity of Magical Rituals

Magnus Secreti Creatoris; it was the first book after Adam, was written in the language of Chaldea and afterwards was translated into Hebrew. It is a noticeable fact that in this work the first section is entitled *Clavis*, and if we may regard the *Sepher Raziel* as antedating the *Claviculæ*, it explains why a Key was attributed to Solomon. The *Clavis* in question is, however, concerned with the magical influences of the stars, "without which we can effect nothing." The second book is called *Ala;* it treats of the virtues of stones, herbs and beasts. The third is *Tractatus Thymiamatum*, the use of which term connects it with the *Sworn Book* of Honorius; it treats of suffumigations. The fourth sets out the times of the year, day and night which are disposed to operation; the fifth embodies the laws regarding lustrations and abstinence; while the sixth, called *Samaim*, expounds the nature of the heavens, of the angels and of the operations of each. The seventh and last book is concerned with the virtues of names. A Latin version of the *Sepher Raziel* occurs in Sloane MS. 3853, ascribed to the same period. It differs from the former in several considerable respects, being also much shorter and full of rare magical symbols.

The MSS. of the third group are all in English, and all of late date.

Sloane 2731 is a very neat MS., begun on January 10, 1676, and containing the entire *Lemegeton, or Lesser Key of Solomon*, in English. Some account of this celebrated work, which has so unaccountably escaped publication, will be found in the third chapter of this part. Sloane 3648 is another manuscript of the *Lemegeton*, also in English, together with the *Ars Notoria*, a book of invocations and prayers attributed to Solomon, of which there are many examples extant in England and on the Continent.[1] It is a work which connects with Magic

---

[1] The printed English translation of Robert Turner is well known to collectors.

without being itself magical, and, in fact, stands in much the same relation to the Key or Clavicle as the *Enchiridion of Pope Leo* to the *Isagoge* of the *Arbatel.* Lastly, the same MS. contains the *Magical Archidoxies* of Paracelsus, but the version seems to be quite distinct from the treatise so entitled in the Geneva folio, containing the collected writings of the German adept.[1] In either case, it is not a work of Ceremonial Magic, its title notwithstanding. Sloane 3805 is a quarto MS., chiefly alchemical and medical, comprising a translation of the forged epistles of Sendivogius, and towards the end the *Lemegeton,* started by the writer apparently with the intention of transcribing all the works attributed to Solomon under the heading of this angelic name. It breaks off, however, at the end of the offices of the thirteenth spirit belonging to the Infernal Hierarchy.

It should be added that the three groups contain materials which are common to all. The independent treatises which follow the *Sepher Raziel* in Sloane 3826 extract matter from the *Sworn Book,* while that entitled *Liber Lunæ,* concerning the intelligences of the mansions of the moon, the squares of the planets, their seals, rings and so forth—which, by the way, seems in this form unknown to modern critics—has given material to other and later collections.

The unprinted literature of Ceremonial Magic offers a considerable field to research, though even in the historical or bibliographical interest it is questionable whether it would repay the pains, unless research of all kinds whatsoever is to be regarded as its own reward. Among the miscellaneous MSS. in the British Museum, it is here only necessary to notice two,

---

[1] The genuine *Archidoxies* are concerned with the alchemical separation of elements, with transcendental Medicine and the Quintessence, with Magisteries and Elixirs. The first complete rendering is in *The Hermetic and Alchemical Writings of Paracelsus,* edited by myself, 2 vols. 4to, 1894.

The Antiquity of Magical Rituals

as they contain materials connected with the present design. Sloane 3884 includes a process in Necromancy—how to call the ghost of a dead body—the invocation of spirits into a crystal—the form for summoning spirits within the circle—and a method of exorcism in the Tuscan language,—all impudently attributed to the author of the *Nullity of Magic*—that is to say, Roger Bacon. In the second part of my present work a special chapter is devoted to Infernal Necromancy, and the MS. here mentioned will be useful for purposes of reference. Sloane 3850 is a MS. of the seventeenth century, which contains transcripts from the fourth book of Cornelius Agrippa and from the *Heptameron* of Peter de Abano in Latin. There is also a *Good and Proved Experiment* for evocation, which uses the *Pater, Ave, Credo* and Litany of the Saints as magical formulæ. Finally, there are processes, mostly in Latin, but some in English, for the discovery of things lost, the recovery of things stolen, for the spirits of the dead who cannot rest in their graves, and for persons possessed by evil spirits. The treatise *De Novem Candariis Salomonis*, containing curious figures and sigils, deserves particular mention, as this again seems unknown to students. Its attribution notwithstanding, it is the work of a Catholic writer.

THE SACRED URÆUS OR BASILISK

CHAPTER II

The Rituals of Transcendental Magic

§ 1. *The Arbatel of Magic*

THE term transcendental must not be interpreted in any exalted or philosophical sense when it is used, informally and conventionally enough, in such a connection as the present. It has not been adopted because it is tolerably appropriate, but rather in the absence of a better word of definition in respect of the claim implied, and because also it has been previously admitted in the same connection. It is perhaps loosely equivalent to the *Haute Magie* of Éliphas Lévi, which I have rendered *Transcendental Magic*, not as a satisfactory equivalent but because there is no current or admitted expression which corresponds more closely. When due allowance has been made for the conceptions which may be presumed to underlie the subject, it must be said that in Ceremonial Magic there is as much and as little Transcendentalism as in the phenomena of modern mediumship. Whatever might be claimed for the intelligences with whom communication is sought to be established, they reveal themselves by their offices, which are either fantasic or frivolous. In such an association it should be understood that material interests are to be included in the second class; in the first would be comprised those which are outside realisation by reason of their extravagance, while at the same time they are unconnected with spiritual aspiration.

Supposing that it were an exact science, there would be

nothing in Practical Magic which interlinks, for example, with a true or with any Mystic Purpose.[1]   Hence, by Rituals of Transcendental Magic there must not be understood a collection of processes by which the Divine in Man is sought to be united with the Divine in the Universe.   The works of St. John of the Cross, of Ruysbroeck, of Eckart, of Molinos, of Saint-Martin, even the *Imitation* of St. Thomas à Kempis—these contain the grand processes of true Transcendental Magic, were it other than desecration to apply a term which is worse than ridiculous to treasures which would be disparaged by the association.   Here there must be understood simply those occult processes and that so-called Theurgic Ceremonial, in which there is at least no explicit connection with Black Magic, which not only contain no dealings with evil spirits for evil purposes, but appear to eschew all such communication, for what purpose soever.   An exception—which, properly understood, is, however, an exception only on the surface—should be made in favour of the procedure adopted by the Church for the expulsion of diabolical powers from persons in the flesh, not because the phenomena of possession are necessarily other than pathological, even in those cases which would appear to be marked and obstinate, but because, on the terms of the ecclesiastical assumption, the Rite of Exorcism is a far more exalted Rite than anything which obtains in Transcendental Magic.   In this matter, as in many other cases of much higher importance, no tolerable justice has been done to the position of the Catholic Church.   It should be observed in addition, that while Ceremonial Magic is concerned with a variety of

[1] By Practical Magic is here intended not certain forms of the putative transcendent science said to be imparted by occult initiation, and to be totally distinct from childish attempts to discover hidden treasure, to obtain the ring of invisibility, and so forth ; the reference is intended solely to the Magic of the Ceremonial Literature.   I believe that the exotic form belongs to the deeps rather than the heights because it is phenomenal procedure, but the distinction—which I have discussed otherwise—is advisable to note here.

processes which may obviously tend to produce in unwary operators the phenomena which characterise possession, there is scarcely a single process in any one of the Rituals—White or Black, Composite or Transcendental—which makes any pretence of relieving persons so afflicted.[1] There is, therefore, no reason to doubt on which side of hallucination the apparatus of the Rituals has been developed, and the sympathies of reasonable students will be with the honourable institution which condemned the practices and sought to liberate the victims, leaving possession itself as an open question, and in this sense as a side issue.

TALISMAN OF ARBATEL

Even with the qualification which I have registered, the putative Transcendental Rituals are exceedingly few. There is — 1. The *Enchiridion* of Pope Leo the Third. 2. The *Arbatel of Magic*. 3. The Celestial Magic of an anonymous German occultist, entitled *Theosophia Pneumatica*, which must be held to represent and to save enumeration of one or two similar handbooks. Of these, the first is included among the Rituals of Ceremonial Magic by the invincible ignorance of almost every person who has undertaken to class it. On the other hand, the

---

[1] There are, of course, innumerable processes for destroying spells and enchantments; among them one occasionally meets with an exorcism to be used in a case of possession. There is one in the edition of the *Grimoire of Honorius* published at Rome in 1760. It is supposed to be efficacious both for men and animals afflicted by Satan. In the edition of 1800 there is another process, which prescribes holy water for aspersion, in the case of a human being, and, in that of an animal, salt exorcised with blood drawn from the bewitched creature. See also my remarks on Sloane MS. 3884.

third borrows all its importance from the second, in which, upon both counts, the interest evidently centres. As regards its origin, its authorship, and even its scope, there is, however, considerable mystery. Within my own knowledge, there are no copies in manuscript, or none at least which are prior to the end of the sixteenth century. It appeared in a tiny volume at Basle and bore the date 1575.[1] Back-dating and imputed authorship are the two crying bibliographical sins of Grimoires and magical handbooks, and the antiquity of the *Arbatel* rests under a certain suspicion on account of its literary connections ; at the same time it would require the knowledge of an expert in typography to pronounce certainly on the reliability of the date indicated. The text is in Latin, but there is a slender possibility in favour of its being the work of an Italian.[2] It makes a reference to Theophrastic Magic, which indicates the influence of Paracelsus, and, although it is difficult to speak with any certainty, seems to hint at an early period of that influence, the period, in fact, of Benedictus Figulus, slightly antedating Rosicrucian enthusiasm, and thus accounting for the omission of all Rosicrucian references, which, in view both of matter and manner, might have been irresistibly expected had the work been posterior to the year 1610.

It should be observed that the *Arbatel* has no connection with the cycle, hereinafter considered, of the Keys of Solomon,

---

[1] Arbatel, *De Magia Veterum*, Basileæ, 1575. The mottoes on the title are *Summum Sapientiæ Studium* and *In omnibus consule Dominum, et nihil cogites, dicas, facias, quod tibi Deus non consuluerit.*

[2] The possibility is warranted by references in the 30th and 31st Aphorisms to some obscure points of Italian history. It is said that by a judgment of the Magicians it was decreed that no Italian should reign over the kingdom of Naples ; now the monarch at the time was an Italian, and he was dethroned in due course. To restore the national dynasty the decree must be annulled by those who made it. A magician of greater power might be able to enforce this, and also the restitution of a certain Book, Jewel and Magic Horn, of which the Treasury of Magic had been despoiled. The mastery of the whole world would pass into the hands of their possessor.

and it is permeated with Christian ideas. The authorship is completely unknown. Arbatel, or ארבעתאל, is probably not an assumed name, but indicative of an instructing or revealing Angel. The use of this Hebrew term is, however, peculiar in connection with the fact that the references to the Old Testament are few and unimportant, while the sayings of Christ, and the New Testament narrative generally, are subjects of continual citation. Solomon, moreover, is not mentioned in the frequent enumerations of adepts and wise men.

So far concerning the origin, authorship and date of the book. It remains to say that it is incomplete. Of the nine " Tomes " into which it purports to be divided, we possess only one. It is not unlikely that the rest were never written, because the author has left us a plan of his entire proposal, and it is evident that his first book more than once overlaps what should have followed. As it stands, the *Arbatel of Magic* is concerned with the most general precepts of Magical Arts—in other words, with the Institutions. It is entitled *Isagoge*, which means essential or fundamental instruction. The missing books are those of Microcosmical Magic, or Spiritual Wisdom; Olympic Magic, that is, the evocation of the Spirits of Olympus; Hesiodiacal and Homeric Magic, being the operations of *Caco-daimones;* Roman or Sibylline Magic, concerning Tutelary Spirits; Pythagorical Magic, dealing with the Genii of the Arts; the Magic of Apollonius, giving power over the enemies of mankind; Hermetic or Egyptian Magic; and that, finally, which depends solely on the Word of God and is called Prophetical Magic.

It is an open question whether all of these books could have been completed without a proportion of that dangerous instruction which makes for open Black Magic. The *Isagoge*, however, must be exempted in part from such charge; the Seven Septenaries of aphorisms of which it consists contain many moral and spiritual exhortations, which, if they are not exactly unhackneyed, are on the surface quite unexceptionable, and might indeed rank among the more exalted of their kind, were it not for the art with which they are connected. The initial groups of these aphorisms serve to introduce the Ritual of the Olympic Spirits, dwelling in the firmament and in the stars of the firmament, between whom the government of the world is distributed. There are 196 [1] Olympic Provinces in the entire universe, so that *Aratron* has 49, *Bethor* 42, *Phaleg* 35, *Och* 28, *Hagith* 21, *Ophiel* 14, and *Phul* 7. These Provinces are termed visible, but even as the *Seven Septenaries of Arbatel* cover the whole ground of reputed Transcendental Magic, so these seven successive multiples of the same mystical number may most probably be taken to indicate powers and offices. It is further said that the Olympic Spirits rule alternately, each for 490 years, which would be mere confusion were separate assemblages of spheres permanently assigned to them.

The powers possessed by these Intelligences are very curiously set forth. They rule naturally over certain departments and operations of the material world, but outside these departments they perform the same operations magically. Thus *Och*, the prince of Solar things, presides over the preparation or development of gold naturally in the veins of the earth—that is to say, he is the Mineralogist in Chief of Nature ; he presides also over the quicker preparation of the same metal by means of chemical art—that is, he is the Prince of Alchemists ; and, finally, he makes gold in a moment by Magic. It is in this way

---

[1] The original edition of the *Arbatel* reads 186, and ascribes 32 provinces to *Bethor*, which breaks the progression of the septenary and is probably a printer's mistake. It is followed, however, by the English and German translators.

that Ceremonial Magic connects with while it assumes to transcend Hermetic Art.[1]

There is another curious instruction, with regard to the names and characters of the Spirits. In opposition to much of the traditional doctrine of Magic, it is affirmed that there is no power in the figure of any character or in the pronunciation of any name, except in so far as there is a virtue or office ordained by God to both. The names, moreover, are not definite, final or real names, whence they differ with different writers accordingly as these have received them. The only effectual names are those which are delivered to an operator by the Spirits themselves, and even then their efficacy seldom endures beyond forty years. It is, therefore, better for the student, says the *Arbatel*, to work only by the offices of the Spirits, without their names; should he be pre-ordained to attain the Art of Magic, the other parts of that Art will offer themselves of their own accord.

The sources of occult wisdom, it proceeds, are, firstly, in God; secondly, in spiritual essences—that is to say, the Angelical Hierarchy; thirdly, in corporeal creatures, the reference being probably to the *signatura rerum* of Paracelsus; fourthly, in Nature—that is to say, in a knowledge of the secret virtues of natural things, as, for example, herbs and precious stones; fifthly, but after a long interval, in the apostate spirits reserved to the last judgment;[2] sixthly, in the administers of punishment in hell, which seems to connect with the classical conception of avenging infernal gods; seventhly, in the people of the elements, that is, the Salamanders, Sylphs, Undines and Gnomes or Pigmies.

[1] It was also by the magical hypothesis a gift from heaven, brought down by the Angel Uriel.

[2] This reference, taken in connection with the matters proposed to be treated in the seventh book, points conclusively to the intention of including the government of Evil Spirits in the scheme of the *Arbatel*.

The Rituals of Transcendental Magic

The secrets deriving from these sources range from the highest achievements of reputed mystical science [1] to the bourgeois ambitions of daily life, from the Regeneration of Enoch and the Knowledge of God, Christ and His Holy Spirit—wherein is the perfection of the Microcosm—to the attainment of honours and dignities, the ingathering of much money, the foundation of a family, good fortune in mercantile pursuits, and successful housewifery both in town and country. The prolongation of life, the transmutation of metals and the talismanic cure of all diseases, with other " paradoxes of the highest science," also figure in the list.

Meditation, inward contemplation and the love of God are the chief aids to the acquisition of Magical Art, together with great faith, strict taciturnity and even justice in the things of daily life. Finally, a true magician is brought forth as such from his mother's womb; others who assume the function will be unhappy. [2]

The powers and offices of the Seven Olympic Spirits are as follows : ARATRON governs those things which are ascribed astrologically to Saturn. He can convert any living organism, plant or animal into stone, and that in a moment of time ; he can also change coals into treasure and treasure into coals; he gives familiars and reconciles subterranean spirits to men ; he teaches Alchemy, Magic and Medicine,

THE CHARACTER OF ARATRON

[1] It should be observed that the mystical achievements are barely mentioned, and that their attainment is imparted by a spirit possessing the office, which is conclusive, as I need not point out, respecting the use of the term. The author of the *Arbatel*, however, considers it good enough Mysticism, as does Éliphas Lévi, to cause oneself "to be worshipped as a god," in virtue of the sigil of *Och*.

[2] When his highest authorities disagree, the occult student is liable to get at the truth, and will find occasionally that it is not at either end, nor yet in the middle. It is edifying to com-

imparts the secret of invisibility, makes the barren fruitful and, lastly, confers long life. He should be invoked on a Saturday, in the first hour of the day,[1] making use of his character, given and confirmed by himself.[2]

The affairs of Jupiter are administered by BETHOR, who responds quickly when called. The person dignified by his character may be exalted to illustrious positions and may obtain large treasures. He reconciles the Spirits of the Air to man, so that they will give true answers, transport precious stones and compose medicines having miraculous effects. BETHOR also grants familiars of the firmament, and can prolong life to seven hundred years, subject to the will of God, which qualification imparts an air of caution.

THE CHARACTER OF BETHOR

pare this express statement of a ruling ceremonial process with another, not less express, which we owe to the reconstruction of all the processes and the reputed recoverer of the true practice of Magic. " Furthermore, certain physical organisations are better adapted than others for the revelations of the occult world ; there are sensitive and sympathetic natures, with whom intuition in the astral light is, so to speak, inborn ; certain afflictions and certain complaints can modify the nervous system, and, independently of the concurrence of the will, may convert it into a divinatory apparatus of less or more perfection ; but these phenomena are exceptional, *and generally magical power should, and can, be acquired by perseverance and labour.*"—" Doctrine and Ritual of Transcendent Magic," by Éliphas Lévi, English translation by A. E. Waite, p. 196. In this case the genius of enlightened differentiation rests entirely upon the later adept. As a matter of fact, occult writers have always recognised that there is the Natural Magician and the Magician according to Art. *Vel sanctum invenit, vel sanctum facit* has been said of Magic, and so also magical knowledge means magical power; where it does not find it, it brings it. I speak, of course, *ex hypothesi.* But such knowledge is not of Rituals or Grimoires, of *Arbatel* or another, nor is the word Magic, nor is the process practical in respect of an external procedure. That which is termed Occultism is the art of desecrating the inmost Sanctuary.

[1] See Part ii. c. 6.

[2] It should be understood that the characters of the so-called Olympic Spirits are, so to speak, their official seals and are not to be confused with the images attributed to the planets. These were of various kinds in correspondence with the variety of influences and were worn as talismans or charms.

PHALEG governs the things that are attributed to Mars. The person who possesses his character is raised by him to great honour in military affairs.

THE CHARACTER OF PHALEG

Solar interests are administered by OCH, who prolongs life to six hundred years, with perfect health therein. He imparts great wisdom, gives excellent (familiar) spirits, composes perfect medicines, converts any substance into the purest of metals, or into precious stones; he also bestows gold and a purse, quaintly described by the English translator of the *Arbatel* as "springing with gold." He causes the possessor of his character to be worshipped as a god by the kings of the whole world.

THE CHARACTER OF OCH

The government of Venereal concerns is entrusted to HAGITH, and the person possessing his character is adorned with all beauty. He converts copper into gold in a moment and gold instantaneously into copper; he also gives faithful serving spirits.

THE CHARACTER OF HAGITH

OPHIEL is the ruler of those things which are attributed to Mercury; he gives familiar spirits, teaches all arts, and enables the possessor of his character to change quicksilver immediately into the Philosopher's Stone.

THE CHARACTER OF OPHIEL

The Book of Ceremonial Magic

Lunary concerns are under the government of PHUL, who truly transmutes all metals into silver, heals dropsy and provides Spirits of the Water, who serve men in a corporal and visible form; he also prolongs life to three hundred years.

Legions of inferior spirits are commanded by each of the Governors, who also have Kings, Princes, Presidents, Dukes and Ministers ruling under them. Ceremonial Magic usually administers the hierarchies upon a colossal scale. The invocation of the Governors is simple. It is performed in the day and hour of the planet which is in correspondence with the Olympic Intelligence by means of the following :—

THE CHARACTER OF PHUL

PRAYER

O Eternal and Omnipotent God, Who hast ordained the whole creation for Thy praise and Thy glory, as also for the salvation of man, I beseech Thee to send Thy Spirit N., of the Solar Race,[1] that he may instruct me concerning those things about which I design to ask him [or—that he may bring me medicine against the dropsy, &c.]. Nevertheless, not my will, but Thine be done, through Jesus Christ, Thine only-begotten Son, Who is our Lord. Amen.

Unless the Spirit, in the words of Robert Turner, be "familiarly addicted" to the operator, he should not be detained above one hour, and should in either case be "licensed to depart" as follows :—

---

[1] This is merely a typical form subject to variations according to the spirit who is evoked.

The Rituals of Transcendental Magic

THE DISCHARGE

Forasmuch as thou camest in peace and quietness, having also answered unto my petitions, I give thanks unto God, in Whose Name thou camest. Now mayst thou depart in peace unto thine own order ; but return unto me again, when I shall call thee by thy name, or by thine order, or by thine office, which is granted from the Creator. Amen. [Then add :] *Be not rash with thy mouth, and let not thine heart be hasty to utter anything before God : for God is in heaven, and thou art upon earth ; therefore let thy words be few. For a dream cometh through the multitude of business, and a fool's voice is known by multitude of words.*—Eccles. v. 3, 4.

§ 2. *Theosophia Pneumatica*

In the year 1686, the *Arbatel* was translated into German, and in the same year—possibly in the same volume—appeared, also in German, a work entitled *The Little Keys of Solomon* or *Theosophia Pneumatica.*[1] There are no examples of these editions in the British Museum, and inquiry has failed to elicit any particulars concerning them. Both are reprinted, together with other specimens of Ancient Magical Literature, to illustrate the Faust legend, in the third volume of Scheible's *Das Kloster.*[2] The translation of the *Arbatel* makes no reference to the previous edition in Latin, and *Theosophia Pneumatica* nowhere states that it is an adaptation of the earlier work. The attribution to Solomon is, of course, wholly contrary to

---

[1] *Clavicula Salomonis, vel Theosophia Pneumatica.*
[2] J. Scheible, *Das Kloster. Weltlich und Geistlich. Meist aus der Altern Deutschen Volks-Literatur*, 12 vols., Stuttgart, 1845–49.

the spirit of the Ritual, and betrays so far the hand of ignorance.

The adapter had, however, been subject to other occult influences besides the *Arbatel*. He applies the term Talmid [1] to the magical aspirant, and this is not used by the original. The adaptation has been well executed and makes for additional clearness. The transcendental portions are slightly accentuated; it is said in one place that the exaltation of prayer is the end of the whole Mystery, and that such exaltation will never be denied to the true seeker, who is recommended on no account to undervalue his own prayers. This is a better presentation of the theory than the corresponding passage in the *Arbatel* itself. There is also an addendum on Transcendental Medicine, which, so far as can be known, is original, and it is as curious as anything in the literature with which we are dealing. [2]

---

[1] There is a curious history attaching to this word, but it can be elucidated only by a Hebrew scholar. It seems to be of late introduction, though it derives from the verb *to learn*. It has been said to represent a stage of initiation in certain occult societies of Islâm.

[2] As it is unlikely that *Theosophia Pneumatica* will ever be printed in English, it may be well to give a summary of its appendix, that is to say, of the only section of this work which differs generically from the *Arbatel*. Affirming that all things are threefold, from the Divine Triad of Father, Son and Holy Ghost, to man, who is composed of the fleshly body, the sensitive soul and the rational spirit, it defines the human principles as follows: The body is of earth; the sensitive soul is of the four elements, but derives through the stars, and is the seat of understanding and genius for arts and sciences; the rational spirit is from God absolutely; the sphere of its activity is celestial and divine, and divine inspiration and influence pass through it to the material body. The body is a house wherein soul and spirit abide and perform their functions, having been married therein by God. At the same time, they strive daily with one another, till the spirit overcomes the soul, and thus attains regeneration. There are two kinds of death—that which results from the destruction of vital physical organs by disease or injury, and that which results from the destruction of the sensitive soul by envenomed astral influences. Physical disintegration and flight of the divine spirit follow in either case. The spirit may also be recalled by the direct action of the will of God, without disease or injury. Man is therefore poised upon three pillars; if one of them fall or break, the man dies. He should preserve and embalm his body against infectious diseases, for the living organism can be embalmed better than a corpse. He should also combat the venomous influences of baleful stars, for Elohim has gifted men with the power to compose characters that will destroy such influences. It is impossible, however, to cure those diseases with which God in His unsearchable compassion may Himself scourge mankind; vain are the best medicines and vain the highest arcana, vain

PLATE II

THE ANGELS AND OLYMPIC SPIRITS OF THE SILVER PLANETS

§ 3. *The Enchiridion of Pope Leo*

We come now to the *Enchiridion of Pope Leo III.*, which, as already indicated, is not a book of Ceremonial Magic; it is necessary, however, to include it in this notice, and to analyse it at some length, so as to establish its true character. Misconceptions and mistakes upon a subject so obscure as Magical Rituals are, speaking generally, excusable enough, but in this case they are found where they are not excusable, namely, among those persons who have undertaken to give account of the work. Catholic bibliographers of the occult sciences, or at least the anonymous author of the occult encyclopædia in Migne's great series, are very angry at the pontifical attribution, and stigmatise the *Enchiridion* as an infamous storehouse of Black Magic. Éliphas Lévi, who may possibly have read it— because occasionally he seems to have glanced at his authors— magnifies its occult importance by stating that it has never been printed with its true figures. In the absence of all evidence on this point, it is impossible to entertain it seriously. The *Enchiridion* is assuredly not a book of Black Magic, nor does it lend itself to the introduction of other figures than those which appear in it, and these are few and simple. Finally, Alfred Maury, in *La Magie et l'Astrologie dans l'Antiquité et au Moyen Age*, describes the *Enchiridion* as a work on Sorcery, bearing traces of Neo-Platonic, and even older, influences. He also evidently had not read it, and is a per-

---

is *p. ex. unicorn.*, vain is the potent *aurum*, vain the *spiritus auri*, vain the *quinta essentia*; *Azoth* itself is useless; the *lapis philosophorum* is made void. The skilled physician will immediately discover such a case in a patient. All other diseases, whether deriving from the planets, from the natural corruption of the earth or from neglect, may be cured by natural remedies—by herbs, balms, spices, oils, metals or preparations of Alchemy. When natural diseases become incurable, it is through the ignorance or indocility of man. This Appendix of *Theosophia Pneumatica* not only indicates the influence but reproduces the terminology of Paracelsus.

sonage of sufficient consequence to deserve severe censure for
following such an evil principle of criticism.

The legend of the *Enchiridion* is as follows. When Charlemagne was leaving Rome after his coronation by Leo III.,
that pontiff presented him with a memorial of the visit in the
shape of a collection of prayers, to which wonderful virtues
were attributed. Whosoever bore the little work upon his
person with the respect due to Holy Scripture, who also recited
it daily to the honour of God, would never be overcome by
his enemies, would pass unscathed through all perils, and the
Divine protection would abide with him to the end of his days.
These things took place in the year 800. In the year 1523
the *Enchiridion* is supposed to have been printed at Rome for
the first time. Thus broadly outlined, there is nothing in this
legend to offend possibility or to raise very serious objection
to the authorship. The reputed connection with occult science
would indeed seem the chief presumption against it, because
there never was a literature so founded in forgery as that of
Magic, except the sister science of physical Alchemy. When
we come, however, to examine the work at first hand, the case
against it assumes a different aspect, and it is condemned out
of its own mouth. While it is not a Ritual of Magic, it is
also certainly not a simple collection of devotions designed to
fortify the person making use of them against dangers of body
and soul by the operation of Divine Grace; it is rather a
collection of charms cast in the form of prayers, and is quite
opposed in its spirit to the devotional spirit of the Church;
furthermore, it is concerned with worldly advantages far more
than with those of a spiritual kind. The work opens with
a characteristic stultification in respect of its own claim, by
pointing out that of all the sovereign princes of past ages there
was none more fortunate than Charlemagne, and the source

of his great prosperity is acknowledged by him in a letter of thanks addressed to Pope Leo, the original of which, it is affirmed, may still be seen in the Library of the Vatican, written with the monarch's own hand. He states therein that since his reception of a little volume entitled *Enchiridion*, filled with special prayers and mysterious figures, sent by His Holiness as a precious gift, he has never ceased to be fortunate, and that of all things in the universe which are capable of harming man, not one has shewn any malignity against him, in gratitude for which he proposes to devote himself and all that is his to the service of his benefactor. The letter is in Latin; the monarch styles himself Carolus Magnus, which appears highly unlikely, and he terms the pontiff *Summus Antistitum Antistes*, but this is not in itself improbable, as the Papal claim to Episcopal supremacy was fully developed at the beginning of the ninth century.

It is needless to say that there is no such document preserved in the Vatican Library; furthermore, there are no letters of Charlemagne extant, and, despite the encouragement he gave to men of learning and the Academy mentioned by Alcuin, it is not at all certain that he could either read or write. Lastly, while it is quite true that his empire included Germany, as it did also Holland, Belgium, Switzerland and part of Italy, after his coronation it is much more probable that he would have styled himself Emperor of the Romans. There is, in fact, no colourable pretence of genuineness about the so-called autograph letter, or to be precise it betrays itself—as I have indeed suggested already.

This fact being established, we may proceed to the consideration of the alleged date of publication—Rome, 1523. This edition is mentioned by Pierre Christian in his *Histoire de la Magie*, and he defends the authenticity of the *Enchiridion* on the ground, among others, that it passed unchallenged in the Eternal City during such a pontificate as that of Clement VII. A second edition is said to have been printed at Rome in 1606; between 1584 and 1633 it appeared four times at Lyons and once at Mayence. In 1660 it was published for the last time at Rome. Unfortunately for the purposes of this criticism, the examples of 1633 and 1660 have been alone available. The first claims to be *nuperrime mendis omnibus purgatum*, but it has been evidently in the hands of a Grimoire maker, and it appears to have been edited and extended in the Grimoire interest.[1] This is certain, but it is impossible to say how much beyond the *Seven Mysterious Orisons* connected with the name of Pope Leo are to be found in the original, or whether the original was antedated. Outside these Orisons the modern accent of the work is unmistakable, and it is difficult to understand how any instructed person, much less a biblio-phile like M. Christian, could have been deceived by it. It is certain, however, that when he approached the secret sciences, their substitutes and their memorials in literature, he depended more on his imagination than on his knowledge or research.

The work itself, as already said, is simply a collection of religious charms, effectual against all the perils to which every sort and condition of men may be made subject on land, on water, from open and secret enemies, from the bites of wild and rabid beasts, from poisons, from fire, from tempests. While it thus ensures against evil, it gives happiness in domestic matters and in the enterprises which contribute to prosperity and to the pleasures of a contented life. The proviso is that

---

[1] This appears more evidently in the last Roman edition, which pretends to be based on all those which preceded it, including impressions published at Parma, Ancona and Frankfort which are now generally unknown. The editor has, moreover, altered and rearranged, omitted and added at choice. He has supplied also a Key to the whole work, which is a short process for the government of evil spirits.

The Rituals of Transcendental Magic

"the instructions must be followed as accurately as human weakness will allow." Fortunately they are more simple than the Grimoires. When a copy of the book has been secured, it must be placed in a small bag of new leather, so that it may be kept clean. A vow must be made to carry it as far as practicable on one's person, and to read with attentive devotion at least one page daily. If a specific danger be apprehended, a page suitable to its nature should be selected. Reading must be done upon the knees, with the face turned to the east: "so did Charlemagne invariably." Furthermore, works of piety must be performed in honour of the celestial genii whose benign influence it is desired to attract; alms also must be given to the poor, "as this is of all things most pleasing unto such spirits, for thereby we become their coadjutors and friends, the economy of the universe being committed to them by the Creator."

Here we have the magical doctrine concerning planetary intelligences which connects the *Enchiridion* with the *Arbatel*, and the hint of "secondary deities" which connects it with Trithemius.[1]

The *In Principio*, or first chapter of the Gospel according to St. John, is declared to be the most potent of all the devotions in the book, and it is to be recited the most frequently. The mysterious figures are said to have been extracted from the rarest manuscripts which antiquity has committed to us, and their virtue is not only highly efficacious, but so easily put in motion, that it is enough for this purpose to carry the work reverently on one's person. "Experience will remove any doubt which may be felt in this respect, while the scruples which may be occasioned by the idea that there is Magic or

[1] Joannis Tritemii, Abbatis Spanheymensis, *De Septem Secundiis, id est, Intelligentiis, sive Spiritibus, Orbes post Deum Moventibus, &c.* Coloniæ, 1567. The treatise is well known, or at least much talked of, and this is the original edition, belonging to the date claimed for it.

superstition herein will be banished by a slight exercise of reason."

As to this latter point, it is said that a little reflection upon the infinite number of secret sympathies and antipathies found in different beings here below will explain how it is that such figures may be in sympathy with the Celestial Intelligences which govern this vast universe.

It will scarcely be necessary to observe that the doctrine of sympathies and antipathies is the very essence of Natural Magic, and connects it with the recondite branches. The mysterious figures referred to were originally nine in number, and in most cases recur several times. The most conspicuous is the *Labarum* of Constantine and the *Tau* symbol, which Lévi connects with the Tarot.

The apparently unmeaning enumeration of various Divine Names is a special characteristic of Ceremonial Magic, and certainly makes the *Enchiridion* interlink with a cycle of literature from which it is otherwise thinly distinct. There is, indeed, little specific difference between the prayers which incorporate them and the Invocations which swarm in the Rituals. It may be added that the use of such Divine Names is supported by a mendacious reference to the Angelical Theology of Dionysius.

The prefatory matter ends at this point. The prose of the Gospel of St. John follows, with versicles and a prayer. Next come the Seven Penitential Psalms, with the Litany of the Saints, after which are the *Mysterious Prayers of Pope Leo*, followed by a multitude of others not less mysterious, and prevailing against human fragility, and so forth. There are prayers for voyages, prayers addressed to the Cross, and then under the Tau symbol, commencing with the curious exclamation, *Per signum ✠ Domini Tau, libera me*, there follows a long conjuration, as express as anything in Magic, designed to prevent the petitioner from injury by any steel weapons whatsoever. Forming part of this ceremony is the pseudo-epistle addressed by Jesus Christ to King Abgar, explaining why our Saviour could not come Himself to that monarch, and promising to send His disciple Thaddeus when He had fulfilled the work given Him by His Father. It goes on to say that Christ has written it with His own hand, and that wheresoever the recipient shall be, in house or field, by sea or stream, *sive in prælio Paganorum seu Christianorum*—such is the stultification thereof—his enemy shall never prevail over him.[1] The king received the epistle with many tears and prayers, all which being duly described, the conjuration of the *baculi, gladii, lanceæ, enses, cultelli, sagittæ, claves, funes, et omnia alia genera armorum*, is continued.

As it is difficult to say where the original *Enchiridion* actually begins, so it is uncertain where it ends. A variety of miscellaneous prayers are, however, attributed to well-known saints quite outside the Carlovingian period, and to Innocent IV. and John XX., without prejudice to a further orison of the great Pope Leo himself. Then come the "curious secrets"—to conciliate and discover one's proper genius, to become invulnerable, to prevent a gun from going off, to behold a future husband or wife, all effected by means of formal prayers—a kind of royal road to the chief ends of Magic, without apparently exceeding the devotional discipline of the Church.

To complete the analysis of this curious collection, its most important practical part is here added, namely :—

---

[1] For this legend, see Fabricius, *Cod. Apoc. N.T.*, I., p. 317.

§ 4. *The Seven Mysterious Orisons*

SUNDAY

Pater noster, &c. Deliver me, O Lord, I beseech Thee, me even, thy creature, N., from all evils past, present and to come, whether of body or soul; grant me peace and health in Thy goodness; incline favourably unto me, Thy creature, by the intercession of the Blessed Virgin Mary and of Thy holy apostles, Peter, Paul, Andrew and of all the saints. Vouchsafe peace unto Thy creature, and health during all my life, so that, strengthened by the mainstay of Thy mercy, I may never be the slave of sin, nor go in fear of any trouble, through the same Jesus Christ Thy Son, our Saviour, Who, being truly God, liveth and reigneth in the unity of the Holy Spirit for ever and ever, Amen. May the peace of the Lord be always with me, Amen. May that peace, O Lord, which Thou didst leave to Thy disciples abide ever with power in my heart, standing always between me and my enemies, both visible and invisible, Amen. May the peace of the Lord, His countenance, His body, His blood, assist, console and protect me, Thy creature, N., in my soul and my body, Amen. Lamb of God, Who didst deign to be born of the Virgin Mary, Who didst cleanse the world from its sins upon the Cross, have pity on my soul and my body. O Christ, Lamb of God, immolated for the salvation of the world, have pity on my soul and my body. Lamb of God, by Whom all the faithful are saved, give unto me Thy peace, to remain with me for ever, both in this life and that which is to come, Amen.

MONDAY

O great God, by Whom all things have been set free, deliver me also from all evil. O great God, Who hast granted Thy consolation unto all beings, grant it even unto me. O great God, Who hast succoured and assisted all things, aid me also; succour me in all my necessities and miseries, my enterprises and dangers; deliver me from all the hindrances and snares of my enemies, both visible and invisible, in the Name of the Father Who created the whole world ✠, in the Name of the Son Who hath redeemed it ✠, in the name of the Holy Ghost Who hath fulfilled the entire law in its perfection. I cast myself utterly into Thine arms, and place myself unreservedly under Thy holy protection, Amen. May the blessing of God the Father Almighty, of the Son and of the Holy Ghost, be always with me ✠, Amen. May the blessing of God the Father, Who by His only Word hath made all things, be with me for ever ✠, Amen. May the blessing of our Lord Jesus Christ, Son of the great living God, be with me for ever ✠, Amen. May the blessing and Seven Gifts of the Holy Spirit be with me for ever ✠, Amen. May the blessing of the Virgin Mary, and of her Son, be with me for ever, Amen.

TUESDAY

May the blessing and consecration of the bread and of the wine, which our Lord Jesus Christ made when He gave them to His disciples and said unto them: Take and eat ye all of this, for this is My body which shall be delivered for you, in remembrance of Me and for the remission of all sins—be with me for ever ✠. May the blessing of the Holy Angels, Archangels, Virtues, Powers, Thrones, Dominations, Cherubim and Seraphim, be with me for ever ✠, Amen. May the blessing of the patriarchs and prophets, apostles, martyrs, confessors, virgins, and of all the saints of God, be with me for ever ✠, Amen. May the blessing of all the heavens of God be with me for ever ✠, Amen. May the majesty of God Omnipotent sustain and protect me; may His eternal goodness lead me; may His boundless charity *inflame me ; may His supreme Divinity direct me ; may the power of the Father preserve me ; may the wisdom of the Son enliven me ; may the virtue of the Holy Ghost stand always between me and my enemies, both visible and invisible. Power of the Father, strengthen me ; wisdom of the Son, enlighten me ; consolation of the Holy Ghost, comfort me. The Father is peace, the Son is life, the Holy Ghost is the consoling and saving remedy, Amen. May the Divinity of God bless me, Amen. May His piety warm me ; may His love preserve me. O Jesus Christ, Son of the living God, have pity upon me a poor sinner.*

WEDNESDAY

O Emmanuel, defend me against the malignant enemy, and against all my enemies, visible and invisible, and deliver me from all evil. Jesus Christ the King hath come in peace, God made man, Who hath suffered patiently for us. May Jesus Christ, the gentle King, stand always for my defence between me and my enemies, Amen. Jesus Christ triumphs, Jesus Christ reigns, Jesus Christ commands. May Jesus Christ deliver me from all evils for ever, Amen. May Jesus Christ vouchsafe me grace to triumph over all my adversaries, Amen. Behold the Cross of our Lord Jesus Christ. Fly, therefore, O my enemies, at the sight thereof ; the Lion of the Tribe of Juda and of the Race of David hath conquered. Alleluia, Alleluia, Alleluia. Saviour of the world, save and succour me. Thou who hast purchased me by Thy Cross and Thy Blood, succour me, I conjure Thee, my God. O Agios, O Theos, Agios, Ischyros, Agios, Athanatos, Elieson, Himas, Holy God, Strong God, Merciful and Immortal God, have pity upon me Thy creature, N. Sustain me, O Lord; forsake me not, reject not my prayers, O Thou, the God of my salvation. Do Thou assist me always, O God of my salvation.

PLATE III

MYSTIC FIGURES OF THE ENCHIRIDION

49   D

THURSDAY

Enlighten mine eyes with true light, that they may never be closed in eternal sleep, lest mine enemy should say : I have prevailed over him. So long as the Lord is with me, I will not fear for malice of my enemies. O most sweet Jesus, preserve me, aid me, save me ; at the Name of Jesus let every knee bow, in heaven, on earth and in hell, and let every tongue confess openly that Jesus Christ is in the glory of His Father, Amen. I know beyond doubt that in what day soever I shall call upon the Lord, in the same hour shall I be saved. O most sweet Lord Jesus Christ, Son of the great living God, Thou hast performed most mighty miracles by the sole power of Thy most precious Name, and hast enriched the poor most abundantly, so that by force thereof the demons flee away, the blind see, the deaf hear, the lame walk erect, the dumb speak, the lepers are cleansed, the sick cured, the dead raised up ; for wheresoever the most sweet Name of Jesus is pronounced, the ear is ravished and the mouth is filled with pleasant savour ; at that one utterance, I repeat, the demons take flight, every knee is bent, all temptations, even the worst, are scattered, all infirmities are healed, all disputes and conflicts between the world, the flesh and the devil are ended, and the soul is filled with every heavenly delight ; for whosoever invoketh or shall invoke this Holy Name of God is and shall be saved—even by this Holy Name, pronounced by the angel even before His conception in the womb of the Holy Virgin.

FRIDAY

O sacred Name, Name which strengthens the heart of man, Name of life, of salvation, of joy, precious Name, resplendent, glorious, agreeable Name, which fortifies the sinner, Name

The Book of Ceremonial Magic

which saves, conserves, leads and rules all. May it please Thee, therefore, most precious Jesus, by the power of this same (Name of) Jesus, to drive away the demon from me; enlighten me, O Lord, for I am blind; remove my deafness; set me upright, who am lame; give me speech, who am dumb; cleanse my leprosy; restore me to health, who am sick; raise me up, for I am dead; give me life once more, and enrich me in all my parts, within and without, so that, furnished and fortified by Thy Holy Name, I may abide always in Thee, praising and honouring Thee, because all is due to Thee, and Thou only art worthy to be glorified, the Lord and Eternal Son of God, in Whom all things rejoice, and by Whom all are governed. Praise, honour and glory, be given Thee for ever and ever, Amen. May Jesus be always in my heart and in my breast, Amen. May our Lord Jesus Christ be ever within me, may He establish me for ever, may He be around me and preserve me; may He be before me and lead me; may He be behind me and guard me; may He be above me and bless me; may He be within me and give me life; may He be near me and rule me; may He be beneath me and fortify me; may He be always with me and deliver me from all the pains of eternal death, Who liveth and reigneth for ever and ever, Amen.

SATURDAY

Jesus, Son of Mary, salvation of the world, may the Lord look favourably upon me, with mildness and propitiation; may He give me a holy and willing spirit, to respect and honour Him only, Who is the Liberator of the World. On Him could no one lay hand, for His hour was not yet come—He Who is, Who was, Who shall remain, God and man, the beginning and the end. May this prayer which I offer unto Him deliver me eternally from my enemies, Amen. Jesus of Nazareth, King

52

of the Jews, honourable title, Son of the Virgin Mary, have pity upon me, a poor sinner, and lead me, according to Thy loving-kindness, in the way of eternal salvation, Amen. Now Jesus, knowing what things must come to pass concerning Him, came forward and said unto them: Whom seek ye? They answered Him: Jesus of Nazareth. But Jesus said unto them: I am He. And Judas, who was to deliver Him, was with them. As soon then as He had said unto them: I am He, they fell backward upon the earth. Then asked He them again: Whom seek ye? And they said: Jesus of Nazareth. Jesus answered: I have told you that I am He; if therefore ye seek Me, let these go their way (speaking of His disciples). The lance, the nails, the cross ✠, the thorns, the death which I have endured, prove that I have effaced and expiated the crimes of the unfortunate. Preserve me, O Lord Jesus Christ, from all afflictions of poverty and from the snares of my enemies. May the five wounds of our Lord be unto me an everlasting remedy. Jesus is the Way ✠, Jesus is the Life ✠, Jesus is the Truth ✠, Jesus has suffered ✠, Jesus has been crucified ✠, Jesus, Son of the living God, have pity on me ✠. Now, Jesus passing went through the midst of them, and no one could place his murderous hand upon Jesus, because His hour was not yet come.

While these prayers are in some respects curious enough, and may not be unreasonably termed pure and simple by their intention, they compare unfavourably with the sublimity and good sense which characterise those of the Roman Liturgy; they are inexact in their references and confused in their method, and no person who seriously considers them will sustain the early date which is claimed for them. Their period is subsequent to the Renaissance, and the ignorance of liturgical formulæ which they shew, in common with all similar forgeries, makes it doubtful whether they are the work of an ecclesiastic at all. In any case, they are clumsy imitations, the product of an unskilful hand.

§ 5. *Summary of Transcendental Magic*

This concludes our examination of the Rituals of so-called Transcendental Magic, comprising all those to which any currency has been given. There are no doubt other treatises which exist only in manuscript and possess no literary history, but they scarcely come within the scope of the present inquiry. I do not believe that anything has remained in obscurity which is more entitled to come into notice than those which have been mentioned briefly in the first chapter. But if I am wrong it signifies nothing, for there has been enough and to spare already.

The general conclusion which must follow from the examination is naturally of a foregone kind. As premised at the outset, the Rituals with which we have been dealing are not worthy of the name Transcendental, nor does it belong to them. We have, on the one hand, a collection of prayers, falsely attributed and modern in their origin, to which no occult significance can be reasonably attached. Devotionally, they are innocent enough; applied after the manner of a charm, they are offices of vain observance. On the other hand, we have a bald rite for the Invocation of Olympic Spirits, which, despite the grandiloquent claims of the unknown author, is rather childish than exalted, for it may be assumed that no person is naïve enough at the present day to take the angelical offices literally, and to believe, for example, that by the evocation of *Aratron* the contents of his coal-cellar will be transformed into real treasures. Transcendental Magic is, therefore, hyperbolical in its promises, while these from the

PLATE IV

MYSTIC FIGURES OF THE ENCHIRIDION

mystical standpoint would be frivolous if they could be construed literally. The occult student will derive no light from such processes, but the subject is at the same time a very curious and fantastic branch of bibliographical research, in which I have been able, moreover, to clear up some doubtful points, and in this sense it has been worth prosecuting. The conclusion, then, in respect of the Rituals of Transcendental Magic is that there are no Transcendental Rituals, and that the truth is not in them.

FROM ST. GEORGE *v.* THE DRAGON. FLEMISH
SCHOOL, LATE FIFTEENTH CENTURY

CHAPTER III

Composite Rituals

§ 1. *The Key of Solomon the King*

BY far the most important class of Magical Rituals is that which incorporates elements both of Black and White procedure—so called. For convenience of treatment these are here termed composite. At the head of all, and, within certain limits, the inspiration and the source of all, stands the *Key of Solomon*, with its complement, in many respects more important than itself, the *Lemegeton, or Lesser Key*, sometimes attributed to Solomon Rabbi ; the Rabbi and the monarch are, however, one and the same—at least in respect of their office, which is the pseudonymous production of impostures. The other Rituals which will be treated in this class are the so-called *Fourth Book* of Cornelius Agrippa and the *Magical Elements* ascribed to Peter of Abano. The occult student—who is commonly led by fools, when not by impostors—has been taught to regard these works as dealing exclusively with White Magic, and it is part of the present design to indicate for the first time the mixed character of their proceedings, even on the surface thereof. The innumerable Rituals of Magic which remain in MS. and are never likely to be printed, belong also, with few exceptions, to the composite class, but, setting the *Lemegeton* aside, to which every prominence should be given, they have had little influence, and being, therefore, of no moment to the history of the occult sciences, will not demand further consideration than has already been accorded some of them in the slight sketch at the close of the first chapter.

Mr. Mathers' presentation of the *Key of Solomon*,[1] which is still in print, though the work of an uncritical hand, must be held to remove the necessity for entering into a detailed account of the contents of that curious work. So far as it has been incorporated by the later makers of Grimoires, it will be found, with its Goëtic variations, in the Second Part. We have here only to consider the question of its antiquity and to establish its true character.

The *Key of Solomon* proper is familiar to scholars in Latin, French, Italian and one or two German MSS. The oldest codex used by the English editor is in contracted Latin, and belongs to the sixteenth century. It is preserved in the British Museum. It is possible that older MSS. may exist in Continental libraries, but those of the Bibliothèque Nationale and of the Arsénal at Paris are of later date.[2] The majority of known MSS. are in the French language. It is, however, claimed that the work was written originally in Hebrew. In this claim there is nothing essentially improbable, but it has the disadvantage of being championed by the last class of persons who hold titles for the expression of an opinion. Assuming that it is well founded, it is not unlikely that the original may

[1] "The Key of Solomon the King (*Clavicula Salomonis*), now first translated and edited from ancient MSS. in the British Museum." By S. Liddell Macgregor Mathers. With plates. George Redway. 1889. It has been reprinted of recent years.

[2] As regards the Arsénal, they are all of the eighteenth century. *Les Clavicules de Rabbi Salomon*, 2346 (72 S.A.F.), claims to be literally translated from the Hebrew text into French. 2348 (75 S.A.F.) is entitled *Livre de la Clavicule de Salomon, Roy des Hébreux*; it is said to have been translated from the Hebrew into Italian by Abraham Colorno, and thence into French. 2349 (77 S.A.F.) reads, *Les Vraies Clavicules du Roy Salomon*, traduitte (*sic*) de l'Hébreux par Armadel. 2350 (78 S.A.F.) is entitled *Le Secret des Secrets, autrement La Clavicule de Salomon, ou le véritable Grimoire*. Finally, there is the *Livre Second de la Clavicule de Salomon*, 2791 (76 S.A.F.).

still exist. The large Hebrew literature of the Middle Ages has been only imperfectly explored, especially in that part which connects with practical Magic. The knavish methods which have ruled in the manufacture of most magical books largely discount the probability with which I am dealing, and the mere affirmation in a manuscript cannot, under these circumstances, be regarded as evidence. No Hebrew scholar is acquainted at the present day with such an original, and three hundred years back the matter, according to P. Christian, was involved in precisely the same uncertainty, for at the end of the sixteenth century the learned Jesuit, Gretser, states that it was unknown, but that there was a Greek translation in the library of the Duke of Bavaria. The present whereabouts of this highly important MS. I have failed to trace, though I must not presume that I have taken especial pains concerning it. In a literature of this class, whether that is best which lies the nearest or not, it is serviceable enough for the practical purpose. I do not propose to be the historian of Magic, whether Black or White, or the classifier of its MSS. All occultism is part of the path of descent, and that which is especially Black may be in one sense the least harmful, as we know where we are in its presence. I will therefore only add in termination of this question that in the eighteenth century the Abbé d'Artigny mentions various examples of the *Key of Solomon* in Latin, and also an edition printed in 1655, which is not only unknown to Mr. Mathers, but seemingly to all modern bibliographers.[1]

[1] Christian's reference is, however, a mere travesty of some information found in the *Nouveaux Mémoires d'Histoire, de Critique, et de Littérature*, par M. l'Abbé d'Artigny, 7 vols., Paris, 1749-1756. The fourth article in the first volume is entitled, " Concerning some pretended Books of Magic, with an Extract from the Clavicles of Solomon." It enumerates three works which, under this title, were current at the time in the French language, and a fourth in Latin, *Clavicula Salomonis ad Filium Roboam*. A *Liber Pentaculorum* is also mentioned, in a way which leaves it to be inferred that it is the *Key of Solomon* under another title, but it

Composite Rituals

Leaving the language of the original an open question, it is clear that, in either case, there is no ground for attributing to the *Key of Solomon* in its present form a higher antiquity than the fourteenth or fifteenth century, at which time Hebrew literature was developing at a rapid rate.[1] If it were first written in Latin, it is, at any rate, permeated with late Jewish ideas, and the corrupt state of the Hebrew in the conjurations and talismans—which is much the same, and that as bad as it can be, in all existing copies—could scarcely have been attained in less than two centuries of careless and ignorant transcription. We may therefore fix the date of its manufacture, or otherwise of its translation, about the period which has been mentioned.

The attribution of the work to Solomon is obvious enough; it could not fail to have suggested itself to a compiler with Kabalistic leanings and with a knowledge of Jewish tradition from the days of the Talmud onward. Further, it is quite

is probably the Latin version of the *Sepher Raziel*. Whether any of these works were printed does not explicitly appear, and the Abbé, like Christian himself, knew very little of his subject. It is he, however, who supplies the information concerning Gretser, but it reads very differently. "Perhaps this (*Liber Pentaculorum*) is the same as the treatise *De Necromantia ad Filium Roboam*, which Father Gretser, a learned German Jesuit, had seen written in Greek in the library of the Duke of Bavaria." The collected works of Gretser are in seventeen folio volumes, and there are limits to research. It may be affirmed, however, that the *Catalogus Codicum Munuscriptorum Bibliothecæ Regiæ Bavariæ, auctore Ignatio Hardt, ejusdem bibliothecæ subpræfecto*, 5 vols., Monarchii, 1806, does not mention such a work. The reference to the printed edition of the Clavicle occurs at pp. 36, 37 of D'Artigny's article, and describes it as consisting of 125 pp. in quarto, without name of place or printer. The frontispiece (? title) reads "Clavicle of Solomon," with a cross within a circle beneath, and below this symbol is the date 1655. The whole work is divided into twelve paragraphs, of which D'Artigny transcribes part of No. 9, an Exorcism of the Spirits of the Air, which most certainly does not occur in any known edition of the *Grand Clavicle*, and is apparently adapted from the *Lemegeton*.

[1] A bibliography of Papus appended to his *Methodical Summary of the Kabalah* enumerates forty-seven separate Kabalistic treatises which appeared in Hebrew between the middle of the thirteenth and the close of the sixteenth century. These are only the most noted, and extra-Kabalistic literature was far larger. I mention this source of reference for the benefit of the occult student, as it may be ready to his hand. The *Magna Bibliotheca Rabbinica* of Bartolocci, forming—with its supplement by another hand—five volumes in folio, is the great and monumental catalogue of literature in Jewry.

consistent with a literature which has done nothing but ascribe falsely. That it should be taken seriously by any well-equipped person at the present day must, of course, be quite inscrutable, and in respect of the English editor, those who feel concerned in the question may account for it in one of two ways :—by a predisposition to accept statements on the faith of occult tradition following upon a conviction as to the reality of occult science ; or, alternatively, by a knowledge derived from the traditions of initiation. The first is regrettable because it is open to abuse, which is stating the case in terms of unstrained mercy ; the second is not likely to exist, because it is injurious to the intelligence of the King of Israel to suppose that he wrote the Clavicle. I do not feel clear, however, that it would be beneath certain storehouses of occult tradition to ratify the ascription or to make archives to support it. In sum, it would be quite in accordance with the mind of occult initiation to transmit a false tradition or to manufacture it.

So far concerning the antiquity of the work and the sovereign mystification of its authorship. It remains now to say something of its character. The *Key of Solomon* can scarcely be judged accurately in the light of its English version, for the translator, preternaturally regarding it as a highly honourable memorial of lawful magic, has excised as much as possible the Goëtic portions, on the ground that they are later interpolations, which is of course arbitrary. He still retains, however, what is generally stigmatised as one of the distinctive marks of Black Magic ; the ritual is permeated with the bloody sacrifice, which Mr. Mathers rightly condemns, but has not seen his way to reject. His version further includes various references to the performance of works of hatred and destruction—that is, works betraying an evil purpose, or a purpose directly connecting with Black Magic. The chapter detailing

Composite Rituals

the method of effecting such objects is omitted, but it is found in five out of the seven codices upon which the version is based. Furthermore, where the intention is not evil, it is frivolous, hyperbolical or paramountly foolish. It is (*a.*) frivolous in such experiments as the detection of stolen goods, by which it is placed on the same level as the pedlar's literature of fortune-telling; it is (*b.*) hyperbolical and fantastic in the experiment of invisibility, in the composition of the Magic Garters and the Magic Staff; it is (*c.*) foolish in such chapters as that on preventing a sportsman from killing any game. Perhaps, however, these distinctions may be held to merge into one another. M. Papus, the mouthpiece of the French occultists, distinguishes between the Keys of Solomon and the impostures of *colportage;* but in what respect, it may be asked, are these processes superior to the chapbooks of *colporteurs?*

The highest ambition of the Clavicles is identical with that of the Grimoires—to become master of a treasure possessed by spirits. It should also be observed that experiments which have for their object an interference with the freewill of another person, such as that of seeking favour and love, are essentially evil experiments.

I have now enumerated all the processes which are set forth in this "fountainhead and storehouse of Kabalistical Magic"; it is for such trumpery purposes that the Magus is directed to undertake his laborious preparation, and for such also to put in motion the powers believed to be inherent in Divine Names, in long pages of pretentious prayers and in "stronger and more powerful" conjurations. However much the justice of the critic may be tempered by the mercy of the familiar explorer towards a memorial of occult science which has been unduly honoured—that is, honoured otherwise than as a literary curiosity—it must be concluded that the

63

Key of Solomon is a grotesque combination of the pompous and ridiculous; it is, in fact, the old story of the mountain and the mouse, but so great is the travail that, in this case, the mouse is brought forth dead.

§ 2. *The Lesser Key of Solomon*

The *Lemegeton, or Lesser Key of Solomon*, Rabbi and King, is a work of far more exalted pretensions, which deploys all the hierarchies and evokes spirits by milliards. About its antiquity there is no need for serious dispute; it claims to be translated from the Hebrew, but its earliest perfect examples are in French of the seventeenth century, and no one has heard of the original. It must have existed, however, in a much earlier form; it is the subject of continual reference by demonologists like Wierus, under the style of the sorcerer's *Liber Spirituum*, and it is from this source that the scornful sceptic who was the pupil of Agrippa, derived his *Pseudo-monarchia Dæmonum*, with, however, significant variations from the known copies.

The *Lemegeton* is divided into four parts, which control the offices of all spirits at the will of the operator, from whom the ordinary conditions are exacted.[1] With the exception of the first part, which gave materials to Wierus, this curious, and in many respects memorable, work has never been printed, although it has been taxed surreptitiously for contributions by most makers of Rituals and Grimoires. It deals, as I have said, with the evocation of all classes of spirits, evil, indifferent and good; its opening Rites are those of Lucifer, Bel, Astaroth and the whole cohort of Infernus; it is entitled *Goëtia*, which sufficiently explains itself,[2] and contains the forms of conjuration

---

[1] See Part ii. c. 1 of the present work.
[2] It is the Greek word γοητεία, *i.e.* Witchcraft.

for seventy-two chief devils and their ministers, with an account of their powers and offices. The second part, or *Theurgia Goëtia*, deals with the spirits of the cardinal points and their inferiors. These are mixed natures, some good and some evil. The third book is called the *Pauline Art*, for the significance of which name I am unable to account. It concerns the Angels of the Hours of the Day and Night and of the Zodiacal Signs. The fourth part, or *Almadel*, enumerates four other choirs of spirits in a somewhat obscure manner. There is one significant point about the entire work —the powers resident in the offices of Infernal Spirits are minutely set forth, but the Ritual is almost silent as to the special benefits which may be expected from intercourse with the higher classes of intelligence ; it is, therefore, obvious to whom the magician would have recourse if he had a definite end in view. It is, indeed, by no means improbable that the first or Goëtic portion constitutes the true *Lemegeton*, and that the other sections, apparently unknown to Wierus, are additions of a later date. This division, in either case, is not only expressly connected with Black Magic, or rather exclusively devoted thereto, but it indubitably divides with the so-called Greater Key the forbidding honour of having been the chief inspiration of all the later handbooks of infernal ceremonial. Devoid of any doctrinal part, it has nothing which calls for citation in this place, but as no Grimoire can pretend to completeness without it, all its hierarchic tabulations and all its evoking processes will be given in the Second Part.

I should state in conclusion that the *Little Key* is ascribed sometimes to Solomon the King and sometimes to a Rabbi of that name. It should be distinguished, however, from the *Key of Rabbi Solomon* proper, which is more especially concerned with the composition, consecration and use of planetary talismans. It pretends to deal only with "good Genies," but it includes the blood sacrifice, and there is the usual anxiety in respect of the form and aspect in which the intelligence may appear. It is, however, especially provided that no seal, pentacle or character shall be applied to the injury of another, and more especially a student of the art. The art, in fine, does not involve any compact, "implicit or explicit." I suppose that this production is later than others of the cycle.

§ 3. *The Pauline Art*

If the intimation of the last section be accepted as a working hypothesis in respect of the *Lemegeton*, and if its third and fourth books be therefore set apart as accretions, there is possibly some colourable pretence for placing *The Pauline Art* among composite Rituals. It is very difficult to speak certainly, as what is offered in the work is the Ritual for the Invocation of the Angels of Day and Night, the Angels of the Twelve Signs and those of the Zodiacal degrees, who are termed Angels of Men. There is, however, no distinct account either of their offices or qualities, except in the case of the last, as to whom it appears that their intervention can be sought only for purposes which are in consonance with the laws of God and the good of mankind generally. It is an arid document largely consisting of name catalogues, but as for this reason it is possible to present it shortly, and as it counts for something in the literature, I shall give it in the following form.

Hours of the Day

The Ruler of the First Hour is SAMAEL, who has 444 serving spirits under eight leaders, namely : *Arniniel, Charpon, Daresiel, Monasiel, Brumiel, Nestoriel, Charmeas, Meresijn.*

Composite Rituals

The Ruler of the Second Hour is ANAEL, who has under his control ten chief and one hundred lesser lords. These in their turn command serving spirits. The chiefs include *Monarchas, Archiel* and *Chardiel;* the subalterns include *Orphiel, Carsiol, Elmoym, Quosiel, Ermosiel, Graniel.*

The Ruler of the Third Hour is VEGUANIEL, under whom are twenty chief officers, two hundred lesser officers and a cloud of serving spirits. The chief officers include *Murriel, Leosiel, Drelmeth, Sardiniel;* among the lesser officers are *Parmiel, Comadiel, Glmarij, Hantiel, Serviel, Furiel.*

The Ruler of the Fourth Hour is VACHMIEL, who has ten chief and one hundred inferior officers, having many serving spirits. The chiefs include *Ammiel, Larmiel, Marfiel, Ormijel, Sardiel,* and the inferiors *Emarfiel, Permiel, Quoriel, Sturbiel, Daniel.*

The Ruler of the Fifth Hour is SAZQUIEL, having ten chief and one hundred lesser officers, each with attendants. The chiefs include *Damiel, Armarele, Maroch, Serapiel, Fustiel,* and the inferiors *Jamersil, Futiniel, Ramisiel, Amisiel, Pubrisiel.*

The Ruler of the Sixth Hour is SAMIL, who has ten chief and one hundred lesser officers, with a vast concourse of serving spirits. Among the chiefs are *Araebel, Charuch, Medussusiel, Nathaniel, Perniel,* and among the subordinates *Jamiel, Joustriel, Sameon, Farsiel, Zamion.*

The Ruler of the Seventh Hour is BARGINIEL, having also ten officers and one hundred subalterns, among whom are *Abrasiel, Farmos, Nosteri, Mamiel, Sagiel,* for the chief, and *Harmiel, Nastoro, Varmaj, Tusmas, Crociel,* as inferior examples.

The Ruler of the Eighth Hour is OSGAEBIAL, who has many chief and subordinate officers and a great cloud of serving spirits. Among the chiefs are *Sarfiel*, *Amatino*, *Choriel*, *Mosiel*, *Lanthros*, and among the subalterns *Demaros*, *Osmajloel*, *Januviel*, *Vernael*, *Thribiel*.

The Ruler of the Ninth Hour is VADRIEL, having ten chief and one hundred lesser officers and serving spirits even as the sands of the sea. The greater include *Astroniel*, *Charms*, *Pamerif*, *Damiel*, *Madriel;* among the lesser are *Kremos*, *Meros*, *Brasiel*, *Nafarin*, *Zoigmiel*.

The Ruler of the Tenth Hour is ORIEL, who has ten cohorts of officers presiding over many serving spirits. These orders include *Armesi*, *Darbiel*, *Panales*, *Mesriel*, *Chorob*, *Lemure*, *Ormas*, *Charnij*, *Zazior*, *Namon*—being one of each choir.

The Ruler of the Eleventh Hour is BARIEL, whose army is similarly divided, and as typical specimens of the ten orders there are *Almariz*, *Pralimiel*, *Chardros*, *Furmiel*, *Lamie*, *Menafiel*, *Demasar*, *Ormary*, *Hevas*, *Zemoel*.

The Ruler of the Twelfth Hour is BERATIEL, whose officers are divided into twelve orders, some greater and some lesser, the examples of each being—in the first class, *Cameron*, *Altrofiel*, *Penatiel*, *Demarae*, *Famaris ;* and in the second, *Pharniel*, *Nerostiel*, *Emarson*, *Voizia*, *Sameron*.

HOURS OF THE NIGHT

The *Negotia perambulantia in tenebris* are more numerous than those of the daylight. They are divided under their respective Supreme Rulers into six chief and six secondary orders, and the serving spirits are proportionately great in number.

The First Hour. Supreme Ruler—GAMIEL. The chief officers include *Moriel*, *Garthiel*, *Sepharon*, *Mousien*, *Arathiel*,

Composite Rituals

Cosel. Lesser officers: *Zanias, Noxin, Tempast, Farion, Glaras, Belsal.*

The Second Hour. Supreme Ruler—FARRIS. The chief officers include *Almodar, Tamarid, Nedros, Ormisiel, Chabril, Praxil.* Lesser officers: *Permaz, Umeroz, Emaril, Fromezin, Ramasiel, Granozin.*

The Third Hour. Supreme Ruler—SARQUAMICH. The chief officers include *Meriarijm, Crusiel, Penarys, Amriel, Dencinoz, Nestozoz.* Lesser officers: *Evanel, Sarmezin, Haglon, Uvabriel, Thymitzod, Fromzon.*

The Fourth Hour. Supreme Ruler—JEFISCHA. The chief officers include *Armesiel, Nedruel, Maneij, Ormael, Phorsiel, Rimezin.* Lesser officers: *Rayziel, Gemezin, Fremiel, Hamayzod, Japnoill, Lamediel.*

The Fifth Hour. Supreme Ruler—ABASDARHON. The chief officers include *Moniel, Charby, Apiniel, Dematron, Nechoxim, Hameriel.* Lesser officers: *Harptzall, Chrymos, Patrozin, Nameton, Barmas, Phatiel.*

The Sixth Hour. Supreme Ruler—ZAAZONASH. The chief officers include *Menorita, Prenostix, Namedor, Cheratiel, Dramazod, Fuleriel.* Lesser officers: *Pammon, Dracon, Gemtzod, Enariel, Rudosor, Salmon.*

The Seventh Hour. Supreme Ruler—MENDRION. The chief officers include *Ammiel, Choriel, Genaritzod, Pendroz, Memsiel, Ventariel.* Lesser officers: *Zacharel, Razziel, Tarmitzod, Anapion, Framoch, Machmay.*

The Eighth Hour. Supreme Ruler—NARCORIEL. The chief officers: *Cambill, Nedarijin, Astrocon, Marifiel, Dramozin, Amelzom.* Lesser officers: *Hanoziz, Gastrion, Thomax, Hebrazym, Zimeloz, Gamsiel.*

The Ninth Hour. Supreme Ruler—NACORIEL. The chief officers, not subdivided: *Adrapen, Chermes, Fenadros, Vema-*

siel, Comary, Demanor, Nameal, Maliel, Hanozoz, Brandiel, Evandiel, Iamariel.

The Tenth Hour : JUSGUARIN. The chief officers ten, including *Lapheriel, Emerziel, Mameroijud.* Lesser officers one hundred, including *Chameray, Hazamil, Vraniel.*

The Eleventh Hour : DARDARIEL. The great officers include *Cardiel, Permon, Armiel, Hastoriel, Casmiros, Dumariel, Tumoriel.* Lesser officers: *Hermas, Druchas, Charman, Elamiz, Ialcoajul, Lamersij, Hamarytzod.*

The Twelfth Hour : SARINDIEL. The chief officers include *Adoniel, Darmosiel, Ambriel,* and the lesser officers *Nefrias, Irmanotzod, Melanos.* There are others cited, but the list is confused in my example and these will serve all purposes of enumeration.

The Angels of the Twelve Signs—classing the latter according to the elementary triplicities—are : *Fiery Triplicity :* Aries—Angel = *Aiel; Leo*—Angel = *Ol;* Sagittarius—Angel = *Sizajasel. Airy Triplicity :* Gemini—Angel = *Giel;* Libra— Angel = *Jael;* Aquarius—Angel = *Ausiul. Watery Triplicity :* Cancer — Angel = *Cael ; Scorpio* — Angel = *Sosol ;* Pisces — Angel = *Pasiel. Earthy Triplicity :* Taurus—Angel = *Tual;* Virgo—Angel = *Voil;* Capricornus—Angel = *Casujoiah.*

But the supreme zodiacal presidency is allocated to the archangels as follows : for the Fiery Triplicity, Michael; for the Airy Triplicity, Raphael; for the Watery Triplicity, Gabriel; for the Earthy Triplicity, Uriel. This follows all the traditional precedents. It is impossible to cite here the so-called angels or genii of men who govern the zodiacal degrees to the number of 360. They are exemplified by the ruling archangels, whose invocation does not seem to be possible, and by the spirits attendant on these, as, for example : *Asajel, Sochiel and Cassiel,* of the Earthy Triplicity ; *Samael,*

Madiel and *Mael*, of the Watery Triplicity; and so forth. These will suffer citation, but the success of the Pauline experiments generally will depend (*a.*) upon the construction of the seals attributed to the twenty-four ruling hours of the day and night, which seals must exhibit the proper astrological signs referable to the day and hour of each intelligence; (*b.*) upon the use, when invocation takes place, of the proper planetary perfumes; (*c.*) upon the astrological seals referable to the chief intelligences of the Twelve Signs under the presidency of the four great archangels; (*d.*) upon a consecrated crystal into which the zodiacal spirits must be called by the operator; and (*e.*) upon the ceremonial use of the invoking formulæ, specimens of which are as follows.

HOURS OF THE DAY AND NIGHT
Invocation of a Supreme Ruler

O mighty and potent prince Samael, who art the ruler and governor of the first hour of the day by the decree of the Most High God, King of Glory; I, the servant of the Most High, do desire and entreat you by three great and potent names of God, ADONAI, AGLAON, TETRAGRAMMATON, *and by the power and virtue thereof, to assist me in my affairs, and by your power and authority to send me, causing to appear before me, all or any of the angels whom I shall call by name, the same being resident under your government. I do further entreat and require that they shall help in all matters which accord with their office, even as I shall desire, and that they shall act for me as for the servant of the Most High. Amen.*

THE INVOCATION OF A GENIUS IN THE CRYSTAL

The ceremony is performed facing towards that quarter of heaven in which the sign is situated.

PRAYER

O thou great and blessed angel N., my angel guardian, vouchsafe to descend from thy holy mansions bringing thy holy influence and presence into this crystal stone, that I may behold thy glory and enjoy thy society and aid, both now and evermore. O thou that art higher than the fourth heaven, thou who knowest the secrets of ELANEL, *thou who ridest on the wings of the wind and art endowed with superlunary motion; do thou descend and be present, I pray thee. If ever I have merited thy society, if my intentions are pure in thy sight, bring hither thine eternal presence; deign to hold commune with me, in the name of the Great God* JEHOVAH, *to Whom the whole choir of heaven continually sings :* O MAPPA LA MAN, *Hallelujah. Amen.*

By the proper observation of the rules laid down in the Pauline Art respecting the Angels of Men, and on the assumption that he is acquainted with the actual minute of his birth, it is said that the operator may attain to all arts and sciences, even to the sum of wisdom. In a word, it is the royal road of knowledge, both in the theoretical and the practical degrees.

Of such is Astronomical Magic, according to the *Lemegeton* and its dependencies. It does not differ essentially from the system of the Enochian Tablets followed by John Dee and Edward Kelley, his skryer, as found in the *Faithful Relation.* The same observation will apply to the content of the next section, which may be permitted to follow without further preface.

§ 4. *The Almadel*

I shall explain in the first place that this scheme of invocation derives its title from the conventional talisman on which the process depends.   It is made of white wax, and is inscribed as hereinafter appears.

This figure is used for the four chief angels whose government extends over the four altitudes of the world, namely, East, West, North and South.   It serves also for their ministers

and inferiors.   As, however, a different colour is attributed to the choir of each quarter, and as this colour must dye the white wax, it follows that those who would traffic with the entire hierarchy must compose four *Almadels*.   Their labour, moreover, will not end here, for each talisman must have four candles made from the same wax and set apart thereto. Finally, there must be provided a seal of gold or silver, on which must be engraved the names HELION, HELLUJON, ADONAI.   It serves for all the choirs.   The candles are provided with waxen feet, and the Almadel rests thereon, being a four-square figure measuring six inches every way. The colour for the Eastern choir is lily white; the others are red, green, and apparently a darkling green which approaches black, but only the first choir is allocated to its distinct quarter of the heaven. The names of the Intelligences are as follows:—

FIRST ALTITUDE: *Alimiel, Gabriel, Borachiel, Lebes, Hellison.* They make all things fruitful in creation.

SECOND ALTITUDE: *Alphariza, Genon, Geron, Armon, Gereinon.* They have power over goods and riches, and can make any man rich or poor. They also cause decrease and barrenness.

THIRD ALTITUDE: *Eliphamasai, Gelomiros, Gedobonai, Saranana, Elomnia.* Their offices are not stated.

FOURTH ALTITUDE: *Barchiel, Gediel, Gebiel, Deliel, Captiel.* In this case also the offices are not stated.

When an Angel of the First Altitude responds to invocation, he carries a banner emblazoned with a white cross, his body is clothed about with a luminous cloud, and he is crowned with roses. He is fair of face, and at his departure leaves a sweet perfume. An Angel of the Second Altitude has the form of a young child in rose-coloured satin, with a crown of red gillyflowers on his head. His face looks towards heaven, and shines with the light of the sun. The perfume which he leaves endures for a long time. An Angel of the Third Altitude appears in the form of a child or little woman in green and silver colours, wearing a crown of bay leaves beset with white flowers. This apparition also leaves sweet perfume. An Angel of the Fourth Altitude appears in the form of a boy or little man, in black or olive garments, crowned with ivy berries. His perfume differs from the rest, but is not less sweet: all the manifestations are beautiful, and, as it is said that they must not be called for anything against God and His laws, it is only the too certain company in which the *Almadel* appears that renders its operations doubtful—I mean, in respect of their intention.

Invocation takes place on a Sunday in the day and hour of the sun. The candles are placed in the candlesticks; the *Almadel* rests—as we have seen—on the projecting feet of the candles, but so that there is a clear space beneath it. There is a hole in each corner, and when the intelligence is about to manifest, an earthen vessel is placed under the talisman containing hot ashes and three grains of mastic in powder. The smoke generated passes through the holes, and when it is smelt by the Angel it is said that he begins to speak.

I should explain, however, that the furniture of the oratory and the vestments worn by the operator must be of the same colour as the *Almadel*. The candles are lighted at the inception, the golden seal is placed in the middle of the talisman, and the Invocant kneels down, holding the Prayer at Calling, which must be written on virgin parchment. The apparition manifests over the *Almadel*, at first in the form of a mist. This clears gradually, and when the incense rises the face of the Angel is turned towards the operator, who is asked in a low voice why the Princes of the particular Choir or Altitude have been thus called. The answer is: "I desire that all my requests may be granted and that which I pray for accomplished, for it appears and is declared by your office that the same is possible to you, if it please God." The particulars are enumerated without fear and without disrespect.

It would seem on the surface of the text as if no preliminary invocation were needed for this work, but that is the confusion of the Ritual which relegates it to the end and to a distinct part of the process.

THE PRAYER AT CALLING

Thou great, mighty and blessed angel of God N., who rulest as the chief and first governing Angel in the first choir or altitude in the East, under the great Prince of the East whom you obey, who also is set over you as King by the Divine Power of God, ADONAI, HELOMI, PINE, *Who is the disposer of all things in heaven, earth and hell : I, the servant of that God,* ADONAI, HELOMI, PINE, *Whom you obey, do invoke, conjure and entreat thee, N., that thou wilt appear forthwith. By the virtue and power of the same God I do command thee from thine order or place of abode to come unto me and shew thyself plainly here before me in thine own proper shape and glory, speaking in a voice intelligible to mine understanding. O thou mighty and blessed Angel N., I, the servant of the same thy God, do entreat and humbly beseech thee to come and shew unto me all things that I shall desire of thee, subject to the power of thine office and the good pleasure of the Lord our God. By the three names of the true God,* ADONAI, HELOMI, PINE, *and by the name* ANA BONA, *I beseech and constrain thee forthwith to appear visibly in thy proper shape, speaking in my ears audibly, that I may have thy blessed, angelical and glorious assistance, familiar friendship, constant society, communication and instruction, now and at all times, herein and in all truths which the Almighty God, King of Kings, Giver of all good gifts, shall be graciously pleased to bestow on me. Therefore, O thou blessed Angel N., be friendly unto me, do for me as God hath empowered thee, whereunto I now adjure thee to appear in power and presence, that I may sing with His Holy Angels :* O MAPPA LAMAN, HALLELUJAH. AMEN.

When he appears, says the Ritual, *give him a kind entertainment ; ask what is lawful, possible and becoming to his office ; and you shall obtain it.* If, however, he should fail to appear, the four candles must be marked with the gold or silver seal, which apparently will ensure obedience.

There are, however, certain planetary considerations connected with this process, on which its success depends. The two first Angels of the First Altitude can only be called on the first and second Sunday in March ; the third and fourth on the Sundays in April ; the fifth after the sun has entered Gemini in May. And so of the rest in succession.

§ 5. *The Fourth Book of Cornelius Agrippa*

It is a matter now almost of general knowledge that a Fourth Book of *Occult Philosophy* is attributed to Cornelius Agrippa, and that it is rejected as spurious. The authenticity of the famous three books has never been questioned and is indeed beyond challenge ; the fourth is perhaps less interesting from the nature of its contents than from this question of its authorship. It is, at the same time, a much more skilful performance than the common run of magical impostures ; it connects with and rises out of the genuine work in a very curious manner ; and, having regard to the special magical complexion of the latter, there might seem no inherent reason why it should not have been the production of Agrippa. The difficulties concerning it may be reduced to three heads. One is of time ; it appeared after the death of the restless speculating philosopher of Nettersheim. Now, a posthumous publication is not necessarily open to suspicion unless it is a treatise on Magic, but a treatise on Magic of the period concerned, not appearing in the lifetime of its writer, is open to the gravest suspicion, because of the scandalous company to which it belongs. The second difficulty is internal, and I do not think that it can be overridden. It is to a considerable extent a *rechauffé* of various portions of the three undisputed books, and, even in the days of Agrippa, it is not likely that any author would have so liberally reproduced himself. The third difficulty is that it was rejected as a forgery by Wierus, the pupil of Agrippa, who must have had a good opportunity of knowing; its rejection by later writers simply follows the lead of Wierus, and is therefore of no moment. The strength of the case against it lies mainly in the third difficulty, but other objections are possible. Though not the work of Agrippa, it was evidently produced in immediate proximity to his period.

The book itself, which is quite informally written, falls into several divisions. There is, firstly, an elaborate treatise on the method of extracting the names of the good and evil spirits referred to the seven planets. This is a further development of a subject treated at some length in the third book of *Occult Philosophy*. The method is of no importance to our inquiry, but those who have sought to unravel it confess that they have been baffled. I ask leave to assure my readers that I have not emulated their zeal by seeking to follow in their footsteps, and, so far as I am concerned, the method therefore remains in the bosom of its proper mystery. Possibly Agrippa and his successor were only fooling their readers, and did not disclose the secret. The treatise on Names is followed by one upon Characters and, depending as it does from the first, this is also not readily intelligible. I have left it to those whom it may concern. Thereafter comes a formal tabulation of all the known shapes familiar to the spirits of the planets, followed by a disquisition upon Pentacles and Sigils, another upon the consecration of instruments used in magical ceremonies, as also of fire, water and so forth. The work concludes with methods for the invocation of good and evil spirits and a short process in Necromancy. As I shall have occasion to cite it frequently in the Second Part, the analysis may here be confined to establishing its connection with diabolism, and the kind of manifestations which are supposed to be obtained by its processes.

Like the *Lemegeton*, it gives specific directions for communicating with evil spirits, and there is no question whatever as to the lawful nature of the experiment, by which I mean that no doubt on the subject entered into the mind of the writer, who offers what he has to the artist without attempting to justify its nature. Refinements of this kind were evidently outside the magic of the fifteenth century. In the following citation I shall depart from my usual custom of translating at first hand, and make use, with some needful prunings, of the version of Robert Turner, which is quite faithful and has, moreover, the pleasant flavour of antiquity.

CONCERNING THE INVOCATION OF EVIL SPIRITS

If we would call any evil Spirit to the circle, it first behoveth us to consider and to know his nature, to which of the planets it agreeth, and what offices are distributed to him from the planet. This being known, let there be sought out a place fit and proper for his invocation, according to the nature of the planet and the quality of the offices of the same Spirit, as near as the same may be done. For example, if his power be over the sea, rivers or floods, then let a place be chosen on the shore, and so of the rest. In like manner, let there be chosen a convenient time, both for the quality of the air—which should be serene, clear, quiet and fitting for the Spirits to assume bodies—and for the quality and nature of the planet, and so too of the Spirit, to wit, on his day, noting the time wherein he ruleth, whether it be fortunate or unfortunate, day or night, as the stars and spirits do require. These things being considered, let there be a circle framed at the place elected, as well for the defence of the invocant as for the confirmation of the Spirit. In the circle itself there are to be written the general Divine Names, and those things which do yield defence unto us; the Divine Names which do rule the said planet, with the offices of the Spirit himself; the names, finally, of the good Spirits which bear rule and are able to bind and constrain that Spirit which we intend to call. If we would further fortify our circle, we may add characters and pentacles agreeing to the work. So also, and within or without the circle, we may frame an angular figure,[1] inscribed with such numbers as are congruent among themselves to our work. Moreover, the operator is to be provided with lights, perfumes, unguents and medicines compounded according to the nature of the planet and Spirit, which do partly agree with the Spirit, by reason of their natural and celestial virtue, and partly are exhibited to the Spirit for religious and superstitious worship. The operator must also be furnished with holy and consecrated things, necessary as well for the defence of the invocant and his fellows as to serve for bonds which shall bind and constrain the Spirits. Such are holy papers, lamens, pictures, pentacles, swords, sceptres, garments of convenient matter and colour, and things of the like sort. When all these are provided, the master and his fellows being in the circle, and all those things which he useth, let him begin to pray with a loud voice and a convenient gesture and countenance. Let him make an oration unto God, and afterwards entreat the good Spirits. I he will read any prayers, psalms or gospels for his defence,

---

[1] Compare the figures of the *Lemegeton*, Part ii. c. 4.

they should take the first place. Thereafter, let him begin to invocate the Spirit which he desireth, with a gentle and loving enchantment to all the coasts of the world, commemorating his own authority and power. Let him then rest a little, looking about him to see if any Spirit do appear, which if he delay, let him repeat his invocation as before, until he hath done it three times. If the Spirit be still pertinacious and will not appear, let him begin to conjure him with Divine Power, but in such a way that all the conjurations and commemorations do agree with the nature and offices of the Spirit himself. Reiterate the same three times, from stronger to stronger, using objurgations, contumelies, cursings, punishments, suspensions from his office and power, and the like.

After all the courses are finished, again cease a little, and if any Spirit shall appear, let the invocant turn towards him, receive him courteously, and, earnestly entreating him, let him require his name. Then proceeding further, let him ask whatsoever he will. But if in anything the Spirit shall shew himself obstinate or lying, let him be bound by convenient conjurations, and if you still doubt of any lie, make outside the circle, with the consecrated sword, the figure of a triangle or pentacle, and compel the Spirit to enter it. If you would have any promise confirmed upon oath, stretch the sword out of the circle, and swear the Spirit by laying his hand upon the sword. Then having obtained of the Spirit that which you desire, or being otherwise contented, license him to depart with courteous words, giving command unto him that he do no hurt. If he will not depart, compel him by powerful conjurations, and, if need require, expel him by exorcism and by making contrary fumigations. When he is departed, go not out of the circle, but stay, making prayer for your defence and conservation, and giving thanks unto God and the good angels. All these things being orderly performed, you may depart.

But if your hopes are frustrated, and no Spirit will appear, yet for this do not despair, but, leaving the circle, return again at other times, doing as before. And if you shall judge that you have erred in anything, then you shall amend by adding or diminishing, for the constancy of reiteration doth often increase your authority and power, and striketh terror into the Spirits, humbling them to obedience.

Hence some do use to make a gate in the circle, whereby they go in and out, which they open and shut as they please, and fortify it with Holy Names and pentacles. This also we are to take notice of, that when no Spirits will appear, but the Master, being wearied, hath determined to cease and give over, let him not therefore depart without licensing the Spirits, for they that do neglect this are very greatly in danger, except they are fortified with some sublime defence. Oftentimes also the Spirits do come, although they be not visible (for to cause terror to him that calls them), either in the thing which he useth or in the operation itself. But this kind of licensing is not given simply, but by a kind of dispensation with suspension, until they shall render themselves obedient.

When we intend to execute any effect by evil Spirits where an apparition is not needful, this is to be done by making the required instrument or subject of the experiment itself, whether it be an image, a ring or a writing, any candle, character or sacrifice, or anything of the like sort. The name of the Spirit is to be written thereon, with his character, according to the exigency of the experiment, either writing with blood or using some perfume agreeable to the Spirit, making also frequent prayers to God and the good angels before we invoke the evil Spirit, and conjuring him by the Divine Power.

Composite Rituals

Over and above the formal diabolism of this process, there are instructions for composing a book of evil spirits, to be prepared ceremonially, according to their name and order. By means of a " holy oath," the ready obedience of the Spirit, whose name is written therein, is supposed to be insured. The book itself must be formed of most pure and clean paper which has never been used previously—a stipulation which may have been of moment in the days of the palimpsest, but is, of course, scarcely necessary in our own. The image of the Spirit must be drawn on the left side, and his character on the right, preceded by the oath which embodies the name of the Spirit, together with his dignity, place, office and power. The operation must be performed on the day and in the hour of the planet to which the Spirit is attributed. When the book has been composed, it must be well bound and emblazoned, being furnished also with markers and seals, for to open it at random after its consecration might endanger the operator. It should be kept reverently and free from profanation, for otherwise it will lose its virtue. Its consecration is a matter of some difficulty, as every Spirit whose name appears therein must be called before the circle, the bonds read over in his presence, and each in succession must be compelled to impose his hand where his respective image and character are drawn, and to "confirm and consecrate the same with a special and common oath." In a word, the document must be regularly and legally delivered as the act and deed of each. During this ceremony the book must be laid within a triangle described outside the circle.

There can be no doubt that these directions are the work of a writer well acquainted with the *Lemegeton*, or that the *Liber Spirituum* in question is identical with that mentioned by Wierus. The forms assumed by the evoked Spirits differ somewhat from those of the *Lesser Key*, which, moreover, at least in its Goëtic portion, has no planetary attribution. According to pseudo-Agrippa, the Spirits of Saturn usually appear with a tall and lean body and an angry countenance, having four faces, of which one is in the usual position, another at the back of the head, and two, with beaks, on either side. They have also a face on each knee, of a shining black. Their motion is like that of the wind, and it is accompanied with a kind of earthquake. Their sign is white earth, "whiter than any snow." Their particular forms are a bearded king riding on a dragon;[1] an old bearded man; an old woman leaning on a staff; a boy; a dragon; an owl; a black garment; a hook or sickle; a juniper-tree. How the three last manifestations are provided with the six visages is a perplexity which must be surrendered to occult commentators.

The Spirits of Jupiter appear with a sanguine and choleric body; they are of middle stature; their motion is "horrible and fearful," but they are mild of countenance and gentle in speech. They are of iron colour, which ought to have connected them with Mars; their motion is that of flashing lightnings, and withal thunderous; their sign is the apparition of men about the circle who seem to be devoured by lions. Their particular forms are a king with drawn sword riding on a lion;[2] a mitred personage in a long vestment; a maid crowned with laurel and adorned by flowers; a bull; a stag; a peacock; an azure garment; a sword; a box-tree.

The Spirits of Mars have a tall body and choleric, a filthy countenance, brown, swarthy or red in colour; they have horns like the hart, claws like a griffin and they bellow like wild

---

[1] Alternatively, the image of a man, having the countenance of a hart and the feet of a camel, a scythe in his right and a dart in his left hand. This also rode upon a dragon.

[2] Also on an eagle or dragon. Another form was that of a naked man crowned, and yet another a man having the head of a lion or ram and the feet of an eagle.

Fig. 1. Fig. 2. Fig. 3.
Fig. 4. Fig. 5. Fig. 6.
Fig. 7. Fig. 8. Fig. 9.
Fig. 10. Fig. 11. Fig. 12.
Fig. 13. Fig. 15.
Fig. 16. Fig. 14. Fig.
Fig. 17. 18.
Fig. 19. Fig. 20. Fig. 21.
Fig. 22. Fig. 23. Fig. 24.
Fig. 25. Fig. 26. Fig. 27.

PLATE V

CHARACTERS OF EVIL SPIRITS

bulls. They have the motion of burning fire, and their sign is thunder and lightning about the circle. Their particular forms are an armed king riding on a wolf ;[1] an armed man ; a woman holding a buckler on her thigh ; a she-goat ; a horse ; a stag ; a red garment ; wool ; a cheestip. Wool of a choleric disposition is perhaps a Goëtic form of gun-cotton.

The Spirits of the Sun are usually large of body and limb, sanguine, gross, and of a gold colour tinctured with blood—which recalls Mrs. Browning's pomegranate. Their motion is that of lightning ; their sign is to produce sweat in the operator, which might, however, be the normal property of all these stellar nondescripts of the world infernal. Their particular forms are a sceptred king riding on a lion ; a crowned king ;[2] a queen with a sceptre ; a bird—not otherwise described, but anything probably except that of paradise ; a lion ; a cock ; a golden garment ; a sceptre ; and lastly, something which Robert Turner wisely left untranslated—*caudatus, i.e.*, tailed.

The Spirits of Venus have a body of medium height and a pleasant visage, of which the upper part is golden and the lower white or green. Their motion is like that of a brilliant star. Their sign is the semblance of maids sporting about the circle and luring the Magician to join them. Their particular forms are a sceptred king riding on a camel ; a naked maid ; a she-goat ; a camel—possibly the atrocious demon of Cazotte ; a dove ; a white or green garment ; the herb savine.[3]

The Spirits of Mercury appear commonly with a body of middle stature, cold, liquid, moist, which sounds redundant, but

[1] Otherwise, on a lion, and armed with a naked sword, while in his left hand is a man's head.

[2] This manifestation seems to have been seated on a throne, with a raven in his breast and a globe under his feet.

[3] Other forms were a woman with the head of a bird and the feet of an eagle, who held a dart in her hand ; also a little maid in long white garments, with a comb in her left hand and flowers in her right.

the reference is to the properties of quicksilver—that is to say, the Mercury of the philosophers was supposed not to wet the hand, but the Mercurial spirits of the sorcerer apparently did. They are withal fair, affable in speech, of human shape and like unto armed knights. They are comparable to silver-coloured clouds in their motion. Their sign is that they cause horror and fear in the operator. Their special shapes are a king riding on a bear;[1] a comely youth; a woman holding a distaff—it is difficult to understand how such an apparition can be like an armed knight, an observation which, if it were worth while, might apply to the remaining modes of manifestation; a dog; a she-bear; a magpie; a garment of many changing colours; a rod; and a little staff.

Finally, the Spirits of the Moon have a large, soft, phlegmatic body, even as a dark cloud in colour. Their countenance is swollen, their head bald, their eyes are red and rheumy, their teeth like those of a wild boar. Their motion is like that of a great tempest sweeping the sea. Their sign is a heavy shower of rain about the circle. Their particular shapes are— a king like an archer riding on a doe; a little boy; a huntress with bow and arrows; a cow; a small doe; a goose; a green or silver-coloured garment; an arrow; a many-footed creature— perhaps a centipede.

The imbecility of this muddled tabulation places the forged Fourth Book in a more absurd light than it otherwise deserves. It really reproduces the manner of Agrippa's treatise with a fidelity which is not unskilful and has quite as much claim to be taken seriously as any of the composite Rituals. It is difficult to say whether it is more especially on the side of the devil or on that of folly, except in so far as these two are one.

[1] There is another riding on a peacock, with eagle's feet and crested head.

Composite Rituals

§ 6. *The Heptameron*

The Fourth Book of Cornelius Agrippa was much too informal, and left too much to the discretion of the operator, to be satisfactory for a science so exact as that of Ceremonial Magic. A form of procedure which bequeathed nothing to the imagination and asked no other skill than the patient exactitude of the rule of thumb was necessary to the weakness of the ordinary sorcerer. The *Heptameron, or Magical Elements* ascribed to Peter de Abano is an attempt to supply the want and to offer to the neophyte a complete wizard's cabinet. Cornelius Agrippa, says the introduction, which might, *ex hypothesi*, be that of a later hand, seems to have written for the learned, for the well-experienced in this art; he does not treat specially of the ceremonies, but mentions them in a general way. Those who have not "tasted magical superstitions" may here find them ready to their hand. "In brief, in this book are kept the principles of magical conveyances." It may be conceded at once that the undertaking is scrupulously fulfilled; what the operator must do and how he should perform it, so as to "draw spirits into discourse," are matters set forth so plainly that the wayfaring man need not err therein. Assuming the sacerdotal office of the operator, or a priest for an accomplice, it is all so simple that failure could not well be ascribed to a blunder on his part.

It would be invidious to suppose that the *Heptameron* is more authentic as regards its attribution than the work to which it is professedly a sequel; its real authorship is involved in much the same kind of obscurity as that of pseudo-Agrippa. There are several grave reasons why the pupil of Trithemius should not have written the spurious Fourth Book, but Peter of Abano is not an unlikely personage to connect with the *Magical*

Elements, if it were not for a trifling chronological disparity of about three hundred years. It is true that Agrippa professedly wrote upon Magic, and the other upon Astrology and Geomancy, unless his imputed works in these departments of occult science are also forgeries; but the *Heptameron* was never heard of for the space which I have mentioned after the death of its reputed author, which occurred in 1316, and it is too obviously later in its tone, too obviously a sequel[1] to a much more recent work, for it to have been possibly a memorial of the fourteenth century.

Peter of Abano, a town in the vicinity of Padua, was born in 1250 and was a learned physician of his period, who attempted to conciliate the different medical systems and is supposed to have been the first European who quoted Averroes. He established himself at Paris, but at the instigation of jealous professional brethren he was accused of heresy and fled to his native place. At Padua a chair of medicine was created for him, but the accusation followed its victim; by some he was charged with denying the existence of demons, by others with obtaining his knowledge from seven imps whom he kept in a bottle. However this may be, the Inquisition instituted a process, but the designed sufferer was delivered by death— as some say, on the eve of his execution. The intervention infuriated the Tribunal, though the testament left behind him by Peter of Abano affirmed his belief in the orthodox faith. The magistrates of the city were ordered, on pain of excommunication, to exhume his body, but it was removed by a faithful servant and buried secretly in another church. The Inquisition clamoured for the punishment of the offender but

[1] A sequel, moreover, which contains several direct references, as, for example: "But after what manner they appear has been described already in the former book of magical ceremonies."— *The Conjuration of the Lord's Day*. This recurs with slight variations throughout the *Heptameron*. It may be advisable to add that Agrippa was of the sixteenth century.

was content in the end to burn the dead physician in effigy. As a counterpoise, a century later his bust was placed in the town-hall of Padua. His undoubted works, which are frankly unreadable, betray no acquaintance with the occult sciences beyond a belief in astrology, which in those days was catholic as Rome and powerful as the Holy Tribunal. He remains, therefore, one of the moral martyrs of Magic, *faussement accusé*, as Gabriel Naudé has it. His accusation and the mode of its prosecution remain also among the lesser glories of the Holy Office.

Accepting the *Heptameron* as a work belonging to the period of its first publication, it is here placed among the Rituals of a composite character, not because it professedly deals with devils, but because the nature of its angels and spirits is indicated by the manner of their conjuration ; in a word, they are described as angels and threatened as demons.

The procedure is divided into two parts—a general method for the evocation of the Spirits of the Air, who are undoubtedly demons, and a set of angelical conjurations proper to each day of the week. The second section presumably belongs to the department of White Magic—if I may adopt this glorious distinction in the ribaldry of a passing moment—as the intelligences concerned are said to be good and great, though their offices are mixed and confusing, including the discovery of treasures, the detection of secrets, fomenting war, opening locks and bolts, procuring the love of women, inclining men to luxury and sowing hatred and evil thought. Obviously, White Magic of this kind is much blacker than it is painted. Though the entire *Heptameron* appears under one attribution, the first part only is ascribed in the text to Peter de Abano. Therein the personal preparation of the operator corresponds to that given in the Second Part of the present work, and the ceremonial itself, which, if cited at all, would have to be printed *in extenso*, as it contains no detachable portions, is much too elaborate to be inserted in this place, more especially as that of the *Lemegeton* will provide later on a fairly complete notion of the scope and purpose of the Composite Rituals, taken in their broad aspect, and will illustrate the fact that all conventional distinctions dissolve therein.

§ 7. *The Sacred Magic of Abramelin the Mage*

The existence of this text had been known to students for a considerable period before it was made available in an English translation by the editor of the *Key of Solomon.* The amateurs of occult science in the more dubious of its practical branches became possessed of this pearl of tradition in 1898, and·I suppose that it is familiar enough in certain circles. I am sorry that it seems necessary to say a few words concerning it in the present place. Mr. Mathers prefixed an introduction which does honour to his especial form of talent—that is to say, it is eloquent as a caution respecting things which should be avoided by an expert in the expression of his views and the mode of writing exercises in English.

The text is preserved in the Arsénal Library at Paris and is a French manuscript belonging to the early part of the eighteenth century; it is also the sole copy which is known certainly to collectors, though there is a rumour of another in Holland. According to its own claim, the work belongs to the year 1458, at which period it was written by one Abraham, the son of Simon and the father of Lamech, for whose benefit it was more especially designed. The original is said to have been in Hebrew, and this statement on the part of the text is naturally accepted by the translator. It is perhaps rendered the more probable from his point of view by the lavish internal evidence that it is the work of a Christian hand, is full of Christian references and allusions to late Grimoires. The point is not worth debating, at least on its own merits, but the references (*a.*) to the " Jewish Sabbath," (*b.*) to the custom of paternal benediction, (*c.*) to those who leave Christianity for Judaism, (*d.*) to the festival of Easter, and otherwise (*e.*) its allusions to the New Testament, (*f.*) its use of the Vulgate, and (*g.*) its hypothesis concerning Guardian Angels are unmistakable proof for those who know what is meant by textual evidence. To conclude on this part of the subject, the date of the work is the date of the known copy, or thereabouts ; it was never written in Hebrew, or by one who was acquainted with Hebrew ; and the claim that the author was a Jew has the same value as the translator's brilliant speculation that the supposed Abraham was a descendant of that other Abraham the Jew, whose mysterious hieroglyphical tract on Alchemy came, as it is alleged, into the hands of Nicholas Flamel, his putative contemporary.

Abramelin the Mage was an instructor of the magical Abraham, who reduced into writing the knowledge which he received from this source, prefixing thereto some account of his own life and occult adventures. There are several respects in which the text differs conspicuously from the common run of the Rituals. It derides, for example, all observations of times and seasons along the usual and accepted lines. Such formalities, it is said, have no power over spirits or virtue in supernatural things. It would follow not unreasonably from this, and is made plain in a special chapter, that the majority of magical books are false and vain. They are also otherwise evil, not only on account of their superstitious attention to celestial signs but from their use of unintelligible words in the processes of conjuration, and so forth. These words are inventions of the devil, or alternatively of wicked men. Stress is laid also on the fact that Rituals of this kind contain no invocations of God, which is demonstrably a libel on the literature.

It will be understood that the hypercritical Abraham is careful on his own part to call upon the Divine aid, but his conjurations are few and simple. He relies, however, on the help of those Guardian Angels which Christian tradition and doctrine attribute to each soul of man. On the other hand, he makes no use of words, figures or pentacles, which he proscribes as abominations invented by diabolical enchanters. He is, therefore, an exponent of Art Magic in the utmost simplification thereof, but that which he saves in ritual he expends in the dramatic elaboration of general *mise en scène*. Looking, however, at his claim, one is tempted to think for a moment that we are in the presence of new modes and even of new intentions in respect of "magical vanity." This time surely, the work is on the side of God, and there is a certain encouragement in the mere title, which says that the content of the book is actually that Holy Magic which God gave unto Moses—to Aaron, David, Solomon—to the other saints, patriarchs and prophets; that it is also the true and the Divine Wisdom, a statement reiterated continually throughout the text itself. It is all for the glory of God, for His high honour, the good of the pious operator and that of the human race.

But when we come to the dealings with spirits, we find that they are Lucifer, Leviathan, Satan and Belial, for the superior princes, and Astaroth, Asmodeus, Beelzebub, *et hoc genus omne*, for the lesser powers. Furthermore, these demons may be summoned indifferently for operations of good or evil, while the objects are the usual objects, the time-long interests, the glorious dedications of White and Black Magic, as established by the concurrent testimony of all the Rituals. The recovery of stolen things, the acquisition of buried treasures, the stirring up of hatred and enmity, the casting of spells and the usual venereal experiments—such are the ends in view. There are even processes in Necromancy, which art is eschewed by all but the most abominable forms of Black Magic.

As the text has been made available, it may be left at this point. No doubt the translator will continue to regard it as a work of great "importance" from the occult standpoint, and its existence in an English form as "a real benefit" to students. I leave it to him.

THE SUN-GOD RA SLAYING THE DRAGON OF DARKNESS.
From the Papyrus of Hunefer, c. B.C. 1370.

95

CHAPTER IV

𝕮𝖍𝖊 𝕽𝖎𝖙𝖚𝖆𝖑𝖘 𝖔𝖋 𝕭𝖑𝖆𝖈𝖐 𝕸𝖆𝖌𝖎𝖈

§ 1. *The Grimorium Verum*

THE four specific and undisguised handbooks of Black Magic, all in the French language, but in three cases, like so much of the Ceremonial literature, possessing Italian connections, real or imputed, are :—

I. GRIMORIUM VERUM, or the Most Approved Keys of Solomon the Hebrew Rabbin, wherein the Most Hidden Secrets, both Natural and Supernatural, are immediately exhibited ; but it is necessary that the Demons should be contented on their part.[1] Translated from the Hebrew by Plaingière, a Dominican Jesuit,[2] with a Collection of Curious Secrets. Published by Alibeck the Egyptian. 1517.[3]

II. TRUE BLACK MAGIC, or the Secret of Secrets, an MS. found at Jerusalem in the Sepulchre of Solomon, containing :

1. Forty-five Talismans with their representation, as also the

---

[1] This is only a conjectural translation. It is impossible to render such a passage as *modo operator per necessaria et contenta facit scia tamen oportit Dæmonum potentia dum taxat per agantur.*

[2] It will be scarcely necessary to advise the reader that a Dominican Jesuit is an absurdity, which might be paralleled by "secular monk," "unordained priest," and so forth. The Order of St. Dominic and the Society of Jesus are totally distinct. A Catholic critic might almost be justified in observing that so gross a blunder would be possible only to a Jew or a heretic ; certainly he would have more reason than would be discoverable in the hypothesis of Papus, that priests are the authors of the Grimoires.

[3] On the reverse of the title :—*The True Clavicles of Solomon.* Memphis. Published by Alibeck the Egyptian.

96

manner of using them, together with their Marvellous Properties. 2. All Magical Characters known unto this day.[1] Translated from the Hebrew of the Magus Iroë-Grego.[2] Rome. In the year of grace, 1750.

III. The Grand Grimoire, with the Powerful Clavicle of Solomon and of Black Magic ; or the Infernal Devices of the Great Agrippa for the Discovery of all Hidden Treasures and the Subjugation of every Denomination of Spirits, together with an Abridgment of all the Magical Arts. (In its earliest edition, without place or date.)

IV. The Constitution of Pope Honorius the Great, wherein may be found the Arcane Conjurations which must be used against the Spirits of Darkness. With a Collection of the Most Rare Secrets. Rome, 1670.

They are all tiny volumes, nominally in duodecimo, but much smaller according to modern measurements.

The date specified in the title of the *Grimorium Verum* is undeniably fraudulent ; the work belongs to the middle of the eighteenth century, and Memphis is Rome. The *Grand Grimoire* is not of higher antiquity. That of Honorius is said to have appeared originally in 1629, but it has been sometimes referred erroneously to the same period of the previous century.

As indicated by the authorship which is attributed to it, the *Grimorium Verum* is based to some extent upon the *Key of Solomon*, the main points of resemblance being in the description of the magical instruments and in some of the forms of prayer. It distinguishes plainly the powers which it is pro-

---

[1] That is, mystic characters for engraving on magical instruments, vessels and vestments. The statement is utterly untrue, for the characters given by the Grimoire are few in number and exceedingly imperfect as well.

[2] Mr. Mathers reads Iohé Grevis. Iroe Gecis is another variation. It is a corruption in any case.

posed to invoke by the name of Devils.[1] At the same time
it refers them nominally to the four elements, which would
connect them with the Sylphs, Salamanders and so forth ; but
the classification in question, somewhat incidentally made, does
not really obtain. There is an account of the Hierarchy of
Spirits, with Lucifer, Beelzebuth and Astaroth as potentates
in chief.[2] A portion of this account is drawn from the *Lemegeton*, perhaps through the *Pseudo-monarchia* of Wierus. The
work purports to be divided into three sections, containing :—
(*a*.) The Characters and Seals of the Demons, with the forms
for their Evocation and Dismissal. (*b*.) A description of the
Natural and Supernatural Secrets which can be operated by
the power of the Demons, and that without any deception.
(*c*.) The Key of the work, and the proper application thereof.
Passing over typographical errors, the MS. from which it has
been printed must have been in a most confused state ; there
are not in reality any distinct divisions, and the little volume
abounds in Latin passages which often defy translation, as, for
example, *sic pro ratione voluntas ; ut illud sit hoc in opere in-
clusum minimo clerum in doctis ; quia amicus fiet capitalis, fiet
inimicus*. So also we have *Sanctum Regum* throughout for
Sanctum Regnum. There are two folding plates of Characters
and Seals, of which many have no reference to the text, while
others essential to the process are missing, the deficiencies
being supplied in the modern Italian versions, which probably follow another edition, also Italian, and the source of

---

[1] "Here beginneth the *Sanctum Regnum*, called the Royalty of Spirits, or the little Keys
of Solomon, a most learned Hebrew nigromancer and Rabbin, containing various combinations
of characters, whereby the Powers, Spirits or, more correctly, Devils are invoked, so that they
are forced to appear whensoever you may determine, each one according to his faculty, and are
compelled to bring whatsoever you may require of them, causing you no kind of annoyance,
provided only that they are contented on their part, for these sorts of creatures give nothing for
nothing."

[2] See Part ii. c. 3.

the French translation, but unknown to the present writer, as indeed to most bibliographers. The work, as it stands, is really in two parts only, the *Grimorium Verum* proper and certain "Rare and Astounding Magical Secrets." The first may be analysed as follows :—(*a*.) Directions for the preparation of the Operator, all of a personal kind and analogous to those of the Clavicle. (*b*.) Instructions for the manufacture of the magical instruments required in the work, also analogous to the Clavicle. (*c*.) The composition of the virgin parchment on which the characters and seals are to be inscribed, shewing distinct variations from the Clavicle. (*d*.) The processes of evocation and the discharge. Beyond the fact that the evoked Spirits are Lucifer, Beelzebuth, Astaroth and the inferiors and ministers of these, this first and chief part is not more repulsive, as it is indeed scarcely more unintelligent, than most of the processes in its prototype.

The second part contains the usual curiosities common to all the later Grimoires, including the *Admirable Secrets* of the pretended Albertus Magnus, the *Little Albert*, &c. In so far as it presents any considerable variations, such variations are usually in the direction of Black Magic. Some are venereal in the more objectionable sense of the term, others merely revolting, while yet others, as that of the Magic Garters, are derived from the Clavicle. Finally, there are certain processes which might claim to be those of White Magic [1] and are concerned with the ceremonial induction of simple clairvoyance.

We may therefore conclude that the *Grimorium Verum* proper is not more diabolical than the first part of the *Lemegeton*, which indeed contains the ceremonial for the evocation of precisely the same spirits.

[1] See Part ii. c. 8, §§ 6, 7, and 8.

§ 2. *True Black Magic*

The Grimoire entitled *True Black Magic* is simply an adapted version of the *Key of Solomon*, with the same preambles, the same ritual, the same talismans, and characters which are analogous when they are not identical. With the moderately intelligible and religiously careful presentation of Mr. Mathers it of course compares very badly; like the *Grimorium Verum*, it is exceedingly confused, and is rendered almost unmeaning by the omission of all the practical part. Its malicious or diabolical element consists, however, more especially in its introduction of the chapter upon works of hatred and destruction, which, as already seen, and as more fully established later on, should undoubtedly be regarded as an integral portion of the original work.

§ 3. *The Grand Grimoire*

The *Grand Grimoire* is the most fantastic of the cycle and is introduced with great pomp by its pretended editor, Antonio Venitiana del Rabina, a personage whose name indicates the Italian origin of the work. By reason of its rarity and the great request in which it is, we are informed that it must be regarded as the veritable *Magnum Opus*—a view which may appear inconsequential, but for which the authority of Rabbinical writers is cited. It is to these authors that we owe the priceless treasure which innumerable charlatans have endeavoured to counterfeit, but have never succeeded in discovering. The copy made use of by Antonio in preparing his edition was transcribed from the genuine writings of the mighty King Solomon, which were obtained by pure chance. "Of a truth, what other man, save this invincible genius, would have had the hardihood to reveal the withering words which God makes use of to strike terror into the rebellious angels and compel them into obedience? Having soared into the celestial altitudes that he might master the secrets and learn the omnipotent words which constitute all the power of a terrible and venerable Deity, the essence of those innermost arcana, made use of by an infinite Divinity, was extracted by this grand king, who passed all the days of his life in the most laborious researches, and in pursuit of the most obscure and hopeless secrets. He succeeded ultimately in all his undertakings, penetrating into the most remote haunts of spirits, whom he bound, one and all, and forced them to obey him by the power of his Talisman or Clavicle. Therein he has discovered unto us the stellar influences, the constellation of the planets and the method for the evocation of all hierarchies of spirits by the recitation of certain sublime Appellations, as they are hereafter set down for you in this book, as well as the true composition and effects of the dreadful Blasting Rod, which causes the spirits to tremble; which God also used to arm his Angel when Adam and Eve were driven out of the Earthly Paradise; wherewith, finally, he smote the rebellious Angels, precipitating their ambitions into the most appalling gulfs by the power of this very Rod—of this Rod which collects the clouds, disperses tempests, averts the lightning, or precipitates each and all upon any portion of the earth at the pleasure of its director."

Such is the preamble of the *Grand Grimoire*. The work is divided into two parts, the first containing the evocation of Lucifuge [1] Rofocale by means of the Blasting Rod, the second

[1] This alteration of the fallen Light-Bearer into Fly-the-Light does not seem to occur in magical literature preceding the *Grand Grimoire*. It was afterwards adopted by Lévi, by whom it has been made popular among occultists, who are, for the most part, quite unaware of its source, as they usually are in such cases.

being that which Antonio inscrutably regards as the *Sanctum Regnum*, namely, the Rite of making Pacts; but one of the most notable characteristics of all the Grimoires is not their diabolical malice, but their unconscious ingenuousness, while the devout, almost laudable, character of all the operations seems to have been held quite sincerely.

The *Grand Grimoire* is, however, regarded as one of the most atrocious of its class; it has a process in Necromancy which is possible, say some occult writers—in the geniality of a lucid interval—only to a dangerous maniac or an irreclaimable criminal. It must be admitted that the Rite is highly unreasonable, but in dealing with such literature it seems unsafe to advance the objection, for it applies much too widely. As to its criminality, this centres in the creation of a disturbance at midnight Mass on Christmas Eve. There is further an account of a poison entitled "The Composition of Death, or Philosophical Stone," which is supposed to indicate an advanced degree of diabolism. Éliphas Lévi says that it pretends to confer the Powder of Projection, the great Mystery of the Sages, but it gives really the Powder of Consecution— as to the significance of which a vague image can alone be invoked. It may, in any case, be added that it cannot well be either, seeing that the composition is a liquid. For the rest, it is simply a stupid recipe, and as no unlawful application is suggested, it is not diabolical at all, unless toxicology, as such, is Satanic, simply because it does not deal in anodynes.

There is, of course, no question that the *Grand Grimoire* is a book of Black Magic, and it is contrary to the nature of things that a book of Black Magic should be otherwise than diabolical. The most objectionable works are not those which openly announce that they are evil, but those which teach evil under the pretence of excellence. The noticeable point, as regards the *Grand Grimoire*, the other works of its class and the White Rituals, is that the diabolism of the confessedly diabolical is often so exceedingly thin, while the angelical element in processes assumed to be angelical borders so often and so perilously on the Satanic side. The first part of the *Grand Grimoire*, like the *Grimorium Verum*, is simply a process for the evocation of evil spirits to obtain the enforced surrender of hidden treasure. In the second part the magician is certainly expected to give himself, body and soul, to the demon who serves him meanwhile, and there can be no hesitation in admitting that this creates a sharp distinction, not only between the *Grand Grimoire* and all the Composite Rituals, but also between the *Grand Grimoire* and the other Liturgies of Black Magic. It is only a palliation to say that the compact is worded as a subterfuge, and in reality gives nothing to the demon, who here, as so frequently in folklore, is bamboozled, receiving the shadow in place of the substance.[1]

§ 4. *The Grimoire of Honorius*

Despite the iniquities of the *Pacta Conventa Dæmonum*, the *Grand Grimoire* has failed, however, to invoke upon itself such severe condemnation as the *Grimoire of Honorius the Great*, otherwise Honorius the Third. It is scarcely too much to say that almost every accusation preferred against this remarkable work is false generally and specifically, the chief distinction between them being that some are the misrepresentations of ignorance and others the false interpretations of prejudgment. The French occultist, Papus, alone seems to take the middle view, though he speaks with some vagueness when

[1] Compare the droll history of the Devil and his Dam, and that concerning the course of Black Magic delivered by the Prince of Darkness at the University of Salamanca.

he says that the sorcery of this Grimoire is more dangerous for weak experimentalists than for the enemies of the sorcerer. Éliphas Lévi observes that the work is not without importance for the students of occult science.[1] At first sight it seems to be nothing but a tissue of repulsive absurdities, but for those who are initiated in the signs and secrets of the Kabalah, it is said that it becomes a veritable monument of human perversity. There was seldom a statement for which there was less foundation; there was never a magical work which less connected with Kabalism; the relation in so far as it exists, and it is confined to a few words which occur in the Conjurations, is common to all Ceremonial Magic, and this is the one Grimoire which is most permeated with Christian elements. Those, however, who are well acquainted with the principles of interpretation which obtain in the writings of Lévi, will not take a charge seriously which depends upon the significance of Kabalistic words or signs, for it is notorious that with the French occultist they meant many things according to his humour, and that he did not know his subject. But Éliphas Lévi was not contented with the general impeachment; in a later work[2] he elaborated a more particular charge. In common with the *Key of Solomon*, and all the Grimoires, the work of Honorius prescribes the sacrifice of a virgin kid, with the object of ensuring the possession of a virgin parchment by the operator. Now, Lévi affirms that when the " abominable author " mentions a kid, he means really a human child. In this interpretation he has not even the excuse of the humorous analogy which has been instituted in vulgar English, for his acquaintance, had he any, with our language was exceedingly slight. There is not a particle of foundation

[1] *Histoire de la Magie*, p. 307.
[2] *La Clef des Grands Mystères*. See also "Thaumaturgical Experiences of Éliphas Lévi" in *The Mysteries of Magic*, by A. E. Waite, second edition.

for the charge; the sacrifice in the case of the *Grimoire of Honorius* means, and can mean, no more than in the case of the *Key of Solomon*. There was a defined purpose in connection with the slaughter of the victim, which was the same in both instances.

So far concerning the misinterpretations of writers who pretend to some first-hand acquaintance with the work under notice. Others who have mentioned it within recent years have been content to follow the French authority without examination. Thus it is that I find Mr. J. H. Slater, in a paper read before the Bibliographical Society, and printed in its Transactions,[1] describing this Grimoire as an advocate of murder and all kinds of crimes. Furthermore, he confuses it throughout with the *Grand Grimoire*.

Taking the work at first hand, the initial question concerning it is the attribution of the authorship. From what we know of magical literature, to say nothing of pontifical dignity, it is antecedently unlikely that it is the work of a Roman bishop, more especially of such a bishop as Honorius. Éliphas Lévi, who rightly sought to vindicate the Church of his childhood, assailed, in the person of one of its sovereign pontiffs, by an unintelligent accusation, but vindicated it badly as usual, took a glance at the history of the time and discovered that during the pontificate of Honorius there was an anti-pope set up by Henry IV. of Germany, and that he was a man of evil life. He immediately conjectured that this personage was the likely author of the objectionable Grimoire. Again there is not a particle of evidence for such a surmise, and it is *un bien vilain procédé*, as M. Papus might say, to increase, without good reason, the responsibility resting upon the memory of the unhappy prelate in question.

[1] "Some Books on Magic." *Transactions of the Bibliographical Society*, Vol. iii. Part 2.

If we come to the facts, they are these. The first edition of the Grimoire is said to have appeared in 1629, and it is not likely that it was forged much earlier than the end of the sixteenth century, being, roughly, nine hundred years after the death of its supposed author. The canonical Pope, it must be confessed, was a voluminous writer; his sermons and his vast correspondence have appeared in two large volumes at Paris,[1] under auspices which were unlikely to admit even a contemptuous reference to the forged constitution. There is none, accordingly, which is to be regretted from the standpoint of bibliography. But the editor has further excluded with the same silence another work much more reasonably attributed, and to which no odium can attach. It is one also which is important to our inquiry, and it is entitled *Honorii Papæ adversus tenebrarum Principem et ejus Angelos Conjurationes ex originale Romæ servato*, Rome, 1529. The authenticity of this work is evidently questioned by its exclusion, and it is impossible to speak certainly concerning it, as, on account of its extreme rarity, few public libraries, none apparently in England, possess an example. But it is evidently the formularies of exorcism, a rite of the Church and possessing a considerable body of literature, to which even a Pope of past ages might not inconceivably have contributed. However this may be, the attribution in the one case will account for it in the other. The book of Black Magic may be merely a perversion of the orthodox conjurations, and if not that, is a reprisal; it is Sorcery revenging herself on a Pope who cast out devils by representing him as the prince of those who dealt with them.

Having said something to justify the Grimoire from groundless condemnation, it is necessary now to add, on the

[1] Horoy's *Bibliotheca Patristica Honorii III. Opera Omnia.* Paris, 1879, 8vo.

authority of its own evidence, that it is a malicious and somewhat clever imposture, which was undeniably calculated to deceive ignorant persons of its period who may have been magically inclined, more especially ignorant priests, since it pretends to convey the express sanction of the Apostolical Seat for the operations of Infernal Magic and Necromancy. The entire claim is set forth most curiously at the beginning of the pseudo-constitution, and must be cited at considerable length to convey its full force.

The Holy Apostolic Chair, unto which the keys of the Kingdom of Heaven were given by those words that Christ Jesus addressed to St. Peter : I give unto thee the Keys of the Kingdom of Heaven, and unto thee alone the power of commanding the Prince of Darkness and his angels, who, as slaves of their Master, do owe him honour, glory and obedience, by those other words of Christ Jesus : Thou shalt worship the Lord thy God, and Him only shalt thou serve—hence by the power of these Keys the Head of the Church has been made the Lord of Hell. But seeing that until this present the Sovereign Pontiffs have alone possessed the power of using invocations and commanding Spirits, His Holiness Honorius the Third, being moved by his pastoral care, has benignly desired to communicate the methods and faculty of invoking and controlling Spirits to his venerable Brethren in Jesus Christ, adding the Conjurations which must be used in such case, the whole being contained in the Bull which here follows.

HONORIUS,

Servant of the Servants of God, unto all and each of our venerable Brethren of the Holy Roman Church, Cardinals, Archbishops, Bishops, Abbots ; unto all and each of our sons in Jesus Christ, Priests, Deacons, Subdeacons, Acolytes, Exorcists, Cantors, Pastors, Clerks both Secular and Regular, Health and Apostolic Benediction. In those days when the Son of God, Saviour of the World, generated in the fulness of time, and born, according to the flesh, of the Race of David, did live on this earth, Whose Most Holy Name is Jesus, before which the heavens, earth and hell do bend the knee; we have seen with what power He commanded demons, which power was also transmitted to St. Peter by that utterance: Upon this rock I will build my Church, and the Gates of Hell shall not prevail against it. These words were addressed to St. Peter as the Head and Foundation of the Church. We then, who, by the mercy of God, and despite the poverty of our merit, have succeeded to the Sovereign Apostolate, and, as lawful successor of St. Peter, have the Keys of the Kingdom of Heaven committed to our hands, desiring to communicate the power of invoking and commanding Spirits, which hath been reserved unto us alone, and our possessors did alone enjoy; wishing, I repeat, by Divine inspiration, to share it with our venerable Brethren and dear sons in Jesus Christ, and fearing lest in the exorcism of the possessed,[1] they might otherwise be appalled at the frightful figures of those rebellious angels who in sin were cast into the abyss, lest also they should be insufficiently learned in those things which must be performed and observed, and that those who have been redeemed by the blood of Jesus Christ may not be tormented by any witchcraft or possessed by the demon, we have included in this Bull the manner of their invocation, which same must be observed inviolably. And because it is meet that the ministers of the Altar should have authority over the rebellious Spirits, we hereby depute unto them all

---

[1] This is an evasion of the Grimoire, which is no wise concerned with the offices of exorcism, but with the conjuration of evil spirits for the usual purposes of magicians.

powers which we possess, in virtue of the Holy Apostolic Chair, and we require them, by our Apostolic authority, to observe what follows inviolably, lest by some negligence unworthy of their character they should draw down on themselves the wrath of the Most High.

The *Grimorium Verum* has once been reprinted in the French language.[1] Of the Italian version there have been two modern editions, both poorly produced.[2] The book of *True Black Magic* is known only by the edition of 1750. The *Grand Grimoire* reappeared at Nismes in 1823 and is, moreover, in all respects identical with the work entitled the *Red Dragon*, of which there are several examples.[3] The *Grimoire of Honorius* is exceedingly rare in the original, but is better known by the reprints of 1660 and 1670, though these also are scarce. There is, finally, an edition dated 1760, and this even commands a high price among collectors. It remains to state that the Abbé d'Artigny was presented about the middle of the last century with an MS. copy of this Grimoire, which was much more complete that the printed editions. He gives no satisfactory account of it, nor can it be traced at this day. Possibly it represented the transition of the *Sworn Book of Honorius* into the Spurious Papal Constitution, which certainly reproduces the motive and moves in the atmosphere of its prototype.

[1] *Les Véritables Clavicules de Salomon. Trésor des Sciences Occultes, suivies d'un Grand Nombre des Secrets, et notamment de la Magie du Papillon Vert.* N.D.

[2] *La Vera Clavicola del Re Salomone, Tesoro delle Scienze Occulte con molti Altri Segreti e principalmonte La Cabala della Farfalla Verde tradotte dalla Lingua Straniera alla Lingua Italiana da Bestetti.* Milano, 1868. Also, with slight variations, Firenze, Armato Muzzi editore, 1880.

[3] For example, *Le Dragon Rouge, ou l'Art de Commander les Esprits célestes, aériens et infernaux.* A Milan, chez Gaspard Buffanelli. And, *Le Véritable Dragon Rouge, plus la Poule Npire, edition augmentée des secrets de la Reine Cleopâtre, secrets pour se rendre invisible, secrets d'Artephius, &c.* This is a reprint of the rare so-called edition of 1521 and is possibly still extant.

§ 5. *Minor and Spurious Rituals of Black Magic*

To distinguish in a mass of forged literature certain books as more spurious than others, seems at first sight a needless ingenuity of criticism. There are, however, some Rituals of Black Magic which are merely the knavish speculations of catchpenny booksellers, and there are others, anterior to the period, and foreign to the centres, of *colportage*, which have never exercised any influence, and are, in fact, generally unknown. Both classes neither possess a history nor have contributed anything to their subject. Yet it does not follow that they offer no points of curiosity or interest, and some account of them must be given in this place.

The *Verus Jesuitarum Libellus*, or " True Magical Work of the Jesuits, containing most powerful conjurations for all evil spirits of whatever state, condition and office they are, and a most powerful and approved conjuration of the Spirit Uriel ;[1] to which is added Cyprian's Invocation of Angels, and his Conjuration of the Spirits guarding Hidden Treasures, together with a form for their dismissal,"—purports. to have been published at Paris in the Latin tongue, and in the year 1508. It was reprinted by Scheible at Stuttgart in 1845, forming part of the curious collection of Faust documents already mentioned. Finally, in the year 1875, the late Major Herbert Irwin made, or procured privately, an English translation, which remains in MS. The date placed on the title-page of the original edition at once betrays the imposture. It will be almost needless to say that in the first decade of

---

[1] The modern reprint of Scheible reads *Usiel* throughout, as does also the MS. English translation. Supposing the latter to have followed the original edition, it would seem conclusive that the blunder—for such it evidently is—occurs also in that.

the sixteenth century there were no Jesuits; the Society originated with St. Ignatius, who died in 1556, being two years
after the confirmation of the Society by Pope Paul III. The
Conjurations are excessively curious. The first is addressed
to a spirit whose name is not indicated, but he is supposed to
have been obedient to Abraham and Isaac, and is directed
to bring the magician, out of the depths of the sea, so many
millions—the number is not specified and depends upon the
cupidity of the operator—of the best Spanish gold; otherwise,
says the Conjuration, I will condemn thy body (*sic*) and thy
soul. In the second formula, the spirit is cited by the knowledge and exorcising power of Agrippa,[1] which again puts
a definite limit to the antiquity of the collection, were it
otherwise necessary. The third Invocation is addressed to
the spirit *Zayariel*, who is conjured by *Agla Scheffert* and the
great *Jehova Podashocheia*. The remainder, to the number
of seven in all, are nearly identical in character and precisely
in purpose, the demon being invariably required to bring that
which is desired by the operator from the depths of the sea,
or from the abyss of the waters, or from the spiritual abyss.
The Discharge or Absolution which concludes the series is
really an additional conjuration.

The *Citation of St. Cyprian* is presumably an experiment
in what is distinguished as White Magic, seeing that it is addressed to an Angel who was the guest of Lot and Abraham.
The object being "help in need," and this in all simplicity,
it is apparently appropriate for every strait in life, and should
be, therefore, noted for reference by those who may think
it worth while; it is too cumbrous and tedious for these pages.
A similar observation would apply only too truly to the *Process
for the Magical Acquisition of Hidden Treasures*, but it is

---

[1] Cornelius Agrippa died in 1535.

much more complete than the rest and has so much connection with the *Summum Bonum*, the desire of the eyes of all Ceremonial Magic, that it may be held necessary to give it. It is, however, an operation of Necromancy and will be found in its proper place in the Second Part.[1] The *Verus Jesuitarum Libellus* closes with a fuliginous conjuration of the entire hierarchy of Infernus, which continues for many pages and contains more unintelligible words than several combined Grimoires. In the absence of all knowledge of its original edition, it is impossible to throw any light upon this singular imposture.

The *Praxis Magica Fausti*, or "Magical Elements of Dr. John Faust, Practitioner of Medicine," claims to have been printed from the original MS. in the Municipal Library of Weimar and is dated 1571, at which period it must be respectfully affirmed that there was no Municipal Library in the birthplace of Goethe. Furthermore, the existing collection does not include the MS. Whether the original edition was antedated cannot be certainly affirmed, as it is exceedingly scarce, and I am acquainted with it only in the reprint of Scheible and in an unprinted transcript by Major Irwin. The work consists of a few curious plates, in the manner of the seventeenth century, and a few unintelligible conjurations, all exceedingly brief. The third of these exhorts the Evil Spirit on the quaint ground that now it is the time of the Great Name *Tetragrammaton*. The purpose of citation is not indicated; the formulæ are Christian, broken up by innumerable crosses and by names and terms which defy conjecture as to their significance. The hierarchy of the spirit is determined by the closing words: "I command thee, O Spirit *Rumoar*, even by Lucifer, thy mighty sovereign."

[1] Part II. c. 9.

The Rituals of Black Magic

§ 6. *The Black Pullet*

The Black Pullet, the *Druid of Menapienne, Red Magic, or the Cream of the Occult Sciences*, with derivatives from the first of these works, such as the *Queen of the Hairy Flies*, the *Green Butterfly*, &c., form a class by themselves, and, with one exception, they are quite unserious publications, which can scarcely be called spurious, as they are almost without pretence.[1] They belong to the late end of the eighteenth century. Dr. Encausse, the head of the French Martinists, suggests that they were all fabricated at Rome and infers—as seen previously —that we owe them to the industry of priests, which seems to follow somewhat loosely from the evidence, is characteristic of himself and his school, and is indeed of much the same value as the statement in *Isis Unveiled*, that the habitual practice of Black Magic at the Vatican could be " easily proved."

The Black Pullet is far the most curious of its class and there is indeed sufficient individuality in its narrative to lift it much above the paltry impostures with which it connects. Its chief occult interest centres in the series of talismanic rings which it incorporates with the text, itself a species of magical romance. It makes no claim to antiquity, except that it embodies its wisdom, and it does not appeal to Solomon. In a book of Black Magic, as it certainly is, though the Goëtic intention is disguised, such modesty makes for virtue. Many of the Talismans seem to be original devices; at least they connect with nothing in occult symbolism known to the present

---

[1] Much depends, however, on the point of view of the critic. A work which, even in its own country, seems almost unknown, *Le Triple Vocabulaire Infernal*, a Manual of Demonomania, by Finellan, defines the Cabala as the art of communicating with elementary spirits, and adds that among the Grand Cabalas are included (1) That called the Green Butterfly; (2) That of the Black Pullet; (3) That of the Queen of Hairy Flies; and (4) That of the Black Screech Owl. The works containing these mysteries are, it is said, exceedingly rare.

writer. At the same time they are constructed in accordance with the rules laid down by the Fourth Book attributed to Cornelius Agrippa as regards infernal signatures.

The Black Pullet reappeared during its own period at various dates, with slight alterations—once as the *Treasure of the Old Man of the Pyramids*, when it was followed by a sequel or companion under the title of the *Black Screech Owl*. It has been reprinted within recent years at Paris in an edition intended for bibliophiles but bearing no indications of bibliographical research. Though modest in the claims which have been specified, the title of the original edition is portentous enough, namely, " The Black Pullet, or the Hen with the Golden Eggs, comprising the Science of Magical Talismans and Rings, the Art of Necromancy and of the Kabalah, for the Conjuration of Ærial and Infernal Spirits, of Sylphs, Undines and Gnomes, serviceable for the acquisition of the Secret Sciences, for the Discovery of Treasures, for obtaining power to command all beings and to unmask all Sciences and Bewitchments. The whole following the Doctrines of Socrates, Pythagoras, Zoroaster, Son of the Grand Aromasis, and other philosophers whose works in MS. escaped the conflagration of the Library of Ptolemy. Translated from the Language of the Magi and that of the Hieroglyphs by the Doctors Mizzaboula-Jabamīa, Danhuzerus, Nehmahmiah, Judahim, and Eliaeb. Rendered into French by A. J. S. D. R. L. G. F." The place of publication is Egypt, which probably stands for Rome, and the date is 740, meaning 1740, which, however, is untrue, as we shall see. It may be said at once that there is no pretence in the text to fulfil the magnificent assurances of the title.

The preface entreats that the *Black Pullet* may not be confounded with the collections of reveries and errors which so many have sought to accredit by announcing supernatural effects. This request, after due consideration, most readers will find it impossible to grant. The work, it has been said, is a romance, and the first thing which it makes clear is that even the addition of a thousand years to the date in the title is insufficient.[1] It is the narrative of a man who " formed part of the expedition to Egypt," and was "an officer in the army of the genius." The reference is, of course, to Napoleon and at best the date of composition is little more than a century ago. While in Egypt, the narrator was sent upon an expedition to the Pyramids, accompanied by some mounted chasseurs. They lunched under the shadow of the "grand colossus," when they were attacked by a horde of Arabs of the desert ; the comrades of the writer were slain and even he was left for dead upon the ground. On returning to consciousness, he surrendered himself to mournful reflections in the immediate anticipation of his end and delivered a valedictory address to the setting sun, when a stone was rolled back in the Pyramid, and a venerable man issued forth, who was proclaimed to be a Turk by his turban. This personage did not fail to discover the corpses which strewed the desert, nor to identify their nation. When the officer in his turn was examined, he manifested life by kissing the hand of the ancient man, who, superior to all prejudices which might have been dictated to the ordinary Mussulman by patriotism or religion, took pity on him, revived him by a wonderful cordial which put the wounded man upon his feet, and he followed his preserver into the Pyramid, wherein was the home of the ancient man and a mighty house of Magic. There were vast halls and endless galleries, subterranean chambers piled with treasures,

---

[1] It is not impossible that the middle of the nineteenth century may be the period to which it should be assigned.

apparitions of blazing lamps, ministering spirits innumerable, magic suppers; above all things there was the Black Pullet. In a word, diurnal life was illustrated throughout by the super-natural; it was a methodised version of Aladdin with an inner meaning by Astaroth. The sage himself proved to be the sole heir of the Magi and the makers of those Egyptian hiero-glyphics which are the "despair of the learned," while, not least, he was himself in quest of an heir, for he felt that he was about to pass away. In fine, the French officer, having acquired the Turkish language by means of a grammar which had its root in sorcery, and being thus enabled to converse with his protector, which on the whole seems superfluous, seeing that his protector possessed a talisman which communi-cated immediate proficiency in all tongues, was instructed in the powers and wonders of twenty-two talismanic figures and the rings corresponding to these, as well as in the secret of the manufacture of the Black Pullet, which possessed more skill in gold-finding than the divining rod in the discovery of water. After these instructions, in spite of many prayers, and the ministries of the genius *Odous*, the just man expired upon a sofa, while the fortunate kinsman in philosophy swooned at the feet of his benefactor. In due course, accompanied by the genius who had been transferred to his service, the French officer managed to depart from Egypt, laden with treasures, and with the ashes of the sage in a costly urn. He took ship for Marseilles, stilled a tempest on the voyage and re-turned to his native country. He made his abode in Provence, spending his days in experiments with the Black Pullet, or in study, meditation and rambling. He undertook at length to write this memorial of his good fortune, in which he threatens the publishers of any pirated edition to adorn them, by means of a talisman, with ears six inches longer than those of

Midas. But this does not seem to have prevented the publishers.

The Black Pullet disclaims all connection with Black Magic and is duly to be identified therewith, firstly by its characters and secondly by their pretended power over evil spirits; though it should be observed that the infernal beings mentioned in the title are not on the surface devils but Salamanders—that is to say, elementary Spirits of Fire. But while it thus transcends Black Magic—if it is requisite to make the distinction—it is not superior to plagiarism and hence incorporates many pages of the *Comte de Gabalis*.

For the evocation of the genii who served the Old Man of the Pyramid it suffices to say : THOMATOS, BENESSER, FLIANTER. You are then liable to be encompassed by thirty-three several intelligences. To obtain their consideration say : LITAN, IZER, OSNAS, and they will bow down before you, individually remarking : NANTHER. The words SOUTRAM, UBARSINENS will cause them to transport you through the air wheresoever you are inclined. Upon the utterance of the one word RABIAM they will return you to your own abode. It is necessary, however, to be fortified by the talismans and rings of the master, but they can be obtained by a cheap process. In the cabinet of the Old Man of the Pyramid they were formed of the precious metals and were resplendent with gems, but they are held to answer all practical purposes if the rings are composed of bronzed steel and the talismans of satin, in strict accordance with the description which here follows.

§ 7. *Talismans of the Sage of the Pyramids*

I. Serves for the conjuration of celestial and infernal powers. It should be embroidered in silver upon sky-blue satin. The evoking words are SIRAS, ETAR, BESANAR, at which multitudes of spirits will appear.

II. Gives the love and complaisance of the entire female sex. It should be embroidered in silver on black satin. The evoking words are NADES, SURADIS, MANINER, pronounced with

<table>
<tr><td>TALISMAN I.</td><td>TALISMAN II.</td></tr>
</table>

The characters should be graven on the inner side of the Ring

The characters should be graven on the inner side of the Ring

the ring—which should be on the middle finger of the left hand—pressed against the lips. This conjuration ensures the manifestation of a genius with rose-coloured wings, who, if addressed with the words SADER, PROSTAS, SOLASTER, will traverse all space to transport you the lady of your heart, though she were the queen of the Caliph's seraglio. At the words MAMMES, LAHER, she will be removed by four slaves. It will be observed that this is occult ribaldry.

The Rituals of Black Magic

III. Discovers all treasures and ensures their possession. The figure of the talisman should be embroidered in gold upon green satin. The words ONAÏM, PERANTÈS, RASONASTOS, will cause the appearance of seven genii *au teint bazané*, each of

TALISMAN III.

The characters should be graven on the inner side of the Ring

whom will pour out golden ducats from great bags of hide at the feet of the sorcerer, the operations of this Grimoire being performed upon a huge scale. *Item*, a black hooded bird will be perched upon the shoulder of each spirit.

IV. Discovers the most hidden secrets and enables its possessor to penetrate everywhere unseen. The talisman

The Book of Ceremonial Magic

should be of violet satin, with the figures embroidered in silver. It must be held in the left hand, on which also the ring should be worn, and should be placed close to the ear, pronouncing the words NITRÆ, RADOU, SUNANDAM, when a distinct voice will utter the desired mystery.

TALISMAN IV.   TALISMAN V.

The characters should be graven on the outer side of the Ring

The characters should be graven on the outer side of the Ring

V. Will make the most taciturn man unbosom himself to its possessor, whose enemies will also be forced to confess all their machinations. The talisman should be of gold-coloured satin with the figures embroidered in gold. By placing the ring on the little finger of the left hand, the talisman against the right ear, and by pronouncing the words NOCTAR, RAIBAN, the most discreet man—as I have indicated—will be compelled to unveil his utterly secret thoughts. The addition of the word

BIRANTHER will force the enemies of the possessor to declare their projects aloud.

VI. Sets to work enough genii for the immediate achievement of any work which the possessor may desire to undertake, and for the stoppage of any which may oppose him. The talis-

TALISMAN VI.   TALISMAN VII.

The characters should be graven on the outer side of the Ring

The characters should be graven on the inner side of the Ring

man should be of lilac satin with the figures embroidered in shaded silk. The magical words are ZORAMI, ZAITUX, ELASTOT.

VII. Has the power to destroy everything; to cause the fall of hail, thunderbolts and stars from heaven; to occasion earthquakes, storms and so forth. At the same time it preserves the friends of the possessor from accidents. The figure of the talisman should be embroidered in silver upon poppy-red satin. The magical words are: (1) DITAU, HURANDOS, for works of destruction; (2) RIDAS, TALIMOL, to command the

121

elements ; (3) ATROSIS, NARPIDA, for the fall of hail, &c.; (4) UUSUR, ITAR, for earthquakes ; (5) HISPEN, TROMADOR, for hurricanes and storms ; (6) PARANTHES, HISTANOS, for the preservation of friends.

VIII. Gives invisibility, even to the eyes of genii, so that

TALISMAN VIII.

*The characters should be graven on the outer
side of the Ring*

God alone shall witness the actions of the possessor. It is accompanied by the power of penetrating everywhere and passing through brick walls. The magical words are BENATIR, CARARKAU, DEDOS, ETINARMI. For each operation the ring must be placed upon a different finger of the right hand. The talisman is of yellow satin embroidered with black silk.

IX. Transports the possessor to any part of the world, and that without danger. The potent words are RADITUS, POLAS-

TRIEN, TERPANDU, OSTRATA, PERICATUR, ERMAS. The talisman is of puce-coloured satin embroidered with gold.

X. Opens all locks at a touch, whatever precautions have been taken to secure them. The magical words are SARITAP,

TALISMAN IX.   TALISMAN X.

The characters should be graven on the inner side of the Ring

The characters should be graven on the outer side of the Ring

PERNISOX, OTTARIM. The talisman is of deep blue satin embroidered with silver.

XI. Sets the possessor in any desired house without the preliminary of entering and reads the thoughts of all persons, so that they can be helped or harmed at pleasure. The talisman is of light grey satin embroidered with gold. To know thoughts, place it on your head, breathe upon the ring, and say : O TAROT, NIZAEL, ESTARNAS, TANTAREZ. To serve those who are worthy : NISTA, SAPER, VISNOS, and they will forthwith

The Book of Ceremonial Magic

enjoy every kind of prosperity. To punish your enemies or evil persons : XATROS, NIFER, ROXAS, TORTOS, and they will be immediately delivered to frightful torments.

XII. Destroys all projects formed against the possessor and compels rebellious spirits. The talisman is of rose-coloured

TALISMAN XI.   TALISMAN XII.

The characters should be graven on the outer side of the Ring   *The characters should be graven on the inner side of the Ring*

satin embroidered with silver. It should be placed upon a table, the left hand imposed upon it ; the ring should be on the middle finger of the right hand, and the operator, with bent head, should repeat in a low voice the words : SENAPOS, TERFITA, ESTAMOS, PERFITER, NOTARIN.

XIII. Endows the possessor with every virtue and talent, as well as with the desire to do good. All substances of evil quality can be rendered excellent by means of it. For the first

The Rituals of Black Magic

advantage, it is sufficient to raise up the talisman, having the ring upon the first joint of the third finger of the right hand, and to pronounce the words : TURAN, ESTONOS, FUZA. For the second, say : VAZOTAS, TESTANAR. The talisman should be of saffron-coloured satin embroidered with silver.

TALISMAN XIII.   TALISMAN XIV.

The characters should be graven on the outer side of the Ring

The characters should be graven on the outer side of the Ring

XIV. Gives the knowledge of all minerals and vegetables, with their virtues and properties ; gives also the universal medicine and the faculty of healing all sick persons. The talisman is of orange-coloured satin embroidered with silver. It should be worn upon the breast and the ring in a locket (kerchief) round the neck, secured by means of a ribbon of flame-coloured silk. The operative words are : RETERREM, SALIBAT, CRATARES, HISATER.

The Book of Ceremonial Magic

XV. Gives immunity from the most ferocious animals ; gives the means of overcoming them ; gives the knowledge of their language ; and drives mad animals away. The talisman should be of deep green satin embroidered with gold. For the first three objects, say : HOCATOS, IMORAD, SURATER, MARKILA. For the last : TRUMANTREM, RICONA, ESTUPIT, OXA.

TALISMAN XV.

TALISMAN XVI.

The characters should be graven on the outer side of the Ring

The characters should be graven on the outer side of the Ring

XVI. Gives discernment for the good or bad intentions of any person. The talisman is of black satin embroidered with gold. It should be placed upon the heart and the ring on the little finger of the right hand. The words are : CROSTES, FURINOT, KATIPA, GARINOS.

XVII. Gives all talents and a profound knowledge of every art, so that the possessor will outshine the toil-worn experts—

though unqualified by scholarship. Hereof are the advantages
of an art which—speaking generally concerning it—is nothing
except practical and the quality of its claims is not strained.
The talisman, which must be carried on the person, should be
of white satin embroidered with black silk. The operative
words are: RITAS, ONALUN, TERSORIT, OMBAS, SERPITAS,

TALISMAN XVII.   TALISMAN XVIII.

The characters should be graven on the inner   *The characters should be graven on the inner*
side of the Ring   *side of the Ring*

QUITATHAR, ZAMARATH, specifying the art which it is desired
to possess.

XVIII. Gives good fortune in any lottery. The talisman
is of cerise-coloured satin embroidered with gold and silver.
It should be bound upon the left arm by means of a white
ribbon, and the ring must be on the little finger of the right
hand. The words are: ROKES for a winning number, PILATUS
for an ambes-ace, ZOTOAS for a denary, TULITAS for a quater-

nary, Xatanitos for a quinary, being careful to pronounce all the words at the quine—an instruction which I do not quite grasp, but if the art or science of the lottery is followed at this day under the old laws, I commend the question to those who are experts therein. This is one of the lesser mysteries of

TALISMAN XIX.   TALISMAN XX.

The characters should be graven on the outer side of the Ring

The characters should be graven on the outer side of the Ring

occultism. At cards the same potent formula should be repeated when shuffling for self or partner. Before beginning, touch your left arm with your right hand in the neighbourhood of the talisman, and kiss the ring. These little contrivances can be effected, says the honest Grimoire, without exciting the notice of your opponent.

XIX. Gives the power of directing all the infernal hosts against the enemies of its possessor. The talisman is of greyish-white satin, shaded. It may be worn in any manner, and the words are : OSTHARIMAN, VISANTIPAROS, NOCTATUR.

XX. Gives the knowledge of the counsels of Infernus and the means of rendering its projects abortive, but whether for the ultimate health and weal of the operator's soul there is no guarantee offered. The talisman is of red satin, with the centre embroidered in gold, the border in silver and the figures in black and white silk. It should be worn upon the breast and the ring on the first joint of the little finger of the left hand. The words are : ACTATOS, CATIPTA, BEJOURAN, ITAPAN, MARNUTUS.

THE MAGIC ROD ACCORDING TO THE BLACK PULLET

These characters should be inscribed upon the Pod with Chinese Ink

The range of human ambition recognised by Ceremonial Magic being always somewhat restricted, it is not surprising that the offices of these talismans frequently overlap one another, or that some of them correspond very closely to the powers ascribed to the Magus by the transcendental science of the *Arbatel*.

THE GOËTIC CIRCLE OF THE BLACK PULLET

The talismans are preceded in the original by the figure of a magical rod, stained, says the letterpress which accompanies it, with the blood of a lamb and having the form of a serpent. The description is somewhat obscure, but the wand must be apparently flexible, so that it can be bent at need, and the mouth and tail joined by means of a golden chain, thus forming a circle. It will be observed that it is the old symbol, the great and mystic symbol, but in what strange company has it fallen! The wand should be six feet long and when bent can be used as a circle of evocation. There is also a figure of the grand magical circle, but it is not described in the text. There are thus twenty-two figures in all, and the inclusion of the word TAROT in the list of evoking terms is not without significance in this connection. A certain correspondence between the talismans and the Tarot Trumps is indeed unmistakable, at least in some instances, and seems to indicate that the work has a more definite occult aspect than would appear at first sight. It is the symbolism of the Trumps Major redirected towards the Powers of the Deep.

§ 8. *The Gold-Finding Hen*

I must pass, however, to the incubation of the gold-finding hen, which is the head and crown of the proceedings. The grand Oromasis, the father of Zoroaster, was the first person who possessed one of these marvellous fowls, which are hatched from an egg in the following manner. Take aromatic woods, such as aloes, cedar, orange, citron, laurel, iris-root, with rose-leaves dried in the sun. Place them in a golden chafing-dish; pour balsamic oil over them; add the finest incense and clear gum. Next say: ATHAS, SOLINAM, ERMINATOS, PASAIM; set a glass over the chafing-dish; direct the rays of the sun thereon, and the wood will kindle, the glass will melt—obviously by the magical power which resides in the operation—a sweet odour will fill the place and the compost will burn speedily to ashes. Place these ashes in a golden egg while still red-hot; lay the egg upon a black cushion ; cover it with a bell-glass of faceted rock-crystal ; then lift up your eyes and stretch your arms towards heaven and cry : O Sanataper, Ismaï, Nontapilus, Ertivaler, Canopistus. Expose the glass to the most fierce rays of the sun till it seems enveloped in flame, till the egg ceases to be visible, till a slight vapour rises. Presently you will discern a black pullet just beginning to move, when if you say : Binusas, Testipas, it will take wings and nestle in your bosom. It is not said that anything disastrous follows, but rather a certain advantage, which will appear in the next paragraph.

While this is the true process of the Pyramids and easy no doubt to an heir direct of Oromasis, it is obvious that it has its difficulties to those born merely under the common moon of sorcery, and, merciful, like all its companions, to human limitations, the Grimoire provides an alternative method suitable to persons of small means. Take an unspotted egg ; expose it to the meridian rays of the sun ; then select the blackest hen that you can meet with ; if it have any coloured feathers, pluck them. Should the Society for the Prevention of Cruelty to Animals not intervene opportunely, contrive to hood this bird with a kind of black bonnet, drawn over the eyes so that it cannot see. Leave it the use of its beak. Shut it up in a box, also lined with some black material, and large enough to hold it comfortably. Place the box in a room where no light of day can penetrate ; give food only in the night to the fowl ; see that no noise disturbs it, and set it to hatch the egg. As everything will be black to the bird, its imagination, which is likely enough, will be overwhelmed by the sense of blackness, and if it should survive the incarceration, it will ultimately incubate a perfectly black chicken, provided only that the operator by his wisdom and virtue is worthy to participate in such sacred and divine mysteries. It does not appear how or why a fowl incubated after this uncomfortable fashion should have a particular instinct for detecting the places wherein gold is hidden, but such is the faculty attributed to it, and it can only be concluded that the *Black Pullet* is a degree more foolish than its idle company of Grimoires.

The simplified process did not, however, in the opinion of sorcery, seem the last word which it was possible to say upon the subject. Despite the threatened vengeance of the heir of Oromasis, the mystery was adapted by the later editors of the *Red Dragon* and reappears as the *Grand Cabala*, without which no other can succeed. In this, its last transformation, it becomes a recipe for evoking the devil which seems to breathe the true spirit of Goëtic genius. Its success, as I must premise, will depend upon a recollected and devotional spirit in the operator, together with a clean conscience ; otherwise, in place of commanding the evil spirit, the latter will command him. This understood, the process itself is simple. You have merely to secure a black hen which has never been crossed by the male bird and to do this in such a manner that it shall not cackle ; it is best therefore to seize it in its sleep, clutching it by the neck, but not more than is necessary to prevent it from crying. You must repair to the highroad, walk till you come to a cross-way and there, on the stroke of midnight, describe a circle with a cypress rod, place yourself in the midst thereof and tear the bird in twain, pronouncing three times the words, *Euphas, Metahīm, frugativi et appellavi.* Next turn to the East, kneel down, recite a prayer and conclude it with the Grand Appellation, when the Unclean Spirit will appear to you in a scarlet surcoat, a yellow vest and breeches of pale green. His head will resemble that of a dog, but his ears will be those of an ass, with two horns above them ; he will have the legs and hoofs of a calf. He will ask for your orders, which you will give as you please, and as he cannot do otherwise than obey, you may become rich on the spot and thus the happiest of men. Such at least is the judgment of the Grimoire. Whether the victim of the process is to be torn in pieces alive does not explicitly

THE APPARITION OF THE GRAND CABALA

appear, but may be inferred from the initial precaution. This being the case, I have so modified the procedure that, in case it should be tried by a fool in these more civilised days, he will have only his pains for the trouble—by the hypothesis of the ceremonial art. This is therefore a word to the fool.

133

DEVIL STRUGGLING WITH ST. PETER.

Hyde Register, British Museum, Eleventh Century.

PLATE VI

THE SABBATIC GOAT

PART II

THE COMPLETE GRIMOIRE

**DEVIL FROM HEARNE'S PRINT OF
THE " DESCENT INTO HELL."**

Engraved by Michael Burghers, c. 1676.

CHAPTER I

The Preparation of the Operator

§ 1. *Concerning the Love of God*

THE rites of so-called Transcendental Magic are, *ex hypothesi*, divine and religious rites, and the counsels, spiritual and moral, which are found in its instructions are, in their meagre and puerile way, the vulgarised counsels of perfection, whatever element of sovereign contra-reason may obtain in its experiments.[1] The Composite Rituals, despite the result of their analysis, also partake largely of the nature of substituted religious observances, at times Judaistic, at times Christian. In both cases this fact is readily intelligible; to communicate with the fabled Spirits of the Firmament and to practise an art which offers to its adepts the regeneration of Enoch, King of the Inferior World,[2] "who was not, for God took him," may well demand a high degree of sanctity from its candidate, to whatever ends it may lead him; while to dominate the so-called Spirits of the Elements, the Kabalistic *Kliphoth* and the Evil Demons, it is reasonable to assume that the

---

[1] The analysis of the *Arbatel of Magic* in Part I. establishes this point, but the following passages may be cited in support of the statement. "In all things call upon the Name of the Lord, and without prayer unto God, through His only-begotten Son, do not thou undertake to do or to think anything." Aph. 2. "Let the word of God never depart from thy mouth." *Ib*. Aph. 3. "Look unto God in all things." *Ib*. Aph. 4. "Desire from God alone." *Ib*. Aph. 11. "Before all things, be watchful in this, that your name be written in Heaven." *Ib*.

[2] The secret of this Regeneration is promised to the adept in *Arbatel*, Aph. 24.

Magus must be free from common weakness, from common vice [1] and must be fortified by the grace and favour of the superior world. Given the magical standpoint in each case, the conditions essential to operation seem, in this respect, above challenge. Its recommendations, however, were more especially of times and seasons; they were for the work of the art in hand rather than for the high and transcendental art of holy life. But it will assuredly appear at first sight a bizarre anomaly that Black Magic should involve also religious observances and should exact similar conditions, both inward and outward, from those who would undertake its enterprises. It is not, as generally supposed, either Christianity *à rebours* or a reversed religion of Israel; it is not the intentional profanation of religious ritual and observance; it is something less outrageous but logically more insensate; so far as it has recourse to such ritual and such observance, it is not to do outrage to God in the interests of diabolism, but to derive power and virtue from above for the more successful control of Evil Spirits, and this obtains indifferently whether the purpose of the operator be otherwise lawful or not.

The Divine Love, says the book of *True Black Magic*,[2] must precede the acquisition of the Science of Solomon, son of King David, who said: The beginning and Key of my Wisdom are the fear of God, to do Him honour, to adore Him with great contrition of heart, and to invoke His aid in all our intentions and aspirations; which fulfilling, God will lead us into the good way.[3]

To account for this anomaly it is insufficient to say that

[1] "To overcome and subjugate the elementary spirits, we must never yield to their characteristic defects. . . . In a word, we must overcome them in their strength without ever being overcome by their weaknesses."—ÉLIPHAS LÉVI, *Rituel de la Haute Magie*, c. 4.

[2] Book I. c. 1.

[3] An adapted rendering of *The Key of Solomon*, Book I. c. 1.

The Preparation of the Operator

the book of *True Black Magic* is simply the *Key of Solomon* adapted to Goëtic intentions. In the first place, as already seen, it is impossible to read the Goëtic intention out of either of the Clavicles; and, in the second place, the same characteristics are found in the Grimoires which derive least of all from the Clavicles, namely, that of Honorius, and that called the *Grand Grimoire*. To meditate continually on the undertaking and to centre every hope in the infinite goodness of the Great Adonai, is the rule established by the latter as the first principle of success.[1]

Nor does the insensate nature of the processes of Black Magic offer explanation by itself. The attempt to propitiate the Deity by means of prayers, sacrifices and abstinence, and thus to obtain the Divine assistance for the successful consummation of hideous offences and preposterous or impossible undertakings, is, of course, madness; for the God acknowledged and invoked by Goëtic Magic is not the Principle of Evil, as the myth of Modern Satanism supposes,[2] but the "terrible and venerable Deity" Who destroyed the power of the rebellious angels—alternatively the Jehovah of the Jewish rituals and the Trinity of the Christian magical cycle. The insane observance followed in reality from the interpretation placed by Goëtic Theurgy on the fundamental doctrine of Practical Magic, namely, the power of Divine words to compel the obedience of all spirits to those who could pronounce them.[3]

---

[1] *Grand Grimoire*, Book I. c. 1.

[2] To do evil because it is pleasing to the Prince of Evil did not enter into the conception of Sorcery. Refinements of this kind are of late date, and mostly of French invention. The sorcerer who sought to do evil and had recourse for assistance to Satan was actuated by no recondite motive; he ministered merely to his own propensities for lust, wealth or revenge. He used Satan as an instrument, treated him and his inferiors as slaves, and always reckoned ultimately to elude the dangers of such dealings.

[3] The doctrine is summarised in a sentence by Éliphas Lévi, when he declares that the virtue of things has created words. Cornelius Agrippa refers it to Platonic teaching, affirming that a certain power or life belonging to the idea underlies the "form of the signification,"

Collections of these words and names were recited as invoking and binding forms, and, incorporated into a suitable setting of official prayers, were used in all magical ceremonies. Black Magic was sometimes their application to more unlawful purposes and sometimes to the same purposes. The utterance of the Divine Name, which was supposed to make the devils tremble and place them at the will of the Magus, was at least equally powerful, it was argued, to enforce their obedience for a purpose in consonance with their own nature. Behind this there lay also the tacit assumption that it was easier to control demons than to persuade angels. Then seeing that prayer to God and the invocation of the Divine Names presuppose a proper spirit of reverence, devotion and love as the condition upon which prayer is heard, it became a condition in Goëtia. The first impossibility required of the adept in Black Magic is therefore that he should love God before he bewitches his neighbour; that he should put all his hopes in God before he makes pact with Satan; that, in a word, he should be good in order to do evil.

§ 2. *Concerning Fortitude*

The spiritual intention of the operator being thus determined, his next step was the acquisition of the mental attitude appropriate to his future work. We may picture him in the traditional state of the sorcerer—poor, proscribed, envious, ambitious, and having no capacity for legitimate enterprises. Unable to earn money, he hankers after hidden treasures, and haunts those spots up and down the country-side which are reputed to conceal them. He has done this presumably for

that is, the voice or word, whence he also says that Magicians regard words as the "rays of things." *De Occulta Philosophia*, Book I. c. 70. Compare also his rendering of the Platonic doctrine that the form comes first from the idea. *Ibid.*, c. 13.

The Preparation of the Operator

a long time before determining to betake himself to Magic, but the earth will not yield up her hoards, for the gnomes and the Earth-Spirits, the Alastors and the Demons of the Solitudes, stand guard over the secrets of dead misers when the human ghost has ceased to walk in the neighbourhood. He does not long hesitate when he learns that the Grimoires of Black Magic are full of darksome rites and fell, mysterious words which compel or expel those guardians. The Church and State may threaten him with a fire for his flesh and a fire for his soul, but by watchfulness and secrecy he hopes to elude the one, and the other is a distant danger. Obviously, however, in order to reach his determination, he must arm himself with intrepidity and prudence, and this is the first counsel of his guides to the *Sanctum Regnum* of Goëtia.

"O men! O impotent mortals!" cries the author of the *Grand Grimoire*,[1] "tremble at your own temerity when you blindly aspire to the possession of a science so profound. Lift up your minds beyond your limited sphere, and learn of me that before you undertake anything it is necessary that you should become firm and immovable, besides being scrupulously attentive in the exact observation, step by step, of all things whatsoever that I shall tell you, without which precautions every operation will turn to your disadvantage, confusion and total destruction; while, on the contrary, by following my injunctions with precision, you will rise from your meanness and poverty, achieving a complete success in all your enterprises. Arm yourselves, therefore, with intrepidity, prudence, wisdom and virtue, as qualifications for this grand and illimitable work, in which I have passed sixty-and-seven years, toiling night and day for the attainment of success in so sublime an object."[2]

[1] Book I. c. 2.
[2] The speaker is pseudo-Solomon.

The Book of Ceremonial Magic

One would think that there were shorter roads to wealth and the satisfaction of the other common appetites.

§ 3. *Concerning Continence and Abstinence*

The *Fourth Book of Occult Philosophy*, referred to Cornelius Agrippa, but composite in character and spurious in attribution, as already seen, gives an exceedingly curious explanation of the rule of sanctity prescribed by all forms of Ceremonial Magic. The instruments used in the Art are ineffective without consecration. The act of consecration is the act by which virtue is imparted to them, and this virtue derives from two sources, the power of sanctification residing in Divine Names and in the prayers which incorporate them, and the power of sanctification residing in the holiness of the person consecrating.[1] An indispensable part of this holiness was the preservacion of chastity for a defined—but, it should be observed, a limited——period preceding operation, and it was to be combined with a fast of graduated severity. In their directions concerning these points the Rituals of Black Magic differ little from their prototypes, the earlier Keys of Solomon, the work of pseudo-Agrippa,[2] or *The Magical Elements* of Peter de Abano. Here is the direction of the Neophyte which occurs in the *Grand*

[1] Here the Fourth Book of Occult Philosophy merely reproduces the instruction of the genuine work. "Consecration is a lifting up of experiments, by which a spiritual soul, being drawn by proportion and conformity, is infused into the matter of our works according to the tradition of Magical Art rightly and lawfully prepared, and our work is vivified by the spirit of understanding. The efficacy of consecration is perfected by two things especially, viz., the virtue of the person himself consecrating and the virtue of the prayer itself. In the person are required holiness of life and a power to consecrate. The former, nature and desert perform ; the latter is acquired by imitation and dignification." Book III. c. 62. The virtue of prayer derives from its institution by God, the ordinance of the Church, or the commemoration which it may make of sacred things.

[2] So also in the Third Book *De Occulta Philosophia*, which is especially devoted to Ceremonial Magic, the student is directed to abstain "from all those things which infect either mind or spirit," and above all from idleness and luxury, "for the soul being suffocated by the

The Preparation of the Operator

Grimoire : "You must abstain during an entire quarter of the moon from the society of females, so as to protect yourself from the possibility of impurity. You must commence your magical quarter at the same moment with that of the luminary itself, by a pledge to the Grand Adonai, who is the Master of all Spirits, to make no more than two collations daily, that is to say, in every twenty-four hours of the said quarter of the Moon, which collations should be taken at noon and midnight, or, if it better please you, at seven o'clock in the morning and at the corresponding hour in the evening, using the following prayer previously to each repast during the whole of the said quarter :—

PRAYER

I implore Thee, O Thou Grand and Powerful ADONAY, *Master of all Spirits ! I beseech Thee, O* ELOIM ! *I implore Thee, O* JEHOVAH ! *O Grand* ADONAY, *I give unto Thee my soul, my heart, my inward parts, my hands, my feet, my desires, my entire being ! O Grand* ADONAY, *deign to be favourable unto me ! So be it. Amen.*

Then take your repast, disrobe as seldom and sleep as little as possible during the whole of the said period, but meditate continually on your undertaking, and centre all your hopes in the infinite goodness of the Great Adonay.[1]

The *Grimoire of Honorius*, which is intended exclusively for persons in Holy Orders, restricts the period of fasting to three

body and the lust thereof, can discern nothing that is celestial," c. 55. The fourth book merely says : "Let the man who would receive an oracle from the good spirits be chaste, pure and confessed." Compare Peter de Abano : "The operator should be clean and purified for the space of nine days before beginning the work ; he should be confessed also, and should receive the Holy Communion."

[1] *Grand Grimoire*, Book I. c. 2.

days, as will be seen later on, and makes no condition of continence in those who are devoted to celibacy. The *Grimorium Verum* prescribes a similar period and adds that the fast should be most austere, that human society and human communications must be avoided as much as possible, but those of women especially. The *Book of True Black Magic* varies the instruction as follows:[1] If the Priest-Exorcist would succeed in operation, he must, when all things else are prepared, abstain from every labour of soul and body, from much eating and drinking, from all luxury, from all vice, and he must meditate on those things which he is about to put in practice for nine complete days before undertaking the work; his assistants—if any—must do in like manner, so that all may be truly fulfilled. Let them begin by the following prayer, which should be recited twice in the night and once in the day.

PRAYER

O Lord God Almighty, be Thou favourable unto us, though unworthy to lift our eyes to Heaven by reason of the multitude of our offences! O God all-merciful, Who willest not the death of a sinner, but rather his true conversion, bestow Thy grace on us! O Lord, O God, full of compassion, aid us in this work which we are about to perform, that Thy Name may be blessed for ever! Amen.[2]

The concluding days of the fast should be additionally

---

[1] An adaptation of the *Key of Solomon*, Book II. c. 4.

[2] The following is added in the Clavicle, *loc. cit.*: O Lord God, Father Eternal! O Thou Who art seated upon Cherubim and Seraphim, Who beholdest the earth and the sea! Unto Thee do I lift up my hands, and beseech Thine aid alone—Thou Who art the fulfilment of good works, Who givest rest unto those who toil, Who humblest the proud, Who art Author of all life and Destroyer of death. Our rest art Thou, Protector of those who call upon Thee; do Thou guard and defend me in this undertaking, O Thou who livest and reignest for ever and ever. Amen.

The Preparation of the Operator

strict, the meals being limited to bread and water, with abstinence from all sin and repetition of the above prayer.

§ 4. *Concerning the External Preparation of the Operator, and firstly Concerning Ablution*

The rite of lustration, being the sacramental mark of inward cleanliness, is prescribed in all magical ceremonies, and is equally important in Goëtic art. The ordinary daily ablution itself becomes symbolical. When the operator rises in the morning, during the preparatory triduum prescribed by the *Grimorium Verum*, his hands and face must be sponged with a clean white cloth, using water which has been previously exorcised according to the indications of the Ritual [1] and reciting the

PREPARATORY PRAYER

Lord God ADONAY, *Who hast formed man out of nothing to Thine own image and likeness, and me also, unworthy sinner as I am, deign, I pray Thee, to bless* ✠ *and sanctify this water, that it may be healthful to my body and soul, that all delusion may depart from me. O Lord God, Almighty and Ineffable, Who didst lead forth Thy people from the land of Egypt, and didst cause them to pass dry-shod over the Red Sea! Grant that I may be cleansed by this water from all my sins and may appear innocent before Thee. Amen.*

The *Book of True Black Magic* observes that the bath is most necessary for Magical Art,[2] and that it must be taken on

---

[1] From these indications it follows literally that such water would hold quicklime in solution. The passage stands thus: "Warning: The said water must be that which was previously exorcised, wherein thy lime was put"—namely, for the dressing of the lambskin. But water consecrated at the same time is most probably intended.

[2] The statement is adapted from the *Key of Solomon*, Book II. c. 5, but the analogy ends with the prescription of warm water; the prayers differ and the whole ceremony is simplified in the Goëtic ritual.

the final day of the fast, when the exorcisor has been cleansed from all sins, when he has written with the pen of the Art, upon virgin paper or parchment, all the conjurations and exorcisms required in the practice, and has performed all the other preparatory ceremonies. From the crown of his head to the soles of his feet he must purify himself with warm exorcised water, saying as he does so: *O Lord Adonay, Who hast formed me in Thine image and in Thy likeness, deign to bless and sanctify this water, so that it may become unto me the salvation of my soul and body, and that no wickedness may ever find place within me.* . . . The Psalms *Dominus illuminatio mea* and *Dixit insipiens in corde suo* should be added.[1] Then he should dry himself.

The prayer following must be repeated—five times during the day and four times during the night—for the space of three days : ASTROSCHIO, ASATH, *à sacra* BEDRIMUBAL, FELUT, ANABOTOS, SERABILEM, SERGEN, GEMEN, DOMOS. *O Lord God, Who art seated above the heavens, Who beholdest the depths, grant me, I pray Thee, that those things which I conceive in my mind may also be executed by me, through Thee, O Great God, Who livest and reignest for ever and ever ! Amen.*

§ 5. *Concerning the External Preparation of the Operator, and secondly Concerning the Vestments*

The use of special garments in the ceremonies of Magic follows reasonably enough from the religious character ascribed to these operations. Peter de Abano recommends a priest's garment if possible, by which an alb may be understood.[2]

---

[1] These Psalms are numbered 13 and 26 in the Vulgate. They were possibly selected on account of the symbolism attaching to these numbers. Thirteen refers to death and resurrection into new life ; it thus connects with the regeneration typified by the bath. Twenty-six is the number of Jehovah. In the Authorised Version the same Psalms appear as 14 and 27.

[2] A long garment of white linen, close before and behind, covering the whole body even to the feet, and cinctured by a girdle—such is the ordinance of pseudo-Agrippa.

The Preparation of the Operator

The Book of Black Magic, following the *Key of Solomon*, and representing the Jewish rite, prescribes an outer vestment like that of the Levites, with the following characters embroidered in red silk upon the breast :—

All garments, even to the shirt, must be of linen cloth,[1] and when assuming them these words should be recited : ANTON, AMATOR, EMITES, THEODONIEL, PONCOR, PAGOR, ANITOR ;[2] *by the virtue of these most holy Angelic Names do I clothe myself, O Lord, in my Sabbath garments, that so I may fulfil, even unto their term, all things which I desire to effect through Thee, Most Holy* ADONAY, *Whose kingdom and rule endure for ever and ever. Amen.*

The shoes and hat should be of white leather, bearing the same characters[3] written in cinnabar diluted with gum-water, the pen of the Art being used. The following names must be written about the hat :[4] JEHOVA, behind ; ADONAY, on the right hand ; ELOY, on the left ; and GIBOR,[5] at the front.

[1] According to the *Key of Solomon* the thread of which they are made should be spun by a young maiden.

[2] The *Key of Solomon* renders these names differently, namely : *Amor, Amator, Amides, Ideodaniach, Pamor, Plaior, Anitor ;* for Sabbath garments it substitutes Vestments of Power.

[3] Special characters are given for the garment and the shoes by the *Clavicle.* They bear no analogy to anything in the Grimoire.

[4] For the hat or bonnet a crown is prescribed in the *Clavicle*, and it should be made of virgin paper.

[5] In place of these words the *Key of Solomon* substitutes *El* and *Elohim.*

CHAPTER II

The Initial Rites and Ceremonies

§ 1. Concerning the Virtues of the Planets

THE *Key of Solomon the King* is the only ordinary
Magical Ritual which regulates the operations of
Magical Art in accordance with a formal attribution
of certain hours in the day and night to the rule and influence
of certain planets, while the Book of *True Black Magic* is
the only Goëtic Grimoire which follows the Clavicle closely in
this as in other respects.[1] The directions given are, however,
exceedingly confused. The common attribution of the seven
days to the seven planets obtains in both cases, and is set
out in the Grimoire as follows :[2]—

Solday	. .	= Saturn	. .	= ♄	. .	= Saturday.
Zedex	. .	= Jupiter	. .	= ♃	. .	= Thursday.
Madime	. .	= Mars	. .	= ♂	. .	= Tuesday.
Zemen	. .	= Sol	. .	= ☉	. .	= Sunday.
Hogos	. .	= Venus	. .	= ♀	. .	= Friday.
Cocao	. .	= Mercury	. .	= ☿	. .	= Wednesday.
Zeveac	. .	= Moon	. .	= ☽	. .	= Monday.

But as there is inequality in the length of the days, says
the Grimoire—that is to say, the comparative duration of day

---

[1] It should be observed, however, that favourable days and hours are occasionally mentioned,
but there is no attempt at a systematic valuation of the times and seasons suitable to different
operations.

[2] The apparently barbarous names given in the table are corruptions of Hebrew words, and
the English editor of *The Key of Solomon* has restored their proper orthography, as follows :—
Shabbathai, Tzedek, Madim, Shemesh, Nogah, Cochab, Lebanah.

and night varies in accordance with the times of sunrise and sunset—so also the hours of the planets are unequal. When the day is, say, fifteen hours in length, to ascertain how many minutes compose an hour of the planet, multiply the fifteen hours by five ; the result is seventy-five, and as many minutes will form the hour of the planet of that day. The corresponding hours of the night are nine ; these multiplied by five produce forty-five, and as many minutes will form the hour of the planet of the night. The same method may be followed through all seasons of the year.

But in any given day of twenty-four hours the number of minutes is 1440, as against 1530 in the above computation, and the method is therefore absurd.[1] The attribution accepted by all writers on Natural Magic, and corresponding with the angelical succession in Peter de Abano, will be found in the following :—

TABLE OF PLANETARY HOURS COMPUTED FROM MIDNIGHT TO MIDNIGHT

HOURS OF THE DAY

	Sunday.	Monday.	Tuesday.	Wednesday.	Thursday.	Friday.	Saturday.
1.	Sun	Moon	Mars	Merc.	Jup.	Venus	Sat.
2.	Venus	Sat.	Sun	Moon	Mars	Merc.	Jup.
3.	Merc.	Jup.	Venus	Sat.	Sun	Moon	Mars
4.	Moon	Mars	Merc.	Jup.	Venus	Sat.	Sun
5.	Sat.	Sun	Moon	Mars	Merc.	Jup.	Venus
6.	Jup.	Venus	Sat.	Sun	Moon	Mars	Merc.
7.	Mars	Merc.	Jup.	Venus	Sat.	Sun	Moon
8.	Sun	Moon	Mars	Merc.	Jup.	Venus	Sat.
9.	Venus	Sat.	Sun	Moon	Mars	Merc.	Jup.
10.	Merc.	Jup.	Venus	Sat.	Sun	Moon	Mars
11.	Moon	Mars	Merc.	Jup.	Venus	Sat.	Sun
12.	Sat.	Sun	Moon	Mars	Merc.	Jup.	Venus

[1] It offers no analogy with the system set forth in the Clavicle, nor can it be definitely traced to any magical authority within my knowledge.

HOURS OF THE NIGHT

1. Jup. . . .	Venus . .	Sat. . . .	Sun . . .	Moon . .	Mars. . .	Merc.
2. Mars. . .	Merc. . .	Jup. . . .	Venus . .	Sat. . . .	Sun . . .	Moon
3. Sun . . .	Moon . .	Mars. . .	Merc. . .	Jup. . . .	Venus . .	Sat.
4. Venus . .	Sat. . . .	Sun . . .	Moon . .	Mars. . .	Merc. . .	Jup.
5. Merc. . .	Jup. . . .	Venus . .	Sat. . . .	Sun . . .	Moon . .	Mars
6. Moon . .	Mars. . .	Merc. . .	Jup. . . .	Venus . .	Sat. . . .	Sun
7. Sat. . . .	Sun . . .	Moon . .	Mars. . .	Merc. . .	Jup. . . .	Venus
8. Jup. . . .	Venus . .	Sat. . . .	Sun . . .	Moon . .	Mars. . .	Merc.
9. Mars. . .	Merc. . .	Jup. . . .	Venus . .	Sat. . . .	Sun . . .	Moon
10. Sun . . .	Moon . .	Mars. . .	Merc. . .	Jup. . . .	Venus . .	Sat.
11. Venus . .	Sat. . . .	Sun . . .	Moon . .	Mars. . .	Merc. . .	Jup.
12. Merc. . .	Jup. . . .	Venus . .	Sat. . . .	Sun . . .	Moon . .	Mars

It will be seen from this table that there is a recurring rule of the planets in unbroken succession through the whole week, after which the sequence recommences in the same order, each planet ruling the first and the eighth of the day hours and the third and the tenth of the night hours of the day referred to that planet. These constitute the planetary hours.

The *Book of Black Magic*, still following and confusing the statements of the Clavicle,[1] lays down that the hours of Saturn, Mars and Venus are good for communion with spirits ; the hour of Saturn serves for invoking souls in hell, and to have news of those who have died naturally. The souls of those who have been slain should be invoked in the hour and also on the day of Mars. It adds that experiments made faithfully and with great diligence, observing all that is laid down, will be invariably verified, but to fail over the smallest part will void perfection in any.

The hours of Saturn and of Mars are also good for preparation, on those days when they are in conjunction with the Moon, or indeed with one another.[2] In a contrary or quadrate aspect

---

[1] In the version that follows, which condenses and summarises the original, there is an attempt to reduce them to order, and to make them consistent, if not intelligible.

[2] The *Key of Solomon* says that the hours of Saturn and of Mars, and also the days in which the Moon is in conjunction with these planets, are admirable for experiments of hatred, enmity and discord. It will be seen in what sense this farrago of villainous nonsense can be regarded as on God's side, as its impossible English editor would doubtless wish us to believe.

they are good for experiences of hatred, lawsuits, enmities, discords and so forth. The hours of the Sun, Jupiter and Venus, especially their planetary hour, are favourable both to ordinary and extraordinary experiments not included in those already mentioned. Those of the Moon are especially suited to the conjuration of spirits, works of necromancy, and the finding of stolen goods; but the luminary must be collocated and in a terrestrial sign—that is to say, (in conjunction) with Mercury for love, favours and invisibility; for works of hatred and discord in a sign belonging to the fiery triplicity—Aries, Leo, Sagittarius; for extraordinary experiences in an aquatic sign—Cancer, Scorpio, or Pisces. Should, however, the observation of these rules seem over-difficult, " do this only "—see that the Moon waxing is in an equal number of degrees with the Sun; it is then very good for the performance of the above experiments. When the full Moon is in opposition to the Sun, it is excellent for warlike, riotous and discordant experiments; in its last quarter it favours works which deal directly with operations of destruction and ruin. The best time for the experiences of death and invisibility is when the Moon is almost deprived of light.

When the Moon is in conjunction with the Sun nothing must be undertaken, because it is an unfortunate time and all things fail therein; but when in its crescent period, acuated with light, any experiences may be prepared and any writings and operations accomplished, especially for conversing with spirits. It must, however, be the day of Mercury and in the hour of that planet, the Moon being in an earthly or aërial sign, as above said, and in a pair number with the Sun.[1]

---

[1] The attribution in the original is throughout this portion not only erroneous. but seems to involve impossible positions. It has been corrected partially, in accordance with the Clavicle.

§ 2. *A General Instruction concerning the Instruments required for the Art*

Most Goëtic rituals specify with considerable minuteness the instruments which are required for the operations, and in these respects, but with variations peculiar to themselves, and distinguishing them also from one another, they follow the authority of the *Key of Solomon*. Peter de Abano tells us nothing concerning them, nor yet pseudo-Agrippa, with the one exception of the sword, which, following a physical analogy, seems to be universal in practical magic. In the Grimoires, however, though sometimes the first weapon to be mentioned, its position is comparatively insignificant, as the knife is a readier instrument. Speaking generally, there is little in the literature to justify the complex modern elaborations of Éliphas Lévi and of Christian.

Among the necessary properties mentioned by the Book of *True Black Magic* are the sword, the staff, the rod, the lancet, the arctrave or hook, the bolline or sickle, the needle, the poniard, a white-handled knife and another knife, with a black handle, used to describe the circle. The most important to make is that called the bolline; it must be forged on the day and in the hour of Jupiter, selecting a small piece of unused steel. Set it thrice in the fire and extinguish it in the blood of a mole mixed with the juice of the pimpernel.[1] Let this be done when the Moon is in her full light and course. On the same day and in the hour of Jupiter, fit a horn handle[2] to the steel,

---

[1] Or, according to the *Key of Solomon*, in the day and hour of Mercury, and substituting the blood of the magpie and the juice of the herb Mercury, the French *Foirole*, from which a so-called Elixir of Long Life was formerly made.

[2] The *Key of Solomon* substitutes white boxwood; it omits the planetary influence, leaving it to be inferred that it should be done in the hour that the steel is forged, which must also be sunrise.

shaping it with a new sword forged thrice as above in the fire. When made and perfected, recite over it this

PRAYER OR CONJURATION

I conjure thee, O form of this instrument, by the authority of God the Father Almighty, by the virtue of Heaven and the stars, by the virtue of the Angels, by that of the elements, by that of stones and herbs, and in like manner by the virtue of snowstorms, thunder and winds, that thou receive all power unto the performance of those things in the perfection of which we are concerned, the whole without trickery, falsehood or deception, by the command of God, Creator of the ages and Emperor of the Angels. Amen.

The ensuing salutations must then be pronounced over the instrument: *Domine, Deus meus, in te speravi; Confitebor tibi, Domine, in toto corde meo: Quemadmodum desiderat cervus ad fontes aquarum,*[1] &c., adding the following words: DAMAHII, LUMECH, GADAL, PANCIA, VELOAS, MEOROD, LAMIDOCH, BALDACH, ANERETHON, MITATRON, *most holy angels, be ye wardens of this instrument, because I shall make use of it for several necessary works.*

Place it in a new wrapper of red silk, making suffumigation with odoriferous perfumes, as will be hereinafter set forth. Take care not to perfect the instrument otherwise than on the day of Venus, and in the hour thereof, when also the needle and other like instruments may be prepared.

Subsequently, on the day of Venus, the Moon being in the sign of Capricorn, or otherwise of the Virgin,[2] if the same be

---

[1] Psalms vii., cx., and xli., according to the computation of the Vulgate.
[2] According to the *Key of Solomon*, it should be on the day and in the hour of Mercury, when Mars is in Aries or Scorpio.

possible, thou shalt make the first knife and shalt steep it in the blood of the mole[1] and the juice of the pimpernel. Let the Moon be in an acute time of course and light, the operation beginning in the first hour of Venus and ending at the ninth hour of the same day. Fit the knife with a handle of white wood cut at a single stroke with a new sword or knife, and on this handle engrave the following characters :—

Fumigate as before, and with this knife do all things needful to the Art, the circle excepted. But if such a knife be too difficult to manufacture, procure one of the same form ready made ; steep it in the blood and juice as above ; fit thereto the same handle bearing the same characters, and upon the blade, proceeding from point to handle, write with a male goose-quill the words : AHARARAT, TŌ. Perfume as before, sprinkle with exorcised water, and place in the silken wrapper already mentioned.[2]

That with the black handle, destined to describe the circle and intimidate the spirits, and for performing other similar things, must be made in every respect like the first, except as regards the day and hour, which should be those of Saturn. The steel should be extinguished in the blood of a cat[3] and the juice of hemlock, while the handle should be of sheep's horn. The

---

[1] Of a gosling, says the Clavicle.

[2] It should be understood that wherever the use of animal blood is prescribed I have made an alteration at some hypothetically essential point, and now give notice, generally and especially, to this effect. The course taken does not mean that I believe in the efficacy of these foolish processes, but that knavish persons may be dissuaded from trying them. It is out of respect to the animals and not consideration to them.

[3] Of a black cat, says the Clavicle, and the weapon when finished should be wrapped in a cloth of black silk, which, however, contradicts Book ii. c. 20, of the same work.

Fig. 1.

Fig. 2.

Fig. 3.

Fig. 4.

Fig. 5.

Fig. 6.

Fig. 7.

Fig. 8.

Fig. 9.

Fig. 10.

Fig. 11.

Fig. 12.

Fig. 13.

PLATE VII

INSTRUMENTS OF BLACK MAGIC

poniard or stiletto and the lancet should be made after the same manner on the day and in the hour of Mercury, and the steel extinguished in the blood of a mole and the juice of the herb Mercury. They should be fitted with horn handles,[1] shaped with a new sword in the day and hour of Mercury, and should bear these characters upon the said handles :—

Fumigate as before, and use in their proper place as required.

The *Grimorium Verum*, which makes for simplicity, reduces the steel instruments to three—namely, knife, graver and lancet. The two first should be made on the day and in the hour of Jupiter, with the waxing Moon in the ascendant, which is at issue with the previous authority. When finished, the following Prayer or Conjuration must, in each case, be recited over them. The knife should be large enough to sever the neck of a kid at one blow; it should be fitted with a haft of wood, made on the same day and in the same hour, and graven with magical characters. The instrument should then be sprinkled, fumigated and preserved for use as required.

CONJURATION

I conjure thee, form of the instrument, N., by God the Father Almighty; by the virtue of Heaven and by all the stars which rule; by the virtue of the four elements; by that of all stones, all plants and all animals whatsoever; by the virtue of hailstorms and winds; to receive such virtue herein that we may

---

[1] White boxwood is prescribed by the *Key of Solomon*.

obtain by thee the perfect issue of all our desires, which also we seek to perform without evil, without deception, by God, the Creator of the Sun and the Angels. Amen.

Recite the Seven [Penitential] Psalms, and add these words : DALMALEY, LAMECK, CADAT, PANCIA, VELOUS, MERROE, LAMIDECK, CALDULECH, ANERETON, MITRATON, *most pure Angels, be ye guardians of these instruments, which are needful for many things.*

The lancet, which is mentioned but not described in the Book of *True Black Magic*, should, according to the *Grimorium Verum*, be made in the day and hour of Mercury, the Moon waxing, and should be conjured after the same manner as the knife and graver. If assistants accompany the operator, each must be provided with his knife, and the like rule obtains concerning the Sword of the Art, which should be polished on the day of Mercury, from the first to the third hour of the night.[1] That designed for the Master or chief operator should bear the words ELOHIM JITOR,[2] proceeding from point to hilt. For that of the first disciple, write the name CARDIEL upon the handle, and upon the blade REGION, proceeding from point to hilt. It should appear on both sides transversely, but add on the one PANORAIM ✠, and on the other HEOMESIM ✠. On the sword of the second disciple write URIEL, SARAION, GAMERIN ✠, DEBALIIN, in the manner before described. On that of the third disciple write DANIEL, IMETON, LAMEDIIN ✠, ERADIN, and fit the same with a handle of white bone.[3]

---

[1] The first or the fifteenth hour is the reading of the *Key*, but there is more reason in the longer period, having regard to the nature of the operation.

[2] *i.e., Elohim Gibor.* The *Key of Solomon* prescribes other Divine Names for the Sword of the Master.

[3] These instructions are terribly confused. Compare the English version of the *Key of Solomon*, wherein the passage is thus amended :— "The first sword should have on the pommel the name *Cardiel* or *Gabriel;* on the Lamen of the Guard, *Region;* on the Blade, *Panoraim Heamesin.* The second should have on the pommel the name *Auriel;* on the Lamen of the

The Initial Rites and Ceremonies

The following Conjuration must be recited secretly over the swords :—*I conjure you, O sword, by the three Holy Names,* ALBROT, ABRACADABRA, JEOVA! *Be thou my fortress and defence against all enemies, visible and invisible, in every magical work. By the Holy Name* SADAY, *which is great in power, and by these other names,* CADOS, CADOS, CADOS, ADONAY, ELOY, ZENA, OTH, OCHIMANUEL, *the First and the Last, Wisdom, Way, Life, Virtue, Chief, Mouth, Speech, Splendour, Light, Sun, Fountain, Glory, Mountain, Vine, Gate, Stone, Staff, Priest, Immortal,* MESSIAH, *Sword, do thou rule in all my affairs and prevail in those things which oppose me. Amen.*

§ 3. *Concerning the Rod and Staff of the Art*

The great mystery of practical magic is supposed to be centred in the Magic Rod, and Éliphas Lévi, who claims to have reconstructed the primitive ceremonial, but seems rather to have over-edited his materials, supplies a highly sensational account of its powers and an elaborate method of its preparation. For him it is the sign of the transmission of the magical priesthood, which has never ceased since the darksome origin of pseudo-transcendent science. The operator is overwhelmed with precautions concerning the secrecy which must be maintained in regard to it and might well be dejected by the difficulties of its consecration. In view of such imputed importance, it is curious that De Abano and pseudo-Agrippa omit all mention of this tremendous instrument, while the *Key of Solomon* dismisses it in a few lines of easy instruction. It would appear, however, that a staff and rod are both necessary, especially in Goëtic operations, though their distinctive provinces are in no

Guard, *Sarion ;* on the Blade, *Gamorin Debalin.* The third sword should have on the pommel the name *Damiel* or *Raphael ;* on the Lamen of the Guard, *Yemeton ;* on the Blade, *Lamedin Eradim.*"

case described. According to the Book of *True Black Magic*, the staff should be of cane and the wand or rod of hazel, both virgin—that is, having no branches or offshoots.[1] They must be cut and trimmed on the day and in the hour of the Sun, while the following characters must be inscribed upon the staff, but on the day and in the hour of Mercury :[2]—

If engraved with the "sacred instrument," it will be so much the better.[3] In either case, let the following words be recited when the writing is finished :—O ADONAY, *most Holy and most Powerful, vouchsafe to consecrate and bless this Staff and this Rod, so that they may possess the required virtue, O most Holy* ADONAY, *to whom be honour and glory for ever and ever. Amen.*

Lastly, the two instruments should be asperged, fumigated and put away in the silken cloth.

The *Grimorium Verum* directs the operator to make two wands of wood which has never borne fruit. The first should be cut at a single stroke from an elder-tree on the day and in the hour of Mercury. The second should be of hazel, free from bud, and cut in the hour of the Sun.[4] The magical characters which must be engraved upon each have been omitted by the printer, but they are supplied—or their substitutes—in

---

[1] The definition of virgin wood differs in the *Key of Solomon*, which says: In all cases the wood should be virgin—that is, of one year's growth only.

[2] According to the *Key of Solomon*, both staff and rod should be cut on the day and in the hour of Mercury at sunrise, which limits the operation to the few days of the middle winter, when the sun rises about eight o'clock.

[3] Presumably, with the burin or graver.

[4] This variation appears to reconcile the *Book of True Black Magic* with the *Key of Solomon*, and is probably the true reading.

the modern Italian versions. They are, for the first, the seal or character of *Frimost* and that of *Klippoth* for the second (see Chap. III., Sec. 2). The prayer of consecration offers no variation of importance from that of *True Black Magic*, and does not need to be reproduced. Aspersion and fumigation are prescribed, as in the previous case.

The *Grand Grimoire* devotes an entire chapter to the true composition of the Mysterious Wand, otherwise the Destroying or Blasting Rod. It mentions no other instrument, and ascribes to it all power in diabolical evocations. It would seem to have supplied Éliphas Lévi with the first hint of his still more potent *Verendum*, to which, however, an allegorial significance may perhaps be attributed. On the eve of the great enterprise, says this Ritual, you must go in search of a wand or rod of wild hazel which has never borne fruit ; its length should be nineteen and a half inches. When you have met with a wand of the required form, touch it not otherwise than with your eyes ; let it stay till the next morning, which is the day of operation ; then must you cut it absolutely at the moment when the sun rises ; strip it of its leaves and lesser branches, if any there be, using the knife of sacrifice stained with the blood of the victim.[1] Begin cutting it when the sun is first rising over this hemisphere, and pronounce the following words :—*I beseech Thee, O Grand* ADONAY, ELOIM, ARIEL *and* JEHOVAM, *to be propitious unto me, and to endow this Wand which I am cutting with the power and virtue of the rods of Jacob, of Moses and of the mighty Joshua ! I also beseech Thee, O Grand* ADONAY, ELOIM, ARIEL *and* JEHOVAM, *to infuse into this Rod the whole strength of Samson, the righteous wrath of* EMANUEL *and the thunders of mighty Zariatnatmik, who will avenge the crimes of men at the Day of Judgment ! Amen.*

[1] See Chapter VI., Sec. 1.

163

Having pronounced these "sublime and terrific words," and still keeping your eyes turned towards the region of the rising sun, you may finish cutting your rod, and may then carry it to your abode. You must next go in search of a piece of ordinary wood, fashion the two ends like those of the genuine rod and take it to an ironsmith, who shall weld the steel blade of the sacrificial knife into two pointed caps and shall affix them to the said ends. This done, you may again return home, and there, with your own hands, affix the steel caps to the joints of the genuine rod. Subsequently, you must obtain a piece of loadstone and magnetise the steel ends, pronouncing the following words:—*By the grand* ADONAY, ELOIM, ARIEL *and* JEHOVAM, *I bid thee join with and attract all substances which I desire, by the power of the sublime* ADONAY, ELOIM, ARIEL *and* JEHOVAM. *I command thee, by the opposition of fire and water, to separate all substances, as they were separated on the day of the world's creation. Amen.*

Finally, you must rejoice in the honour and glory of the sublime Adonay, being convinced that you are in possession of a most priceless Treasure of the Light.[1]

§ 4. *Concerning the Pen and Ink of the Art*

Preliminary magical ceremonial seems to have as its chief object the personal consecration of every article, great or small, indispensable or occasional, which is connected with the several processes. The pen and ink with which characters and names

---

[1] Another method of preparing a Magic Rod ordains that it shall be a branch of the hazel-tree put forth during the year of operation. It must be cut on the first Wednesday after the new moon, between 11 P.M. and midnight. The knife must be new and the branch severed by a downward stroke. The rod must then be blessed; at the stouter end must be written the word AGLA ✠, in the centre ON ✠, and towards the point TETRAGRAMMATON ✠. Lastly, say over it : *Conjuro te cito mihi obedire*—I conjure thee to obey me forthwith.

are written must both be specially prepared. Take a new quill, says the *Grimorium Verum;* asperge and fumigate it after the manner of the other instruments ; when you hold it in your hand to shape it, say the following words :—ABABALOY, SAMOY, ESCAVOR, ADONAY : *I have expelled all illusion from this pen, that it may retain efficaciously within it the virtue necessary for all things which are used in this Art, as well for operations as for characters and conjurations. Amen.*

In like manner, a horn or ink-well must be bought on the day and in the hour of Mercury, and in the same hour the following names of God must be written about it :—JOD, HE, VAU, HE, METATRON, JOD,[1] CADOS,[2] ELOYM,[3] SABAOTH. It must then be filled with fresh ink which has been exorcised as follows :—

EXORCISM OF THE INK

I exorcise thee, creature of Ink, by ANSTON, CERRETON, STIMULATOR,[4] ADONAY, *and by the name of Him Whose one Word created all and can achieve all, that so thou shalt assist me in my work, that my work may be accomplished by my will, and fulfilled with the permission of God, Who ruleth in all things and through all things, everywhere and for ever. Amen.*

BENEDICTION OF THE INK

Lord God Almighty, Who rulest all and reignest through all eternity, Who dost fulfil great wonders in Thy creatures, grant unto us the grace of Thy Holy Spirit by means of this ink. Bless it ✠ *, sanctify it* ✠ *and confer upon it a peculiar*

---

[1] The *Key of Solomon* substitutes the Divine Name, *Jah*, thrice repeated.
[2] *i.e.*, *Kadosh*.   [3] *i.e.*, *Elohim*.
[4] The *Key of Solomon* reads *Anaireton, Simulator.*

virtue, so that whatsoever is said, whatsoever we desire to do and to write herewith, may succeed through Thee, Most Holy Prince ADONAY. *Amen.*[1]

Then asperge, fumigate and exorcise.

The Book of True Black Magic, on the other hand, directs the operator to pluck the third feather from the right wing of a male goose[2] and to say when extracting it : ABRACHAY, ARATON, SAMATOY, SCAVER, ADONAY! *Expel all evil from this feather, so that it may possess full power to write whatsoever I will.*

Then shape it with the Knife of the Art, namely, that having a white handle ; incense also and asperge it. Lastly, take a new earthen cornicle or inkhorn, made on the day and in the hour of Venus, and write about it these names with the exorcised lancet of the Art : JOD, HE, VAU, HE, MITATRON, JAE,[3] JAE, JAE, CADOS, ELOYN, ZEVAO.[4] Then dip the pen therein, pronouncing the following words :—*I exorcise thee, creature of the feather kind, by* ETERETON,[5] *by* STIMULATON[5] *and by the name* ADONAY. *Do thou aid me in all my works.*

The instruction continues :—As it is sometimes necessary to write with coloured inks, have several horns containing white inks, in which infuse thy colours for the pentacles and characters. The colours must be diluted with the blessed water which we term exorcised, and with gum arabic. Lastly, perfume them. Let this be done with all devotion, humility and

---

[1] This prayer, like many others in the Grimoires which derive from the Clavicle, is the introduction of a Christian compiler. The *Key of Solomon* has no Trinitarian references and no crosses.

[2] This process is identical with that of the Clavicle, the names only being mutilated.

[3] *i.e., Jah.*

[4] *i.e., Elohim Tzabaoth.*

[5] As before, *Anaireton* and *Simulator.*

faith, wanting which nothing can be accomplished, says the Grimoire.

The same work gives particulars concerning the extraction of the sword-feather from the right wing of a swallow, preceding the action with the words *Yin He*. It should then be made into a pen by means of the Knife of the Art, and the name Anereton must be written on it with the goose-quill, after which the Psalms *Ecce quam bonum et quam jucundum* and *Laudate Dominum omnes gentes* [1] are to be recited over it, followed by aspersion and fumigation.

It is not to be supposed that any ordinary ink could be suitable for so serious a business as that of engrossing pacts. Even the consecrations previously given are inadequate in such a case. It is understood that the signature is written with the blood of the operator, but the deed itself requires a special preparation, as follows :—Place river-water in a new, varnished earthenware pot, together with the powder hereinafter described. Then take sprigs of fern gathered on the Eve of St. John and vine twigs cut in the full moon of March. Kindle this wood by means of virgin paper, and when the water boils the ink will be made. It must be changed each time that there is occasion to write, that is to say, whensoever the appellation of a spirit is undertaken.

Powder for Pact-Ink

℞ Gall-nuts . . . . . . 10 oz.
Roman Vitriol or Green Copperas . . 3 oz.
Rock Alum or Gum Arabic . . . 3 oz.

Make an impalpable powder, and when you would compose the ink, use as above described.

The authorities for this process are not the Grimoires proper

[1] Psalms cxxxii. and cxvi. of the Vulgate.

but the collections of Magical Secrets which are sometimes appended to them but sometimes form independent works.

§ 5. *Concerning Virgin Wax or Virgin Earth* [1]

The candles used in evocation or in other magical experiences, and the images required for bewitchment, must be composed of virgin wax or virgin earth—that is to say, the substances in question must not have been applied previously to another purpose.[2] Before operating the following words must be recited over the material :—ENTABOR, NATABOR, *Si tacibor*, ADONAY, AN, LAYAMON, TINARMES, EOS PHILODES.[3] *Angels of God, be ye present! I invoke you in my work, that I may obtain virtue by your mediation and may be perfected very surely.* Then recite the Psalms *Domine, non est exaltatum cor meum* and *Domine, quis habitabit*,[4] adding these words : *I exorcise thee, creature of wax [or earth], and, by the Creator and God Almighty, Who created all things from nothing by His Most Holy Name, and by His angels, I ordain thee to receive virtue and benediction in His Name, that so thou mayst be sanctified and blessed, thus obtaining that virtue which we desire, by the Most Holy Name* ADONAY, *which is the life of all creatures, Amen.* Asperge the substance with the holy water of the Art, after which preserve it, to make use thereof when needed. So doing, says *True Black Magic*, thou shalt obtain a sure result in all which thou undertakest.[5]

---

[1] This process is adapted from the *Key of Solomon*, Book ii. c. 8.

[2] The virginity of the wax and the earth is more perfectly ensured by the directions of the *Key of Solomon*, in accordance with which the operator must dig up the earth with his own hands and reduce it to a paste, using no instrument in case of defilement. The wax must be taken from bees who have made it for the first time.

[3] These names differ from those in the *Key of Solomon*, which, however, are, for the most part, equally unintelligible.

[4] Ps. cxxx. and Ps. xiv. in the Vulgate.

[5] The *Key of Solomon* directs that the earth should be freshly dug up on each occasion that it is required.

The Initial Rites and Ceremonies

§ 6. *Concerning the Silken Cloth*[1]

When all the instruments belonging to the Art have been properly consecrated and exorcised, they must be gathered into a costly cloth of silk, as Solomon ordains—says the testament—whereby they may be preserved clean and pure and may thus be more efficacious. So it be not black or brown, the colour is indifferent, but the following characters must be written upon it in pigeon's blood with the male goose-quill proper to the Art.

Add these names : ADONAY, AMMASTIUS, ANARETON, COSBOS, ELOYM. Then fumigate and asperge, reciting subsequently the Psalms *Domine, Dominus noster, Deus Judicium tuum Regi da* and *Ecce nunc dimittis.*[2] Place, lastly, all the magical instruments in this silken cloth. " So shalt thou use them at will and shalt learn their effect," says the Magus, Iroë-Grego. But the pledge has a savour of the salt which is called prudence.

§ 7. *Concerning the Victim of the Art*

It is usually supposed that the offering of a bloody sacrifice is an essential condition of success in Black Magic and that the embrutement of the operator is the chief purpose of the ordination. It is true that such an offering is in most cases enjoined, but its object is simple and commonplace rather than diabolical or recondite, and the practice itself is based on the so-called White Magic of the *Key of Solomon*. It offers

---

[1] This process is adapted from the *Key of Solomon*, Book ii. c. 20. There, however, the use of blood is omitted.

[2] Psalm viii. and Psalm lxxi. in the Vulgate, together with the Canticle of Simeon.

another instance that if this text be the head and fount of the Art, it is also the root of its diabolism. The Art—I should explain—has its victim, not because blood is required in the one case more than the other, but because it was customary for pacts and pentacles to be written on parchment or vellum, and, in view of that doctrine of personal consecration already explained, the Black Magician had, as far as possible, to dispense with outside labour, to be his own whitesmith, his own penmaker, and hence also his own tanner. *Alterius non sit qui suus esse potest* was the maxim of Paracelsus, and it was carried further in Goëtia than mere intellectual independence. Make yourself what you want; do not trust it to others; it will not only possess more of your personal virtue, but you will be sure of the article—such might be the commentary of the Grimoires upon the aphorism of the sage of Hohenheim, and there is the more reason in the counsel because even the accessible substances required by the operator had usually some awkward conditions attached to them, which might remain unfulfilled unless he himself was actively present in their preparation. A particular case in point is the parchment used in the Art. The magician was required to slay a lamb or kid with his own hands, not because there was any symbolical importance attached to the act of destruction—the Grimoires make no such ascription—not because the blood was used—for its use is seldom prescribed—but to insure that the animal was one from which virgin parchment or virgin vellum could be prepared.

That is called virgin, says the *Book of True Black Magic*, which is made from animals that have never engendered, males above all,[1]—from which definition it is obvious that recourse

[1] The *Key of Solomon*, Book ii. c. 17, distinguishes between virgin parchment and unborn parchment; the latter is obtained from an animal which has been taken before its time from the womb of its mother.

to the professional tanner might jeopardise the entire injunction. But seeing that every operation undertaken in the Art assumed a religious aspect, the slaughter of the animal became a sacrifice [1] and had its accompanying ceremonies, prayers and invocations, each ritual possessing its own variants.

The preparation of the virgin parchment is given as follows in the *Grimorium Verum* : [2]—

CONCERNING THE VICTIM OF THE ART [3]

Take your kid ; place it on a block with the throat turned upward, so that it may be easier for you to cut it ; be ready with your knife, and cut the throat at a single stroke, pronouncing the name of the Spirit whom you wish to invoke. For example, say : *I slay thee, N., in the name and to the honour of N. . . .* Have a care that two blows be not needed, but let it die at the first ; then skin it with the knife, and while skinning it make the following

INVOCATION

ADIRAM, DALMAY, LAUDAY, TETRAGRAMMATON, ANERETON, [4] *and all ye holy angels of God, be ye here and deign to impart*

---

[1] It is fair to state that there is a form of evocation given in the *Vocabulaire Infernal* in which a sacrifice *per se* is prescribed. The source from which it is derived is not cited. "Whosoever would evoke the devil must sacrifice to him a dog, a cat and a hen ; these animals must be the property of the operator, who must also pledge himself to eternal fidelity and obedience, and must receive a special mark upon his body impressed by the devil himself. His recompense is an absolute control over three infernal spirits, respectively of earth, water and air." Some obscure demonologist is most likely the authority for this process, which is unknown to the Grimoires. It should be added that the *Vocabulaire Infernal* was compiled in the Catholic interest—though it looks as if that interest had been in traffic with Satan.

[2] This preparation being one of the most important preliminaries of Goëtic Art, will be given with all its variations as they are found in the four chief Grimoires. For the sacrificial portions of the *Grand Grimoire* and that of Honorius, see Chapters VI. and VII.

[3] The process in the *Grimorium Verum* is an adaptation of that in the *Key of Solomon*.

[4] The English edition of the Clavicle reads, *Zohar, Zio, Talmaï, Adonai, Shaddai, Tetragrammaton.*

virtue unto this skin, that it may be properly conserved, and that all things thereon written may attain their perfection.

After the skinning, take salt well pounded; stretch the skin; strew your salt upon it so as to cover the whole surface. But first let the salt be blest in the following manner:—

EXORCISM OF THE SALT

I exorcise thee, creature of salt, by the living God, by the God of gods and the Lord of lords, that all illusions may depart from thee, and that so thou mayst serve to make the virgin chart.

BENEDICTION OF THE SALT

God of gods and Lord of lords, Who hast created all things out of nothing, and hast specially designed salt for human health, bless ✠ *and sanctify this salt, and may I so use it that all things which are in this circle may receive the required virtue for that effect which we desire. Amen.*

This ended, place your salted skin in the rays of the sun for the space of one day. Then prepare a vessel of glazed clay and write the characters of Guland and Surgat (Chap. III. Sec. 2) about it with the pen and ink of the Art. Set quick-lime slaked with exorcised water in the pot, and while it is liquid place your skin therein, and so leave it till it peels of itself. When the hair is ready to fall at the touch of a finger, take it from the pot and peel it with a knife of hazel-wood, over which you have pronounced these words: *Most Holy* ABOEZRA, *be pleased to impart such virtue unto this wood that I may cleanse this skin therewith, through Thy Holy Name* AGASON. *Amen.*

This done, and the skin being also cleansed, stretch the same upon a board of new wood, and round about it set stones of the same length as the sides of the skin. But first say over them the prayer which here follows :—

PRAYER

O ADONAY, *most strong and powerful God, grant that these stones may stretch this skin, and do Thou remove from them all illusion, so that by Thy power they may possess the virtue which we desire. Amen.*

This done, the skin may be left to dry, but before quitting it recite the following

PRAYER

JE, AGLA, JOD, HOI, HE, EMMANUEL, *be ye guardians of this parchment or skin, so that no phantoms may possess it.*

This finished, leave it in the air until it be dried,[1] taking care that the place is clean and has been asperged while reciting the following holy words : *In the name of the immortal God, may God asperge thee and cleanse thee from all delusion and from all wickedness ; so shalt thou be whiter than snow. Amen.*

When the skin is dry, take it from the board, bless it with aspersion and fumigation, and preserve it for use. It must not be seen by women, especially in their times, for it will lose its virtue, and whosoever makes this parchment must be, in like manner, most pure and clean and chaste. Let him say a Mass of the Nativity, whether it be the day of the Feast or another

---

[1] Which should be in the space of three days, according to the Clavicle.

day, and note that all the instruments must be generally on the Altar.[1]

The Book of True Black Magic reproduces with further variations the process of the genuine Clavicle :—Secure the animal which is to furnish the parchment in a secret place, where no one dwells or can behold it. Then take a virgin rod ; shape it into the form of a knife with the white-handled Knife of the Art, paring it neatly of all branches. Over this say : *I conjure thee, Rod, by the Creator of the Universe and the King of Angels, Whose name is* HELSADAY![2] *Receive thou power and virtue to skin this animal for the making of the parchment, that so all things which I shall write thereon may prosper, by God Almighty, Who liveth and reigneth for ever and ever. Amen.* When shaping this knife recite the Psalm *Deus, judicium tuum Regi da.*[3] Then write these words upon the Rod : AGLA, ADONAY, ELOE,[4] *may the work of this wooden Knife be accomplished by you!* Say also over it : CARA, CHERNA, SITO, CIRNA.[5] Next, skin the animal with the same wooden knife, saying : ADIRAM, DAHNAY, SADAY, TETRAGRAMMATON, ANERETON, ANERETON, CURETON,[6] *Holy Angels of God, be ye present and give virtue to this parchment. May it be consecrated by you, and thus may all things which shall be written therein acquire the virtue needful for the attainment of the desired end. . . .*

When you have skinned it, take salt and say over it : *God of gods, vouchsafe to bless and sanctify this salt, so that it may cleanse the parchment which I am about to prepare therewith, and that both may obtain virtue, power and effect. . . .* Salt the

---

[1] The *Grimorium Verum* exhibits the transition of the Rituals from the purely Jewish elements of the *Key of Solomon* to the purely Christian materials of the Grimoire of Honorius.
[2] *i.e.*, *El Shaddai.*   [3] Psalm lxxi. of the Vulgate.   [4] *i.e.*, *Elohim*, or *Eloah.*
[5] These words are peculiar to the Grimoire, and their significance is beyond conjecture.
[6] See Note on p. 171.

skin and set it in the sun for fifteen days; next take a pot of glazed clay and write these characters about it; place a large

⊶ᒋ℘ᴡᒍᕼᒍ⏑ᶗᕼᕮᒷ�904E

piece of quicklime with some blessed water in this vessel, and when the lime is slaked, steep the skin for the space of nine whole days therein, after which it must be extracted and scraped with a wooden knife to remove the hair. Let it dry for eight days in the shade, but when setting it to dry, asperge it and say : *In the Name of the Great Eternal God, I asperge thee. Be thou cleansed from all vice and iniquity!* [When dry] perfume it with sweet-smelling herbs; wrap it in the silken cloth with the other instruments of the Art; and take notice that if it be seen by a woman in her times, it will lose all its virtue.

But if this kind of parchment be too difficult to prepare,[1] take virgin parchment of any animal; exorcise it as before; place lighted coal in a new glazed pot; mix good perfumes therewith; and hold your parchment above the vessel to receive them. Before all, however, write these characters about the pot[2] with the instruments of the Art.

ᛏᴑᒍᗡᏕᏕᏕᏟᏫᴡᒷᘞᏗᗱ

So long as the fumigation goes on, say : *Angels of God, be my help, and by you be my work accomplished!* . . . When it is finished, say : LAZAY, SALMAY, DALMAY, ANEPATON, CENDRION, ANITOR, ENCHEION,[3] *Holy Angels of God, be ye present and*

---

[1] The shorter process is not so good, says the *Clavicle.*

[2] The *Key of Solomon* provides characters for the parchment but not for the pot. They are, moreover, entirely different.

[3] The *Key of Solomon* reads : *Zazaii, Zalmaii, Dalmaï, Adonai, Anaphaxeton, Cedrion, Cripon, Prion, Anaireton, Elion, Octinomon, Zevanion, Alazaion, Zideon, Agla, On, Yod He Vau He, Artor, Dinotor.*

give virtue to this parchment, so that it may in turn acquire that of all characters with which it shall be inscribed, by the help of the pious and merciful God. . . . Recite the Psalms *Deus, judicium tuum Regi da* and *Laudate Dominum omnes gentes*, adding the following

CONJURATION

I conjure thee, creature of parchment, by all the names of God, that nothing which shall be written within thee may ever be blotted from truth.

Lastly, asperge it and place it in the silken cloth, as above.

The *Grimorium Verum* indulges the weak pupil by a further simplification, as follows :—If you are unable to prepare the parchment yourself, buy a new one and conjure it ; asperge also and fumigate it three times. The sacrifice, with its delays and unpleasantness, is thus abrogated, and the operator can proceed at once to the practical mystery of the *Sanctum Regnum*. It would also appear that parchment or vellum proper may be dispensed with in favour of :—(*a.*) The skin of some other animal, which would, however, involve a like process ; or (*b.*) the caul of a new-born child, which would, of course, possess the requisite virgin character, and was simply consecrated according to the following instructions, as found in *True Black Magic.*[1]

When you have succeeded in obtaining the caul of a new-born child, perfume the same with sweet odours and sprinkle it, after which say the following Psalms : *Domine, exaudi orationem meam*, and *Domine, Deus meus, respice in me*, with the conjuration hereunto attached :—BOSMELETIC, JEYSMY, ETH,

---

[1] The *Key of Solomon* merely observes that the cauls of newly-born children, duly consecrated, may be used instead of virgin parchment, and that paper, satin, or silk may also be employed in operations of less importance.

The Initial Rites and Ceremonies

HODOMOS, BELUREOS. *O Lord, Who didst make all things in wisdom; Who didst choose Abraham, Thy first believer, and his seed hath multiplied like the stars of heaven; Who didst appear unto Moses, Thy servant, surrounded with flaming fire, and didst make known to him Thy names, which are* HEIE, ACER, HEIE[1]—*that is to say, I am that I am; Who didst also lead forth Thy people dry-shod over the Red Sea; Who unto Moses, Thy servant, didst give the Law of Salvation on Mount Sinai; Who unto Solomon didst impart wisdom above the measure of men : I humbly adore Thy majesty and beseech Thy mercy, praying Thee to consecrate this skin by Thy virtue, O Most Holy* ADONAY, *Whose reign endureth for ever. Amen.*

Asperge the caul with the blessed water of the Art, place it in the silken cloth, and when working the exorcisms, the requisitions made to the spirits must be written on this skin, which should be fumigated with stinking odours.

§ 8. *Concerning Aspersion and Cleansing*

In the preparation of the instruments, as already abundantly evident, and in the more important works which follow it. the ceremonies of aspersion and fumigation, that is, of purifying and consecrating, are continually enjoined. Sprinkling is performed with the *Aspergillus*, which, according to the *Grimorium Verum*, should be composed of mint, marjory and rosemary, bound about with a thread woven by a virgin girl. It should be made on the day and in the hour of Mercury, the moon waxing. The ewer, in the canons of procedure established by *True Black Magic*, should be a pot of glazed earth,[2] filled with fresh spring

---

[1] The mutilations of the Divine Names in the Grimoires are part of the distinguishing characteristics of these works, and hence they are preserved in the text. It may scarcely be necessary to inform the student that the words mentioned should read AHIH, ASHR, AHIH.

[2] The *Key of Solomon* offers choice between a vessel of brass, of lead varnished within and without, and of earth.

M

water, in which some salt has been cast. The following Psalms should be recited over it :—*Domine, ne in furore tuo arguas me*, and *Domine, exaudi orationem meam*,[1] with the addition of this

PRAYER

O Thou most powerful Lord, my God, my rest, and my life! Do Thou help me, Most Holy Father! In Thee I place my hope, Who art the God of Abraham, God of Isaac, God of Jacob, God of the Angels and Archangels, God of the Prophets, and God the Creator of all things. In all humility, and with the invocation of Thy Holy Name, I pray that Thou wilt vouchsafe to bless this water, that in whatsoever place it shall be cast it may sanctify our bodies and our souls, through Thee, Most Holy ADONAY, *Whose reign is without end. Amen.*

The *Aspergillus* recommended by this Ritual differs somewhat from the former, being of vervain, periwinkle, sage, mint, valerian, ash and basil, taking care not to use hyssop[2] but rosemary in place thereof. It should be fitted with a handle of virgin hazel, three palms in length, and bound as before. The following characters should be engraved on one side of the said handle :—

This *Aspergillus* may be used on any occasion with perfect assurance that all phantoms will be expelled from every place which shall be sprinkled thereby with water duly exorcised. The prayer to be used at sprinkling is thus given by the

---

[1] Psalm vi. and Psalm xlii. in the Vulgate.
[2] The plant here condemned is prescribed by the *Key of Solomon*.

The Initial Rites and Ceremonies

Grimorium Verum:—In the Name of God Immortal, may God asperge thee, N., and cleanse thee from all illusion and from all wickedness, and thou shalt be whiter than snow.

When asperging add also: *In the Name of the Father* ✠ *and of the Son* ✠ *and of the Holy Ghost* ✠. Amen.

Concerning Incense and Fumigation

The *Grimorium Verum* prescribes a cruse or chafing-dish for fumigation, adding, with a decorative redundance corresponding to its impossible spirit, that it should be filled with freshly kindled coal and fresh fire, the whole blazing. Place aromatics thereon, and perfume what you would, saying : *Angels of God, be our help, and by you be our work fulfilled !* ZAZAY, SALMAY, DALMAY, ANGERECTON, LEDRION, AMISOR, EUCHEY, OR ! *Great Angels ! And do Thou also, O* ADONAY, *be present and impart hereto such virtue that this creature may receive a form, whereby our work may be accomplished ! In the Name of the Father* ✠ *and of the Son* ✠ *and of the Holy Ghost.* ✠ *Amen.* . . . Recite the Seven Psalms which follow *Judicium tuum Regi da* and *Laudate Dominum omnes gentes.*[1]

The perfumes are aloes wood and incense for most occasions, and mace for the fumigation of the circle. The *Book of True Black Magic* omits mace but substitutes benzoin and storax, and any others at choice, without specific distinction as to the circle. The following Prayers, Exorcisms and Benedictions, to be said over the aromatic perfumes, occur in the two Rituals, the first and third being common to both, and borrowed from the *Key of Solomon ;* the second, also referable to the same source, is not found in the *Grimorium Verum.*

---

[1] As these Psalms, lxxi. and cxvi. in the Vulgate, are widely separated from each other, and so also in the Authorised Version, it is difficult to determine those which are referred to in the text.

FIRST EXORCISM

O God of Abraham ✠, *God of Isaac* ✠, *and God of Jacob* ✠, *vouchsafe to bless and sanctify these creatures, of whatsoever species they may be, so that they may obtain virtue and power to discern good spirits from bad, even phantoms and enemies, through Thee, O* ADONAY, *Who livest and reignest for ever and ever. Amen.*

SECOND EXORCISM

I exorcise thee, O impure Spirit, who art the phantom of the Enemy. In the Name of God Almighty, come out from this kind, with all thy falsehood and wickedness, so that it may become sanctified and exorcised, in the Name of God Almighty; that all virtues may inspire those who partake of this odour; that the Spirit of God may descend, and the virtue of the Lord manifest, in the burning of this species; and that no phantom may dare to accost it. Through the Ineffable Name of God Almighty. Amen.

THIRD EXORCISM

Deign, O Lord, to sanctify this creature, so that it may become a signal remedy for the human race, and the salvation of our souls and bodies, through the invocation of Thy Most Holy Name, that so all creatures which inhale the smoke of this kind may have health of body and soul. Through that Lord Who hath created the ages of ages. So be it.

This done, sprinkle the perfumes with exorcised water, and set them aside in the silken cloth for use as prescribed. When you would fumigate anything, take new coal which has not been kindled, set it alight, and while it is still black, exorcise it, saying :

EXORCISM OF THE LIGHTED COAL

I exorcise thee, O creature of Fire, by Him Who hath made all things ! Do thou expel from thee all phantoms, so that they may in no wise harm or trouble us in our work, by the invocation of the Most High Creator. Amen. O Saviour, Almighty and merciful, bless Thy creature of this kind, so that no harm may come to him who shall make use of it. Amen.

In concluding this portion of its ceremonial, the *Book of True Black Magic* states that there are occasions on which perfumes of a stinking or malodorous kind must be used. As the first point of their preparation, the operator must say over them : ADONAY, LAZAY, DELMAY, AMAY, SADAY, ELOY,[1] *by the invocation, O Saviour, of Thy Most Holy Name, vouchsafe us, through this kind, the help of Thy grace, and may it assist us in all things which we need to fulfil; may all malice pass out herefrom, may it be blessed and sanctified in Thy most powerful Name. Amen.*

Asperge the stinking perfume with exorcised water, place it in the silken cloth and use it as needed, but always in the name of the Most Holy ADONAY. So doing, thou shalt obtain thy desire, says the " Manuscript discovered at Jerusalem in the Sepulchre of Solomon."[2]

[1] The names given in the *Key of Solomon* are *Adonai, Lazai, Dalmai, Aima, Elohi.*

[2] A short way to Magic by means of perfumes is given by Nyrauld in his work on Lycanthropy. To discern future events, fumigate yourself with linseed and seed of psellium, or with roots of violets and wild parsley. To drive away evil spirits and phantoms, make a perfume of calamon, peony, mint and *palma Christi.* To attract serpents, burn the windpipe of a stag ; to expel them, burn a horn of the same animal. Make a perfume with gall of fish, thyme, roses and aloe wood. When kindled, sprinkle with water or blood, and presently the whole house will seem full of water or of blood, as the case may be. Add earth which has been turned up by a ploughshare, and the ground will appear to tremble. The enumeration might be continued almost indefinitely.

§ 9. *Concerning the Time of Operation*

When the sacrifice of the Art or its substitute has once been completed, the operator is in possession of all the materials that he will require *ex hypothesi* for the performance of Goëtic works as described in. the *Book of True Black Magic* or the *Grimorium Verum*. But as the first of these Rituals ordains that the preparation of the artist shall be made in accordance with certain planetary influences, so in like manner does it regulate the time of operation or accomplishment. The instructions still follow, and still in a confused manner, the authority of the Clavicle. It will be well to reproduce them here in a succinct analysis, though the piecemeal nature of the treatise attributed to Iroë-Grego leaves the rules without much practical value, while no attention is paid to them by other makers of Grimoires :—

An experiment of speaking with spirits or conjuring them should be operated in the day and hour of Mercury, which hour may be the first or the eighth, but the fifteenth or twenty-second of the same night will be still better, for spirits appear more easily in the silence of the dark hours. A certain atmospheric condition is also required for the experiment of calling spirits, and an obscure uninhabited place congruous to such an art is even more necessary, for so only will it be accomplished and educed. But if the experiment be concerned with a theft,[1] it should be performed in the hour of the Moon and on her day —if it be possible, in the crescent Moon—from the first to the eighth hour, or, failing this, at ten o'clock in the night. It is better, however, in the day, because the light has more corre-

---

[1] An experiment of this kind is reproduced by the Grimoire from the *Key of Solomon*, but does not call for inclusion either by its connection with Black Magic—for there is no connection, or by any inherent interest—for there is again none.

spondence to the intention, that is, to the manifestation of hidden things. The experience of invisibility[1] should be operated when the Moon is in Pisces. Experiments of love, favour and grace[2] should be accomplished on the day and in the hour of the Sun or Venus, from the first to the eighth hour, with the Moon in Pisces. Works of destruction, hatred and desolation[3] should be performed on the day and in the hour of Saturn, from the first or eighth to the fifteenth or twenty-second hour of the night; they are then certain. Burlesque and amusing experiments are performed on the day of Venus, in the first and the eighth hour, or in the fifteenth and twenty-second hour of the night. Extraordinary experiences should be operated in corresponding hours on the day of Jupiter.[4]

[1] See Chapter VIII.
[2] See Venereal Experiments in Chapter VIII.
[3] See Chapter VIII.
[4] The chapter on Extraordinary Experiments in the *Key of Solomon* is rendered unintelligible by want of details. It reappears in the Grimoire, but is omitted from this translation for the reason indicated.

SATAN BOUND. ON PRE-NORMAN CROSS
SHAFT AT KIRKBY STEPHEN,
WESTMORLAND.

CHAPTER III

Concerning the Descending Hierarchy

§ 1. *The Names and Offices of Evil Spirits*

IN all matters of ceremonial the inspiration of the Grimoires must be sought in the *Key of Solomon* proper, but for the names and offices of the demons it must be sought in the *Lesser Key*. The hierarchy, according to the *Lemegeton*, with its accompanying evoking processes, will be given in the fourth chapter, as there is no special reason for separating it from the practical context. I shall therefore deal in this place with the simpler though later summaries, which will prevent these curious issues from being confused.

The *Book of True Black Magic*, like its prototype the original *Clavicle*, gives no account of the nature of the Spirits with which it professes to deal, and, as already seen, it breaks off abruptly at the point where the conjuring formulæ should follow to complete the work. This *Secret of Secrets*, as the Grimoires term the methods for raising and discharging spirits, being omitted, it may now be dismissed from consideration till we come to the minor processes of Ceremonial Magic, chiefly venereal and fantastic, which are grouped in the eighth chapter.

The *Grimoire of Honorius* mentions by name four kings, referred to the cardinal points, and seven lesser spirits to be invoked on the days of the week, but as will appear later on, there is no explicit notice of the Descending Hierarchy. These

Concerning the Descending Hierarchy

deficiencies are supplied by the *Grimorium Verum* and the *Grand Grimoire*.

THE SEAL AND CHARACTERS OF LUCIFER   THE SEAL AND CHARACTERS OF BEELZEBUTH

As regards spirits, says the former, some are superior and others inferior. The three superior are Lucifer, Beelzebuth and Astaroth. According to the latter, Lucifer is Emperor; Beelzebuth, Prince; and Astaroth, Grand Duke. They must be invoked by means of the characters which they themselves have made known, and these characters must be written with the blood of the operator, or with that of a sea-tortoise. Failing this, they may be engraved on an emerald or ruby, for both these stones have great sympathy with spirits, especially with those of the solar race, who are wiser,

THE SEAL AND CHARACTERS
OF ASTAROTH

185

better and more friendly than the rest.[1] The character must
be worn upon the person ; in the case of a male, it should be
placed in the right pocket, but a female must carry it between
the breasts, towards the left side, like a reliquary. It should
be graven or written on the day and in the hour of Mars for
both sexes, and apparently in the case of each of the three
spirits.

The lord commands the servants, so the Grimoire proceeds,
and these three spirits can do all things. But the operator is
advised that he shall obey those who obey him, because the
exalted and powerful spirits serve only their confidants and intimate friends. He is further grimly warned to keep upon his
guard lest any spirit should seize him unawares. Each of the
rulers has two chief officers, who announce to the subjects all
things which their lord hath commanded throughout the world,
and ordain all that is to be done. The inferiors of Lucifer are
Put Satanachia and *Agaliarept ;* they inhabit Europe and Asia.
Those of Beelzebuth are *Tarchimache* and *Fleurety ;* they dwell
in Africa. Those of Astaroth are *Sargatanas* and *Nebiros,*
whose asylum is America, so that this kind of Magic is presumably post-Columbian.

The *Grand Grimoire* does not distribute the six subordinate
spirits among three rulers, but enumerates them somewhat
differently, together with their dignities, as follows :[2]—

---

[1] The attribution is somewhat confused ; the ruby is a solar stone, but Albertus Parvus
attributes the emerald to the Moon, which would establish its connection with evocation.

[2] The Hierarchy according to Wierus is at variance with both the Rituals, and may be
worth quoting on account of its curious details :—

PRINCES AND GRAND DIGNITARIES.—*Beelzebuth*, Supreme Chief of the Infernal Empire,
founder of the Order of the Fly. *Satan*, Leader of the Opposition. *Euronymous*, Prince of
Death, Grand Cross of the Order of the Fly. *Moloch*, Prince of the Land of Tears, Grand
Cross of the Order. *Pluto*, Prince of Fire. *Leonard*, Grand Master of Sabbaths, Knight of
the Fly. *Baalberith*, Minister of Treaties. *Proserpine*, Arch-she-devil, Sovereign Princess of
Mischievous Spirits. MINISTERS.—*Adramelek*, Lord High Chancellor, Grand Cross of the
Order of the Fly. *Astaroth*, Grand Treasurer. *Nergal*, Chief of the Secret Police. *Baal*,

Concerning the Descending Hierarchy

LUCIFUGE ROFOCALE.—Prime Minister.
SATANACHIA.—Commander-in-Chief.
AGALIAREPT.—Another Commander.
FLEURETY.—Lieutenant-General.
SARGATANAS.—Brigadier-Major.
NEBIROS.—Field-Marshal and Inspector-General.

It will be seen that the principalities of Infernus are chiefly represented in the light of a standing army, yet their interference in earthly matters is not of a military kind. LUCIFUGE ROFOCALE has the control, with which Lucifer has invested him, over all the wealth and treasures of the world. His subordinates are *Baal*,[1] *Agares*[2] and *Marbas*.[3] The grand SATANACHIA has the power of subjecting all wives and maidens to his wishes, and of doing with them as he wills. His subordinates are *Pruslas*, *Aamon*[4] and *Barbatos*.[5] AGALIAREPT has the faculty of discovering arcane secrets in all the courts and council-chambers of the world; he also unveils the most sublime mysteries. He commands the Second Legion of Spirits, and his subordinates are *Buer*,[6] *Gusoyn*[7] and *Botis*.[8] FLEURETY has the power to perform any labour during the night and to cause hailstones

Commander-in-Chief of the Infernal Armies, Grand Cross of the Order of the Fly. AMBAS-SADORS.—*Belphegor* in France, *Mammon* in England, *Belial* in Turkey, *Rimmon* in Russia, *Thamuz* in Spain, *Hutgin* in Italy, *Martinet* in Switzerland. JUDGES.—*Lucifer*, Lord Chief Justice. *Alastor*, Commissioner of Public Works. ROYAL HOUSEHOLD.—*Verdelet*, Master of Ceremonies. *Succor Benoth*, Chief of the Eunuchs. *Chamos*, Lord High Chamberlain, Knight of the Fly. *Melchom*, Paymaster. *Misroch*, Grand Steward. *Behemoth*, Grand Cup-Bearer. *Dagon*, Grand Pantler. *Mullin*, First Gentleman of the Bedchamber. MASTERS OF THE REVELS.—*Kobal*, Stage Manager. *Asmodeus*, Superintendent of Casinos. *Nybbas*, Chief Mimic. *Antichrist*, Juggler and Mimic.

[1] *Baal* is the first Spirit of the *Lemegeton*, and a King ruling in the East.
[2] The second Spirit of the *Lemegeton*.
[3] The fifth Spirit of the *Lemegeton*.
[4] Possibly *Paimon*, ninth Spirit of the *Lemegeton*.
[5] The eighth Spirit of the *Lemegeton*.
[6] The tenth Spirit of the *Lemegeton*.
[7] Eleventh Spirit of the *Lemegeton*.
[8] The seventeenth Spirit of the *Lemegeton*.

in any required place. He controls a prodigious army of spirits, and has *Bathsin*[1] (or *Bathim*), *Pursan* and *Eligor*[2] as his subordinates. SARGATANAS has the power to make any person invisible, to transport him anywhere, to open all locks, to reveal whatsoever is taking place in private houses, to teach all the arts of the shepherds. He commands several Brigades of Spirits, and has *Zoray*, *Valefar* and *Faraii* for his immediate inferiors. NEBIROS has the power to inflict evil on whomsoever he will; he discovers the Hand of Glory and reveals every virtue of metals, minerals, vegetables, as also of all animals, both pure and impure. He possesses the art of predicting things to come, being one of the greatest Necromancers in all the Infernal Hierarchies; he goes to and fro everywhere and inspects the hordes of perdition. His immediate subordinates are *Ayperos*, *Naberrs* and *Glassyalabolas*.

It is added that there are millions of other spirits in subjection to those which have been mentioned, but their enumeration serves no purpose, as they are required only when it pleases the superiors to employ them in their own place, for the latter make use of all the inferior Intelligences like workmen or slaves.

The *Grimorium Verum*, however, mentions seventeen of the most important subordinate spirits, who seem to correspond

CHARACTER OF CLAUNECK

with the ministers of the six great leaders mentioned above, but there is little unanimity among makers of magical rituals, whether white or black.

CLAUNECK has power over goods and riches; he can discover hidden treasures to him

---

[1] The eighteenth Spirit of the *Lemegeton*.
[2] The fifteenth Spirit of the *Lemegeton*.

who makes pact with him ; he can bestow great wealth, for he is well loved by Lucifer. He brings money from a distance. Obey him, and he will obey thee.

MUSISIN has power over great lords ; he instructs them in all that passes in the Republics and the realms of the Allies.

CHARACTER OF MUSISIN   CHARACTER OF BECHARD

BECHARD has power over winds and tempests, over lightning, hail and rain, by means of a charm with toads and other things of this nature, &c.

CHARACTER OF FRIMOST

FRIMOST has power over wives and maids, and will help thee to enjoy them.

KHIL occasions great earthquakes.

CHARACTER OF KHIL

CHARACTER OF MERSILDE

MERSILDE can transport thee instantaneously wheresoever may be desired.

189

The Book of Ceremonial Magic

CLISTHERET makes day or night about thee at pleasure.

CHARACTER OF CLISTHERET

SIRCHADE has power to shew thee all kinds of animals, of whatsoever nature they may be.

CHARACTER OF SIRCHADE

CHARACTER OF SEGAL

SEGAL causes all manner of prodigies visibly, both natural and supernatural.

HIEPACTH will bring thee a distant person in an instant.

CHARACTER OF HIEPACTH

CHARACTER OF HUMOTS

HUMOTS can transport all manner of books for thy pleasure.

190

Concerning the Descending Hierarchy

FRUCISSIERE brings the dead to life.

CHARACTER OF FRUCISSIERE

GULAND can cause all varieties of disease.

CHARACTER OF GULAND

CHARACTER OF SURGAT

SURGAT opens all locks.

CHARACTER OF MORAIL

MORAIL has the power to make everything in the world invisible.

FRUTIMIERE dights thee all kinds of festivals.

HUICTIIGARA occasions sleep and waking in some, and afflicts others with insomnia.

SATANACHIA and SATANICIÆ govern forty-five, or, as some say, fifty-four demons, four of whom are *Sergutthy*, *Heramael*, *Trimasel* and *Sustugriel*. Two of these rank as chief. The rest are of no great importance.

These are serviceable spirits, who act easily and quickly,

CHARACTER OF HUICTIIGARA

CHARACTER OF FRUTIMIERE

provided that they are content with the operator. *Sergutthy* has power over wives and virgins, when the occasion is favourable. *Heramael* teaches the art of medicine, gives absolute knowledge of all diseases, with their full and radical cure, makes known all plants in general, the places where they grow, the times of their gathering, their virtues also and their composition for the attainment of a perfect cure. *Trimasel* teaches chemistry and all sleight of hand. He imparts the true secret for confecting the powder of projection which changes imperfect metals—lead, iron, pewter, copper and quicksilver—into true good silver and good gold, namely, Sun and Moon, according to the ferment thereof. Only he must be satisfied with the operator, if the operator would be satisfied with him. *Sustugriel* teaches magical art; he gives familiar spirits for all things that can be desired, and furnishes mandragores.

Agalierept and *Tarihimal* govern *Elelogap*, whose power is over water. The two *Nebirots* rule *Hael* and *Sergulath*. *Hael* instructs in the art of writing all kinds of letters, gives an immediate power of speaking all kinds of tongues and explains the most secret things. *Sergulath* furnishes every manner of speculation, teaches tactics and the breaking of hostile ranks. They have eight powerful inferiors. 1. *Proculo*, who gives sleep for twenty-four hours, with knowledge of the spheres of sleep. 2. *Haristum*, who gives the power of passing unsinged through the fire. 3. *Brulefer*, who makes one loved by women. 4. *Pentagnony*, who renders invisible and also beloved by great lords. 5. *Aglasis*, who transports through the whole world. 6. *Sidragrosam*, who makes girls dance stark naked. 7. *Minoson*, who insures winning in all games. 8. *Bucon*, who has the power to excite hatred and jealousy between the two sexes.

§ 2. *Concerning the Forms of Infernal Spirits in their Manifestations*

Having regard to the nature and antecedents of the Intelligences with which Black Magic professes to be concerned, it must be highly important that the operator should know the kind of apparitions which may be expected, when, despite the incredulity of Horatio, the spirits from the vasty deep do respond to conjuration. The majority of the Grimoires leave it to be inferred from their silence that they come in human shape —possibly in " a neat surcoat and snow-white linen," like the Adonay of the sorcerer in the *Thaumaturgic Experiences* of Éliphas Lévi. With the Composite Rituals it is always a subject of apprehension, and a peaceable manifestation is earnestly bargained for.

According to the *Grimorium Verum*, the spirits do not invariably manifest under the same forms, and we have had some surprising specimens of their mutations in the earlier texts ; being disengaged from all matter, they must of necessity borrow a body in order to appear before us,[1] and then they assume any shape and figure which seems good to them. Beware, however, lest they affright thee—is another pregnant warning. Lucifer appears under the form and figure of a comely boy ; when angered, he is shewn with a ruddy countenance, but there is nothing monstrous in his shape. Beelzebuth appears occasionally under monstrous forms, such as the figure of a misshapen calf, or that of a goat having a long tail ; at the same time he manifests most frequently under the semblance of an enormous fly.[2] When angered, he vomits floods of water and howls like a wolf. Astaroth appears of a black and white colour, usually under a human figure, but occasionally in the likeness of an ass.

The subject of Infernal Manifestations is, however, fully treated in the next chapter. The indications in the present section are merely the later variants.

[1] A portion of this statement is derived from the *Key of Solomon ;* but whereas it is put clearly in the Grimoire, it is incomplete and inconsequent in the original. It is the alternative aspect of the Kabalistic principle that the spirit clothes itself to come down and divests itself to return upward. When the abyss gives up forms its capacity of manifestation is Protean, but the most beloved tendency is monstrous. And the forms disrobe for the abyss to open and receive them when they go back to their cover.

[2] A giant, a serpent, a woman, are also other modes of his manifestation, according to the discretion of demonologists.

CHAPTER IV

The Mysteries of Goëtic Theurgy according to the Lesser Key of Solomon the King

§ 1. *Concerning the Spirits of the Brazen Vessel, otherwise called the False Monarchy of Demons*

THE Goëtic Art |of Solomon [1] gives instructions for the evocation of the seventy-two spirits whom the King of Israel, according to a well-known legend, shut up in a brass vessel and cast into a deep lake. When the vessel was discovered by the Babylonians, it was supposed to contain a great treasure and was accordingly broken open. The spirits who were thus set at liberty, together with their legions, returned to their former places, Belial excepted, who entered into a certain image, and gave oracles to the people of the country in return for sacrifices and divine honours, by which there is corrupt Kabalistic authority for concluding that demons were assuaged and sustained. Their names and offices are as follows :—

---

[1] Though a work of considerable length, this *Lesser Key*, so far as it concerns our inquiry, admits of reduction into a manageable compass by the omission of tiresome and egregious particulars as to the number of spirits who are subject to a particular Lord, Prince or Emperor, and are liable to appear in his company. It should be understood in a general way that there are hundreds and thousands and millions, according to the dignity of the hierarch ; they must have been a source of considerable inconvenience, and even of dismay, to the operator !

The Book of Ceremonial Magic

I. Baal, a king ruling in the East, who imparts invisibility and wisdom. He appears with a human head, or with that of a toad or cat,[1] but sometimes with all at once. He speaks with a hoarse voice.[2]

II. Agares, a duke ruling in the East, who appears in the form of a comely old man, ambling upon a crocodile and carrying a goshawk on his wrist. He makes those who run

THE SEAL OF AGARES   THE SEAL OF VASSAGO   SEAL OF VASSAGO USED IN WHITE MAGIC

stand still, brings back runaways, teaches all languages, destroys spiritual and temporal dignities and causes earthquakes.[3] He is of the Order of the Virtues.[4]

---

[1] The cat is the traditional domestic favourite, not only of those who diabolise, but of the diabolical world itself, which shews that after all there is a strong link with humanity in the cohorts of Lucifer. The reader will remember that the cat falls on its feet, not by natural good luck, but by the special dispensation of Mohammed, and that the favourite of the Prophet is in Paradise, no doubt on the best terms with the dog of the Seven Sleepers.

[2] Another codex says that he manifests with three heads—the first like a toad, the second like a man and the third like a cat.

[3] According to the *Vocabulaire Infernal*, the special province of *Agares* is to put to flight the enemies of those whom he protects.

[4] That is, he belonged to this choir during the first estate of the Fallen Angels.

The Mysteries of Goëtic Theurgy

III. VASSAGO, a mighty prince, of the nature of *Agares*, who declares things past, present and future, and discovers what has been lost or hidden. He is good by nature.[1]

IV. GAMYGYN, a great marquis, appearing in the form of a small horse or ass, but afterwards in human shape. He speaks hoarsely, teaching the liberal sciences, and giving news of souls who have died in sin.[2]

V. MARBAS,[3] a president, who appears as a mighty lion,

THE SEAL OF GAMYGYN   THE SEAL OF MARBAS   THE SEAL OF VALEFOR

and then in human shape.[4] He answers truly concerning all things hidden or secret, causes and cures diseases, imparts skill in mechanics, and changes men into various shapes.[5]

VI. VALEFOR,[6] a powerful duke, appearing as a many-headed lion.[7] He leads those with whom he is familiar into theft.

[1] This may account for his invocation, especially in Ceremonial Crystallomancy, by the putative adepts of White Magic—as the most dubious of all arts is called in the scorn of its professors.

[2] According to Wierus, he summons into the presence of the exorcist the souls of drowned men and of those detained in Purgatory, called magically *Cartagra*—that is, the affliction of souls. They assume an aërial body, are visible to sight and reply to questions. Another version says that *Gamygyn* tarries with the exorcist till he has accomplished his desires.

[3] Or *Barbas*.

[4] At the request of the operator (Wierus).

[5] He is the third spirit in the Hierarchy of Wierus.

[6] Or *Malaphar*.

[7] With the head of a hunter or a thief, says Wierus. He shews friendship to his familiars till they are caught in the trap.

VII. AMON, a strong and powerful marquis, who appears like a wolf with a serpent's head[1] and vomiting flame. When so ordered, he assumes a human shape, but with the teeth of a dog.[2] He discerns past and future, procures love and reconciles friends and foes.

THE SEAL OF AMON

VIII. BARBATOS, a great count and duke, who appears when the sun is in Sagittarius with four noble kings and three companies of troops; he gives instruction in all the sciences, reveals treasures concealed by enchantment, knows the past and future, reconciles friends and those in power, and is

THE SEAL OF BARBATOS

of the Order of the Virtues.[3]

IX. PAIMON, a great king, very obedient to Lucifer.[4] He appears like a crowned man seated on a dromedary, preceded by all manner of musicians. He speaks with a roaring voice, teaches all arts, sciences and secrets, gives and confirms dignities, makes men sub-

THE SEAL OF PAIMON

ject to the will of the Magician, provides good familiars. He is observed towards the North-West, and is of the Order of Dominions.[5]

[1] *Cauda serpentis*, says Wierus.

[2] And, according to another MS., "a great head like to a mighty raven."

[3] He also understands the songs of birds and the language of all other animals (Wierus).

[4] A longer recension says : By Lucifer is here to be understood he that was drowned in the depths of his knowledge. He would needs be like God and for his pride and arrogancy was thrown out into destruction. Of him it is said—Every precious stone is thy covering. The last reference is to the panegyric of the Prince of Tyre in Ezekiel : its occurrence in this place is most remarkable.

[5] It appears from Wierus that the operator may fail to understand this spirit, in which case he must stretch forth the character belonging to him and command him to speak clearly.

X. BUER,[1] a great president, who appears when the sun is in Sagittarius and teaches philosophy, logic, the virtues of herbs, &c. He heals all diseases and gives good familiars.

THE SEAL OF BUER   THE SEAL OF GUSION

XI. GUSION,[2] a mighty duke, who appears like a cyno-cephalus, discerns the past, present and future, answers all questions, reconciles enemies and gives honour and dignities.

XII. SYTRY, a great prince, who appears with a leopard's

THE SEAL OF SYTRY   THE SEAL OF BELETH

head and the wings of a griffin, but assumes a beautiful human form at the Magician's command. He procures love between the two sexes, and causes women to shew themselves naked.[3]

XIII. BELETH,[4] a terrible and mighty king, riding on a pale horse, preceded by all manner of musicians. He is very

---

[1] The seventh spirit of the *Pseudo-Monarchia*. He is also an exponent of ethics.

[2] Otherwise, *Gusayn*, the eighth spirit of Wierus, and Pirsoyn, according to the variant of another MS.

[3] *Jussus secreta libenter detegit feminarum, eas ridens ludificansque ut se luxorise nudent.* —*Wierus.*

[4] Otherwise, *Byleth.* Some codices give considerable space to this demon and the precautions to be taken concerning him.

furious when first summoned, and must be commanded into a triangle or circle with the hazel wand of the Magician pointed to the South-East. He must be received courteously and with homage, but a silver ring must be worn on the middle finger of the left hand, which must he held against the face.

THE SEAL OF LERAJIE

THE SEAL OF ELIGOR

He procures love between man and woman and is of the Order of the Powers.[1]

XIV. LERAJIE, a powerful marquis, coming in the likeness of an archer, clad in green and bearing bow and quiver. He occasions battles and causes arrow-wounds to putrefy.

XV. ELIGOR, a great duke, appearing as a goodly knight

THE SEAL OF ZEPAR

THE SEAL OF BOTIS

carrying a lance, pennon and sceptre. He discovers hidden things, causes war, marshals armies, kindles love and lust.[2]

XVI. ZEPAR, a great duke, who appears in red apparel and armed like a soldier. He inflames women with love for men

---

[1] He yet hopes to be restored to the Seventh Thrones—"which is not altogether credible," according to one of the versions.

[2] Alternatively, he procures the favour of lords and knights.

and can transform them into other shapes till they have been enjoyed by their lovers.[1]

XVII. BOTIS, a great president and earl, who appears like a horrid viper, but, when commanded, assumes a human shape, with large teeth and horns. He bears a sharp sword in his hand, discerns past, present and future, reconciles friends and foes.

XVIII. BATHIN,[2] a mighty duke, who appears like a strong man with a serpent's tail, riding on a pale horse. He knows the virtues of herbs and precious stones, and can transport men swiftly from one country to another.

THE SEAL OF BATHIN

XIX. SALEOS,[3] a great duke, who appears like a brave soldier, riding on a crocodile and wearing a duke's crown. He promotes love between the sexes.

THE SEAL OF SALEOS

XX. PURSON,[4] a great king, who appears like a lion-headed man, carrying a viper in his hand and riding on a bear, preceded by many trumpeters. He conceals and discovers treasure, discerns past, present and future, gives true answers respecting

THE SEAL OF PURSON

things human and divine, and provides good familiars.[5]

---

[1] The last statement is on the authority of Wierus. According to another reading, *Zepar* makes women barren.

[2] Otherwise, *Bathym* or *Marthim.*   [3] Called also *Zaleos.*   [4] Otherwise, *Curson.*

[5] He also utters sound doctrine concerning the creation of the world.

THE SEAL OF MORAX

XXI. MORAX,[1] a great earl and president, who appears like a human-headed bull, and gives skill in astronomy and the liberal sciences, with good familiars. He knows the virtues of all herbs and precious stones.

THE SEAL OF IPOS

XXII. IPOS,[2] a mighty earl and prince, appearing as an angel with a lion's head,[3] the webbed feet of a goose and a hare's tail. He knows the past and future, and imparts wit and courage.

XXIII. AINI,[4] a strong duke, who appears with the body of a handsome man but having three heads, the first like a serpent, the second like a man with two stars on the forehead and the third like a cat.

THE SEAL OF AINI

He rides on a viper and carries a blazing firebrand, with which he spreads destruction. He imparts much cunning and gives true answers concerning private matters.

THE SEAL OF NABERIUS

XXIV. NABERIUS,[5] a valiant marquis, who appears in the form of a crowing cock and flutters about the circle. He speaks hoarsely, gives skill in arts and sciences, especially rhetoric, and restores lost dignities and honours.[6]

[1] This spirit is named *Foraii* by Wierus. Another variant is *Forfax*.

[2] Otherwise, *Ipes, Ayporos* or *Aypeos*.

[3] According to Wierus, sometimes in the form of an angel and sometimes in that of a crafty and evil lion. He is termed filthy and obscene, even in the angelic mask.

[4] Called *Aym* or *Haborym* by Wierus.   [5] *i.e., Cerberus.*

[6] Another codex reverses this, saying that he procures the loss of prelacies and dignities.

XXV. GLASYALABOLAS,[1] a mighty president, who comes in the form of a dog, but winged like a griffin. He teaches all arts and sciences instantaneously, incites to bloodshed, is the leader of all homicides, discerns past and future, and makes men invisible.

THE SEAL OF GLASYALABOLAS

XXVI. BUNE, a strong duke, who appears as a three-headed dragon, the heads being respectively those of a dog, griffin and man. He has a pleasant voice ; he changes the places of the dead, causes demons to crowd round sepulchres, gives riches, makes men wise and eloquent, answers questions truly.

THE SEAL OF BUNE

XXVII. RONOBE,[2] a great marquis and earl, appears in a monstrous form ; he teaches rhetoric and the arts, gives a good understanding, the knowledge of tongues and favour of friends and foes.

THE SEAL OF RONOBE

XXVIII. BERITH,[3] a terrible duke, appearing in the form

---

[1] *Alias, Caacrinolaas* or *Caassimola.*

[2] Otherwise, *Roneve* and *Ronove.*

[3] This spirit, says Wierus, is by some called *Beal,* but by the Jews *Berith* and by necromancers *Bofi* or *Bolfry.*

of a soldier in red apparel, with a golden crown, and bestriding

THE SEAL OF BERITH

a red horse. The ring used for *Berith* is required for his evocation. He gives true answers of things past, present and to come, turns all metals into gold, gives and confirms dignities. He speaks in a clear and persuasive voice, but is a great liar and his advice must not be trusted.

XXIX. ASTAROTH, a great and powerful duke, appears like

THE SEAL OF ASTAROTH

a beautiful angel [1] riding on an infernal dragon and carrying a viper in his right hand. He must not be permitted to approach on account of his stinking breath, and the magician must defend his face with the magic ring. *Astaroth* answers truly concerning past, present and future, discovers all secrets and gives great skill in the liberal sciences. He will also discourse willingly concerning the fall of spirits. [2]

XXX. FORNEUS, a great marquis, appears as a sea-monster.

THE SEAL OF FORNEUS

He teaches all arts and sciences, including rhetoric, gives a

[1] Another version says "a foul angel."
[2] But pretends that he himself was exempt from their lapse (Wierus).

good reputation and the knowledge of tongues, and causes men to be loved by their enemies even as by their friends.

XXXI. FORAS,[1] a great president, who appears in the form of a strong man and teaches the virtues of all herbs and precious stones, as well as logic and ethics; he makes men invisible, imparts wit, wisdom and eloquence, discovers treasures and restores things lost.

THE SEAL OF FORAS

XXXII. ASMODAY,[2] a strong and powerful king, appears with three heads, the first like a bull, the second like a man and the third like a ram. He has a serpent's tail, the webbed feet of a goose and he vomits fire. He rides an infernal dragon, carries lance and pennon and is the chief of the power of *Amaymon*. He must be invoked bareheaded,[3] for otherwise he will deceive. He gives the ring of virtues, teaches arithmetic,

THE SEAL OF ASMODAY

geomancy and all handicrafts, answers all questions, makes men invisible, indicates the places of concealed treasures and guards them, if within the dominion of *Amaymon*.

XXXIII. GAAP,[4] a great president and prince, appears when the sun is in the southern signs, coming in a human shape and preceded by four powerful kings. He teaches philo-

---

[1] Otherwise, *Forcas*.
[2] Called also *Sydonay*.
[3] And in a standing position (Wierus).
[4] *Alias*, *Tap* and *Goap*.

The Book of Ceremonial Magic

sophy and the liberal sciences, excites love and hatred, makes

THE SEAL OF GAAP

men insensible, gives instruction in the consecration of those things which belong to the divination of *Amaymon*, his king, delivers familiars out of the custody of other Magicians, gives true answers as to past, present and future, transports and returns men speedily from place to place at the will of the exorcist. He was of the Order of the Powers.[1]

XXXIV. FURFUR, a great earl, appears in the form of a

THE SEAL OF FURFUR

hart, with a fiery tail, and will not open his mouth till compelled within the triangle.[2] He then assumes the form of an angel, speaking with a hoarse voice. He causes love between man and wife,

raises thunder, lightning and great winds, gives true answers about secret and divine things.

THE SEAL OF MARCHOSIAS

XXXV. MARCHOSIAS, a mighty marquis, appears in the form of a wolf[3] with the wings of a griffin, a serpent's tail and fire issuing from his mouth. At the command of the operator he assumes a human form. He is strong in battle, gives true answers to all questions and is extremely

[1] A longer codex says that there were certain exorcists who offered burnt sacrifices to *Gaap* and invoked him according to formulæ which they pretended to derive from Solomon, but their real author was Cham, the first who after the flood began to invoke evil spirits.

[2] According to Wierus, he will speak outside the triangle, but what he says will be false.

[3] Otherwise, a cruel she-wolf.

faithful to the exorcist. He belongs to the Order of Domi-nations.[1]

XXXVI. SOLAS or STOLAS, a powerful prince, appears in the likeness of a raven and then as a man. He teaches the art of astronomy and the virtues of herbs and stones.

THE SEAL OF SOLAS

THE SEAL OF PHŒNIX

XXXVII. PHŒNIX, a great marquis, appears like the bird of that name, singing dulcet notes in a child's voice.[2] When he assumes human shape at the will of the Magician, he speaks marvellously of all sciences, proves an excellent poet and fulfils

THE SEAL OF HALPAS

THE SEAL OF MALPAS

orders admirably. He hopes to return to the Seventh Thrones in 1200 years.

XXXVIII. HALPAS, a great earl, appears in the form of a stockdove, speaking with a hoarse voice. He burns towns,[3]

---

[1] And expects to return to the Seventh Thrones after 1200 years, but is deceived therein (Wierus).

[2] But this is the voice of the syren, so the exorcist must beware, and those also who are with him.

[3] Or, according to Wierus, builds them and fills them with armed men.

visits the wicked with the sword and can send men to fields of war or to other places.

XXXIX. MALPAS, a powerful president, appears at first like a crow, but afterwards, when so commanded, assumes a human form, speaking with a hoarse voice. He brings artificers swiftly from all parts of the world, destroys the desires and thoughts[1] of enemies, gives good familiars and receives a sacrifice kindly, but will deceive him who offers it.

XL. RAUM,[2] a great earl, appears in the form of a crow,

THE SEAL OF RAUM

but assumes human shape when bidden. He steals treasure, even out of the King's house, and carries it where commanded; he destroys cities and dignities; he discerns past, present and future; he causes love between friends and foes. Finally, he is of the Order of the Thrones.

XLI. FOCALOR, a strong duke, appears in the form of a

THE SEAL OF FOCALOR   THE SEAL OF SABNACK

man with the wings of a griffin. He drowns men, sinks war-

---

[1] The reading of Wierus is preferable, *i.e.*, Temples and Towers. But the reference is to the edifices of enemies. On his own part, he builds houses and high towers wonderfully.

[2] Or *Raym.*

ships and has power over the winds and the sea, but he will not hurt any one if commanded to forbear by the exorcist. He hopes to return to the Seventh Thrones in 1050 years.[1]

XLII. SABNACK,[2] a mighty marquis, appears in the form of an armed soldier, having a lion's head and riding on a pale-coloured horse. He builds towers, camps and cities, fortifies the same, torments men with wounds and putrid sores swarming with worms;[3] he also gives good familiars.

XLIII. VEPAR,[4] a great duke, appears as a mermaid. He guides the waters and battleships; he occasions storms at sea, when so commanded by the Magician. He also causes the sea to seem

THE SAL OF VEPAR

full of ships; he occasions death in three days by means of putrefying sores and worm-eaten wounds.

XLIV. SHAX,[5] a great marquis, comes in the form of a

THE SEAL OF SHAX

THE SEAL OF VINE

stockdove,[6] speaking with a hoarse voice. He destroys the sight, hearing and understanding of any man or woman at the will of the exorcist, steals money from the king's exchequer

---

[1] He is deceived, says Wierus, and so say other codices.   [2] Alias, *Saburac*.
[3] At the command of the magician (Wierus).
[4] Otherwise, *Separ*.   [5] Also *Chax* or *Scox*.   [6] Otherwise, a stork.

and returns it in 1200 years. He will transport anything, but must first be commanded into the triangle; otherwise he will deceive the operator. He discovers all hidden things which are not in the keeping of wicked spirits and gives good familars.[1]

XLV. VINE, a great king and earl, appears in a monstrous

THE SEAL OF BIFRONS   THE SEAL OF VUAL

form,[2] but assumes human shape when commanded. He discerns things hidden, reveals witches and makes known the past, present and future. At the command of the exorcist he will build towers, demolish walls and make the waters stormy.

XLVI. BIFRONS, a great earl, appears in a monstrous form but assumes the human shape when commanded. He gives

THE SEAL OF HAGENTI

proficiency in astrology, geometry and other mathematical arts; he teaches the virtue of herbs, precious stones and woods; he changes dead bodies, puts them in other places and lights phantom candles on their graves.

XLVII. VUAL, a great duke, comes at first as an enormous dromedary, but afterwards assumes human form and speaks in the Egyptian tongue. He procures the love of women, discerns

---

[1] He is also a horse-stealer, when so desired by the exorcist.
[2] Or as a lion seated on a black horse and holding a viper in his hand.

past, present and future, and excites friendship even between foes. He was of the Order of the Powers.

XLVIII. HAGENTI, a great president, appears in the shape of a gigantic bull with the wings of a griffin, but will duly put on human form. He gives wisdom, transmutes all metals into gold and turns wine into water.

XLIX. PROCEL[1] appears in the form of an angel, and is a great and strong duke. He speaks mysti-cally of hidden things, teaches geometry and the liberal sciences, and at the com-mand of the operator will make a great commotion, like that of running waters; he also warms waters and tempers baths.[2] He was of the Order of the Powers before his fall.

THE SEAL OF PROCEL

L. FURCAS, a great duke, appears in the form of a cruel old man, with long beard and hoary hair. He is seated on a

THE SEAL OF FURCAS   THE SEAL OF BALAM

pale horse and has a sharp spear in his hand. He teaches philosophy, rhetoric, astronomy, logic, chiromancy and pyro-mancy—perfectly in all their parts.

LI. BALAM, a terrible and powerful king, appears with three

---

[1] Otherwise, *Pucel*.   [2] *i.e.*, the thermal springs frequented by sick people.

heads, the first like that of a bull, the second like that of a man and the third like a ram's. With the tail of a serpent and eyes flaming fire, he rides upon a furious bear, carrying a goshawk on his wrist and speaking with a hoarse voice. He gives true answers as to past, present and future, makes men go invisible, and imparts wit.[1]

LII. ALLOCEN,[2] a strong duke, appears in the form of a soldier, mounted on a great horse, his face like that of a lion,

THE SEAL OF ALLOCEN   THE SEAL OF CAIM

exceedingly red, his eyes flaming fire, his speech hoarse and loud. He teaches astronomy and the liberal sciences, and gives a good familiar.

LIII. CAIM, a great president, appears in the form of a thrush,[3] but afterwards in that of a man bearing a sharp sword and seeming—as it is said fantastically—to answer in burning ashes. He is a keen disputant; he imparts to men the understanding of birds' songs, the lowing of cattle, the barking of dogs and the voice of waters. He gives true answers concerning things to come and was once of the Order of Angels.

LIV. MURMUR, a great duke and earl, appears in the form of a soldier, riding on a griffin and having a duke's crown on

---

[1] He is of the Order of the Dominations.
[2] Otherwise, *Alloien* and *Allocer*.   [3] Or of a blackbird.

his head. He is preceded by two ministers sounding trumpets. He teaches philosophy perfectly; he constrains the souls of the dead to appear and to answer questions. He was partly of the Order of Thrones and partly of Angels.

LV. OROBAS, a great prince, appears first like a horse but,

THE SEAL OF MURMUR

THE SEAL OF OROBAS

when commanded, in human form. He discovers past, present and future; he gives good dignities and advancements, with the favour of friends and foes; he will reply concerning the creation

THE SEAL OF GOMORY

THE SEAL OF OSE

of the world and Divinity; he is very faithful to the exorcist and defends him from temptation by any spirit.

LVI. GOMORY, a powerful duke, appears like a beautiful woman, wearing a ducal crown.[1] He discovers past, present and future, as also the whereabouts of hidden treasures; he procures the love of women and especially of girls.

LVII. OSE, a great president, appears at first like a leopard

[1] And riding on a camel (Wierus).

and then in human shape. He gives skill in all liberal sciences
and true answers concerning divine and secret things. He can

THE SEAL OF AMY

change men into any shape that the exorcist may desire, and
he that is changed will not know it.[1]

LVIII. AMY, a great president, comes first as a great
flaming fire and then as a man. He gives perfect knowledge

THE SEAL OF ORIAS

of astrology and the liberal sciences, with good familiars, and
can betray treasures that are kept by spirits.[2]

LIX. ORIAS, a great marquis, appears in the form of a

---

[1] He can also reduce them to such a state of insanity that they will believe their identity
changed, that they are kings and so forth. The delusion, however, will only endure for one
hour (Wierus).

[2] He is partly of the Order of the Angels and partly of that of the Powers. He hopes to
return to the Seventh Thrones in 1200 years, which is incredible, says Wierus.

lion bestriding a strong horse; he has a serpent's tail and holds two enormous, hissing snakes in his right hand. He teaches the virtues of the planets and the mansions thereof; he transforms men, gives dignities, prelacies and confirmations, with the favour of friends and foes.

LX. VAPULA, a strong duke, comes in the form of a lion

THE SEAL OF VAPULA

with griffin's wings. He gives skill not only in manual professions but also in philosophy and the sciences contained in books —I suppose, as distinguished from the secret sciences.

LXI. ZAGAN, a great king and president, appears at first in the form of a bull, with the wings of a griffin, but after in

THE SEAL OF ZAGAN

human shape. He makes men witty, turns water into wine, blood into oil and oil into water;[1] he can change any metal into coin of the realm and can make fools wise.

---

[1] Otherwise, wine into water or into blood.

The Book of Ceremonial Magic

LXII. Valac, a great president, comes as a little boy with

THE SEAL OF VALAC

the wings of an angel and riding on a two-headed dragon. He gives true answers concerning hidden treasures, tells where serpents may be seen and will deliver them helpless to the exorcist.

LXIII. Andras, a great marquis, comes in the form of an angel, with the head of a black night-raven, riding upon a strong black wolf and having a sharp bright sword gleaming in his hands. He sows discord and will kill the unwary.[1]

LXIV. Flauros, a great duke, appears at first like a

THE SEAL OF ANDRAS

THE SEAL OF FLAUROS

terrible leopard, but at the command of the exorcist he puts on the shape of a man, with fiery eyes and terrible countenance. He gives true answers of things past, present and future, but unless commanded into the triangle he will deceive the exorcist. He converses gladly of divinity and the creation of the world, as also of the fall of spirits, his own included. If desired, he will destroy and burn the enemies of the operator, nor will he suffer him to be tempted, by spirits or otherwise.

[1] Another codex says frankly that he can kill the Master and all his Assistants.

LXV. ANDREALPHUS, a mighty marquis, appears at first in the form of a peacock, with a great noise, but after puts on human shape. He teaches geometry perfectly and all that belongs to measurements, astronomy included. He can transform men into the likeness of a bird.

THE SEAL OF ANDREALPHUS   THE SEAL OF CIMERIES

LXVI. CIMERIES, a powerful marquis, appears like a valiant soldier on a black horse. He rules the spirits in the parts of Africa; he teaches grammar, logic and rhetoric, discovers buried treasures and things lost and hidden; he can make a man appear like a soldier of his own kind.

THE SEAL OF AMDUSCIAS

LXVII. AMDUSCIAS, a great duke, comes first like an unicorn, but will stand up at request in human shape, causing all manner of musical instruments to be heard but not seen. He makes trees fall at the will of the operator and gives excellent familiars.

LXVIII. BELIAL, a mighty king, created next after Lucifer, appears in the form of a beautiful angel, seated in a chariot of fire and speaking with a pleasant voice. He fell first amongst the superior angels who went before Michael and other heavenly angels. He distributes preferences for senatorships,

THE SEAL OF BELIAL

causes favours of friends and foes and gives excellent familiars. He must have offerings and sacrifices made to him.[1]

THE SEAL OF DECARABIA

LXIX. DECARABIA, a marquis, comes in the form of a star in a pentacle, but puts on the image of man at command. He discovers the virtues of herbs and precious stones, makes birds seem to fly before the exorcist and remain with him as familiars, singing and eating like other birds.

THE SEAL OF SEERE

LXX. SEERE, a mighty prince under *Amaymon*, King of the East, appears in the form of a beautiful man on a strong, winged horse. He brings all things to pass suddenly, transports to any place in the twinkling of an eye and discovers all thefts. He is indifferently good or bad, and will do the will of the operator.

---

[1] He is partly of the Order of the Virtues and partly of that of the Angels. Unless he be constrained by Divine Power, he will not remain one hour in the truth. He was one of the vast cohort shut up by Solomon in a brazen vessel and released subsequently by the Babylonians.

The Mysteries of Goëtic Theurgy

LXXI. DANTALIAN, a mighty duke, appears in the form of a man with many faces of men and women; he has a book in his right hand. He teaches all arts and sciences, declares all secret counsels, for he knows all human thoughts and can change them at his will. He kindles love and shews the similitude of any person in a vision, wheresoever they may be.

LXXII. ANDROMALIUS, a great duke and earl, appears in the form of a man holding a serpent in his hand. He returns

THE SEAL OF DANTALIAN   THE SEAL OF ANDROMALIUS

stolen goods, reveals the thief, discovers all wickedness and underhand dealing, as also hidden treasures.

Such are the prime mysteries of *Goëtia* according to the tradition of the *Lemegeton;* such is the work which has been described in the interest of White Magic as distinct from the *Key of Solomon*, but highly important and valuable in its own department.[1] Viewed in the light of these two-and-seventy methods of accomplishing all abominations, it would seem that the three "analogical realms of occult philosophy" are the three kingdoms which we have known under other names from our childhood—as "the world, the flesh and the devil." It

---

[1] That is the discriminating judgment of Mr. Mathers, who forbears, however, to specify. I do think that the *Lemegeton* is very curious and in this sense important, but not for the reasons which actuated Mr. Mathers presumably.

will be unnecessary after their enumeration to argue any longer upon the distinction between Black and White Magic as it appears in one of the oldest and best of the Rituals. There is no longer any need to inquire whether the operator is saved by his intention, for we are acquainted with the nature of the intentions which govern procedure in one of the most reputable memorials of White Magic which is now extant. The evocation of Lucifer and Astaroth, whatever the pretext, must be

THE TRIANGLE OF SOLOMON

the first step towards Satanism ; but here we have Satanism undiluted, *plus* all the mysteries of the impure Venus. To dismiss, therefore, the definition which no longer perplexes, let us establish that the distinction between White and Black Magic is the distinction between the *Lemegeton* and the *Grimoire of Honorius,*—in other words, between cipher and zero.

§ 2. *Concerning the Rite of Conjuration, from the Lemegeton*

In communicating with the seventy-two spirits, the age of the Moon should be observed, for it is affirmed on the authority of Solomon that all days are profitable save the second, fourth, sixth, ninth, tenth, twelfth or fourteenth of that luminary.

The Mysteries of Goëtic Theurgy

The seals must be made of metals; those of the chief kings should be of gold; marquises, of silver; dukes, of copper; prelates, of tin or silver; knights, of lead; presidents, of fixed quicksilver;[1] and earls, of silver and copper in equal parts. The entire cohort is governed by AMAYMON, King of the

THE DOUBLE SEAL OF SOLOMON

East; CORSON, King of the West; ZIMINAR, King of the North; and GAAP, King of the South. These may be bound from 9 A.M. till noon, but, except on occasions of great importance, should not be invoked themselves, as they act commonly by their inferiors. Marquises may be bound from 3 to 9 P.M. and from sunset to sunrise; dukes from sunrise till noon, in

[1] Numerous experiments of the alchemists are concerned with congealing and fixing quicksilver, but there are also "cabalistic" processes by which this substance was prepared expressly for the construction of talismans, and these must not be confused with the more sober—if not more successful—recipes of Hermetic Art. On this point see *Les Secrets du Petit Albert*, Lyons edition, 1775, pp. 63–65.

The Book of Ceremonial Magic

clear weather; prelates in any hour of the day; knights only from dawn till sunrise, or from 4 P.M. till sunset; presidents in any daylight hour up to the evening twilight; counts and earls in any hour of the day, but it must be in the woods and forests, or in a place that is free from noise and far from the resort of

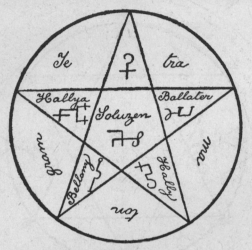

THE PENTAGRAM OF SOLOMON

men. The ceremonial circle must be drawn towards that side to which the spirit who is to be called is attributed.[1] The triangle into which Solomon summoned the rebellious demons must be made two feet outside this circle and three feet over it. The double seal and pentagram of Solomon must be drawn on a parchment of calf-skin, or otherwise on gold or silver,

[1] The chief consecrations of the circle are summarised by Francis Barrett in *The Key to Ceremonial Magic* as follows : Therefore when you would consecrate any place or circle, you should take the Prayer of Solomon used in the dedication and consecration of the Temple ; you must likewise bless the place by sprinkling with holy water and with suffumigations, and commemorate in the benediction holy mysteries, such as these : the sanctification of the throne of God, of Mount Sinai, of the Tabernacle of the Covenant, of the Holy of Holies. . . . And by invoking all Divine Names which are significant to this.

PLATE VIII

THE MAGICAL CIRCLE

and should be worn upon the white vestment of the operator, together with the seal of the spirit, which must be exhibited on his appearance—to compel obedience and assumption of the human form. In addition to these characters, the secret seal of Solomon must be drawn with the blood of a black cock that has never engendered, on virgin parchment, the operator himself being clean within and without, having abstained from sexual intercourse for the space of one month and having

MAGICAL SWORDS AND WAND

obtained pardon for his sins by means of fasting and prayer.[1] It is to be composed on a Tuesday or Saturday at midnight, with the Moon increasing in Virgo, and with burning of perfumes of aloes, resin, cedar and alum.

The other directions correspond broadly to those prescribed in the second chapter. There is the rod or sceptre; the sword; the mitre or cap; a long robe of white linen; a girdle of lion's skin, three inches wide and inscribed with the names which appear in the outer circle of practice; material for the

[1] I do not think that an intentional profanation of the sacraments and holy offices of the Church was here intended. This would be ascribing a depth to the motive of the Grimoires which they never possessed.

fumigations; oil to anoint the temples and eyes; and clean water for the ablution. The Prayer at Lustration is simply the versicle of David:—*Thou shalt purge me with hyssop,*

THE SECRET SEAL OF SOLOMON

O Lord, and I shall be cleansed; Thou shalt wash me and I shall be made whiter than snow.

PRAYER AT VESTING

By the figurative mystery of this holy vestment, I will clothe me with the armour of salvation in the strength of the Most High, ANCOR, AMICAR, AMIDES, THEODONIAS, ANITOR, *that so the end which I desire may be effected, O* ADONAI, *through Thy strength, to Whom be praise and glory for ever and ever.*[1]

[1] VARIANT: *Anoor, Amacor, Amides, Theodonias, Anitor;* by the merits of the angels, O Lord, I will put on the garment of salvation, that this which I desire I may bring to effect, through Thee, the Most Holy Adonai, Whose Kingdom endureth for ever and ever. Amen.

The Mysteries of Goëtic Theurgy

Prayers should also be offered in harmony with the intention of the operator before pronouncing the forms of evocation, as follows :—

FIRST CONJURATION

I invoke and conjure thee, O Spirit N., and, fortified with the power of the Supreme Majesty, I strongly command thee by BARALAMENSIS, BALDACHIENSIS, PAUMACHIE, APOLORESEDES *and the most potent princes* GENIO, LIACHIDE, *Ministers of the Tartarean Seat, chief princes of the seat of* APOLOGIA *in the ninth region; I exorcise and command thee, O Spirit N., by Him Who spake and it was done, by the Most Holy and glorious Names* ADONAI, EL, ELOHIM, ELOHE, ZEBAOTH, ELION, ESCHERCE, JAH, TETRAGRAMMATON, SADAI : *do thou forthwith appear and shew thyself unto me, here before this circle, in a fair and human shape, without any deformity or horror; do thou come forthwith, from whatever part of the world, and make rational answers to my questions; come presently, come visibly, come affably, manifest that which I desire, being conjured by the Name of the Eternal, Living and True God,* HELIOREM ; *I conjure thee also by the particular and true Name of thy God to whom thou owest thine obedience; by the name of the King who rules over thee, do thou come without tarrying; come, fulfil my desires; persist unto the end, according to mine intentions.*

THE RING OF THE EXORCIST

I conjure thee by Him to Whom all creatures are obedient, by this ineffable Name, Tetragrammaton Jehovah, *by which the elements are overthrown, the air is shaken, the sea turns back, the fire is generated, the earth moves and all the hosts of things celestial, of things terrestrial, of things infernal, do tremble and are confounded together; speak unto me visibly and affably in a clear, intelligible voice, free from ambiguity. Come therefore in the name* Adonai Zebaoth; *come, why dost thou tarry?* Adonai Saday, *King of kings, commands thee.*

This being repeated frequently, if the spirit do not yet appear, say as follows :—

SECOND CONJURATION

I invoke, conjure and command thee, O Spirit N., to appear and shew thyself visibly before this circle, in fair and comely shape, without deformity or guile, by the Name of On; *by the Name Y and V, which Adam heard and spake; by the Name of* Joth, *which Jacob learned from the Angel on the night of his wrestling and was delivered from the hands of his brother Esau; by the Name of God* Agla, *which Lot heard and was saved with his family; by the Name* Anehexeton, *which Aaron spake and was made wise; by the Name* Schemes Amathia, *which Joshua invoked and the Sun stayed upon his course; by the Name* Emmanuel, *which the three children, Shadrach, Meshach and Abednego, chanted in the midst of the fiery furnace, and they were delivered; by the Name* Alpha *and* Omega, *which Daniel uttered, and destroyed Bel and the Dragon; by the Name* Zebaoth, *which Moses named, and all the rivers and waters in the land of Egypt brought forth frogs, which ascended into the houses of the Egyptians, destroying all things; by the Name* ESCERCHIE ARISTON, *which also Moses named, and the rivers and waters in the land of Egypt were turned into blood; by the Name* ELION, *on which Moses called, and there fell a great hail, such as never was seen since the creation of the world; by the Name* ADONAI, *which Moses named, and there came up locusts over all the land of Egypt and devoured what the hail had left; by the Name* HAGIOS, *by the Seal of* ADONAI, *by those others, which are* JETROS, ATHENOROS, PARACLETUS; *by the three Holy and Secret Names,* AGLA, ON, TETRAGRAMMATON; *by the dreadful Day of Judgment; by the changing Sea of Glass which is before the face of the Divine Majesty, mighty and powerful; by the four beasts before the Throne, having eyes before and behind; by the fire which is about the Throne, by the Holy Angels of Heaven, by the Mighty Wisdom of God; by the Seal of* BASDATHEA, *by this Name* PRIMEMATUM, *which Moses named, and the earth opened and swallowed Corah, Dathan and Abiram; do thou make faithful answers unto all my demands, and perform all my desires, so far as thine office shall permit. Come therefore peaceably and affably; come visibly and without delay; manifest that which I desire; speak with a clear and intelligible voice, that I may understand thee.*

If he come not at the rehearsing of these Conjurations, as without doubt he will, proceed as follows, it being a Constraint :—

THIRD CONJURATION

I conjure thee, O Spirit N., by all the most glorious and efficacious Names of the Great and Incomparable Lord the God of Hosts, come quickly and without delay, from whatsoever part of the world thou art in; make rational answers to my demands; come visibly, speak affably, speak intelligibly to my understanding. I conjure and constrain thee, O Spirit N., by all the aforesaid Names, as also by those seven other Names wherewith Solomon bound thee and thy fellows in the brazen vessel, to wit, ADONAI, PRERAI, TETRAGRAMMATON, ANEXHEXETON, INESSENSATOAL, PATHUMATON and ITEMON ; do thou manifest before this circle, fulfil my will in all things that may seem good to me. Be disobedient, refuse to come, and by the power of the Supreme Being, the everlasting Lord, that God Who created thee and me, the whole world, with all contained therein, in the space of six days ; by EYE, by SARAY, by the virtue of the Name PRIMEMATUM, which commands the whole host of Heaven; be disobedient, and behold I will curse and deprive thee of thine office, thy joy and thy place; I will bind thee in the depths of the bottomless pit, there to remain until the Day of the Last Judgment. I will chain thee in the Lake of Eternal Fire, in the Lake of Fire and Brimstone, unless thou come quickly, appearing before this circle, to do my will. Come, therefore, in the Holy Names ADONAI, ZEBAOTH, AMIORAM ; come, ADONAI commands thee.

Should he still fail to appear, you may be sure that he has been sent by his King to some other place. Invoke, therefore, the King to despatch his servant as follows :—

INVOCATION OF THE KING

O thou great and powerful King AMAYMON, who rulest by the power of the Supreme God, EL, over all Spirits, superior and inferior, but especially over the Infernal Order in the Dominion of the East, I invoke and command thee by the

The Mysteries of Goëtic Theurgy

particular and true Name of God, by the God Whom thou dost worship, by the Seal of thy creation, by the most mighty and powerful Name of God, JEHOVAH, TETRAGRAMMATON, Who cast thee out of Heaven with the rest of the Infernal Spirits; by all the other potent and great Names of God, Creator of Heaven, Earth and Hell, of all contained therein; by their powers and virtues; by the Name PRIMEMATUM, which commands the whole host of Heaven. Do thou force and compel the Spirit N. here before this circle, in a fair and comely shape, without injury to myself or to any creature, that he may give me true and faithful answer, so that I may accomplish my desired end, whatsoever it be, provided that it is proper to his office, by the power of God, EL, Who hath created and doth dispose of all things, celestial, aërial, terrestrial and infernal.

Having twice or thrice invoked the King in this manner, again conjure the spirit, using the previous forms, and rehearsing them several times, whereupon he will come assuredly. Yet should he fail, be convinced that he is bound with chains in hell, and is not in the custody of his King. To set him free it is necessary to recite

THE CHAIN CURSE

O thou wicked and disobedient N., because thou hast not obeyed or regarded the words which I have rehearsed, the glorious and incomprehensible Names of the true God, Maker of all things in the world, now I, by the power of these Names, which no creature can resist, do curse thee into the depths of the Bottomless Pit, to remain until the Day of Doom, in the Hell of unquenchable fire and brimstone, unless thou shalt forthwith appear in this triangle, before this circle, to do my will. Come, therefore, quickly and peaceably, by the Names ADONAI, ZEBAOTH, ADONAI, AMIORAM. *Come, come,* ADONAI, *King of Kings, commands thee.*

Having read so far, if he come not, write his seal on parchment; put it in a black box, with brimstone, assafœtida and other stinking perfumes; bind the said box with iron wire, hang it on the point of your sword, hold it over the fire of charcoal, which shall have been placed towards that quarter whence the spirit will come, and say first unto the Fire :—*I conjure thee, O Fire, by Him Who made thee, and all other creatures in the world, to torment, burn, and consume this Spirit N. everlastingly.*

TO THE SPIRIT

Because thou art disobedient, and obeyst not my command-ments nor the precepts of the Lord thy God, now I, who am the servant of the Most High and Imperial Lord God of Hosts, JEHOVAH, *having His celestial power and permission, for this thine averseness and contempt, thy great disobedience and re-bellion, will excommunicate thee, will destroy thy name and seal, which I have in this box, will burn them with unquenchable fire and bury them in unending oblivion, unless thou comest immedi-ately, visibly and affably, here before this circle, within this triangle, assuming a fair and comely form, without doing harm unto myself or any creature whatsoever, but giving reasonable answer to my requests and performing my desire in all things.*

If he appear not at this point, say as follows :—

Thou art still pernicious and disobedient, willing not to appear and inform me upon that which I desire to know; now therefore, in the Name and by the power and dignity of the

The Mysteries of Goëtic Theurgy

Omnipotent and Immortal Lord God of Hosts, JEHOVAH TETRA-
GRAMMATON, *sole Creator of Heaven, Earth and Hell, with all
contained therein, the marvellous Disposer of all things visible
and invisible, I do hereby curse and deprive thee of all thine
office, power and place; I bind thee in the depth of the Bottomless Pit, there to remain unto the Day of Judgment, in the Lake
of Fire and Brimstone, prepared for the rebellious Spirits. May
all the Company of Heaven curse thee; may the Sun, the Moon,
the Stars, the Light of the Hosts of Heaven, curse thee into fire
unquenchable, into torments unspeakable; and even as thy name
and seal are bound up in this box, to be choked with sulphureous
and stinking substances and to burn in this material fire, so, in
the Name of* JEHOVAH, *and by the power and dignity of the three
Names,* TETRAGRAMMATON, ANEXHEXETON, PRIMEMATUM, *may
all these drive thee, O thou disobedient Spirit N., into the Lake
of Fire, prepared for the damned and accursed Spirits, there to
remain until the Day of Doom, remembered no more before the
face of that God Who shall come to judge the quick and the
dead, with the whole world, by fire.*

Set the box in the flame, whereupon he will appear; when
he comes, quench the fire, make sweet perfumes, give him
good entertainment, shewing him the pentacle on the hem
of your vestment covered with a linen cloth, and saying :—
*Behold thy confusion, if thou be disobedient. Behold the Pen-
tacle of Solomon which I have brought into thy presence. Behold
the person of the Exorcist, who is called* OCTINIMOES, *in the
midst of the Exorcism, armed by God and fearless, potently
invoking and calling. Make, therefore, reasonable answers to
my demands; be obedient to me, thy Master, in the Name of
the Lord* BATHAL, *rushing upon* ABRAC, ABEOR, *coming upon*
BEROR.

He will become obedient and bid you ask what you will, for he is made subject by God to your purpose. When he shews himself humble and meek, say :—*Welcome, Spirit (or, most noble King), welcome art thou unto me ; I have called thee through Him Who created Heaven, Earth and Hell, with all contained therein, and thou hast obeyed, also by the like power. I bind thee to remain affably and visibly before this circle, within this triangle, so long as I need thee, to depart not without my license, till thou hast truly and faithfully fulfilled all that I shall require.*

THE LICENSE TO DEPART

O Spirit N., because thou hast diligently answered my demands, I do hereby license thee to depart, without injury to man or beast. Depart, I say, and be thou willing and ready to come, whensoever duly exorcised and conjured by the Sacred Rites of Magic. I conjure thee to withdraw peaceably and quietly, and may the peace of God continue for ever between me and thee. Amen.

Go not out of the circle till he be gone, but make prayers to God for the great blessing He has bestowed upon you by thus granting your desires and delivering you from the malice of the enemy.

For these verbose and tiresome conjurations the Latin version of Wierus substitutes one general form of citation, in the Name of the Christian Trinity, which is not really an especial anachronism, for the compiler of the *Lemegeton* was acquainted at least with the books of the New Testament. This is proved by the references in the Second Conjuration

234

to the Living Creatures of the Apocalypse, and it leaves the attribution to Solomon in precisely that state which our respect for a prince in Israel would naturally desire. No doubt, however, the English editor of The Key Major of Magic would see no reason to question the attribution and would explain the anachronism very simply as a late interpolation.

HELL MOUTH AND THE DEVIL CHAINED.

From Cædmon.

CHAPTER V

Concerning the Mystery of the Sanctum Regnum, or the Government of Evil Spirits; being the Rite of Conjuration according to the Grimorium Verum

THE preparations of the operator prescribed by the *Grimorium Verum* are fully represented in the earlier chapters, but they may be summed here as follows :— 1. An austere fast of three days ; 2. Retreat or isolation from human society ; 3. Abstinence from sexual intercourse ; 4. The recitation of certain prayers and the performance of certain ablutions ; 5. The composition of the required instruments. He must further devote himself to the invocations, lest memory fail him at the moment set apart for the work, and to insure mastery of the practice. He should also recite the following prayer daily [1]—at Prime once, at Tierce twice, at Sext three times, at Nones four times, at Vespers five times, and six times before going to rest. It is explained that these hours are planetary and unequal.[2] Prime is reckoned at the rising of the sun, Tierce at three hours after, Sext at mid-day, Nones at three in the afternoon and Vespers at sunset.

---

[1] This portion of the process offers some analogy with the *Key of Solomon*, Book ii. c. 2.

[2] *i.e.*, they are governed by the times of sunrise and sunset. Sext and Nones would not, however, be variable.

236

The Mystery of the Sanctum Regnum

PRAYER [1]

ASTRACHIOS, ASACH, ASARCA, ABEDUMABAL, SILAT, ANA-
BOTAS, JESUBILIN, SCIGIN, GENEON, DOMOL, Lord God, *Who
dwellest above the heavens, Whose glance searchest the abyss ;
grant me, I pray Thee, the power to conceive in my mind and
to execute that which I desire to do, the end of which I would
attain by Thy help, O God Almighty, Who livest and reignest
for ever and ever. Amen.*

These things being done, says the Grimoire, it remains only
to follow the invocations and to compose the characters, to
which end the operator shall proceed as follows :—On the day
and in the hour of Mars, the Moon waxing, and at the first
hour of the day, which begins automatically fifteen minutes
before the rising of the Sun, a piece of virgin parchment must
be prepared, containing all the characters and invocations of
the spirits on whom it is desired to call. On the day and in
the hour aforesaid, let the operator bind the little finger of the
(left) hand, which is the finger of Mercury, with a thread
woven by a virgin girl ; let him pierce that finger with the
lancet of the Art, so as to draw blood, and form therewith
the character of *Scirlin*, from whom all other spirits depend,
since he is their messenger and can compel them to appear
despite themselves, because he has the power of the Emperor
to him deputed. His invocation, which must be written, is
as follows :—

---

[1] This prayer is similar to that in the *Key of Solomon*, Book ii. c. 2, with the exception of
the names, which are much mutilated in the Grimoire ; these should read :—*Herachio, Asac,
Asacro, Bedrimulael, Tilath, Arabonas, Ierahlem, Ideodoc, Archarzel, Zophiel, Blautel, Bara-
cata, Edoniel, Elohim, Emagro, Abragateh, Samoel, Geburahel, Cadato, Era, Elohi, Achsah,
Ebmisha, Imachedel, Daniel, Dama, Elamos, Izachel, Bael, Segon, Gemon, Demas.* But the
majority of these are unintelligible.

The Invocation of Scirlin

Helon ✠, Taul ✠, Varf ✠, Pan ✠, Heon ✠, Homono-reum ✠, Clemialh ✠, Serugeath ✠, Agla ✠, Tetragram-maton ✠, Casoly ✠.

With the confusion so common in the Grimoires, the character of *Scirlin* is not given, whence the operator who followed the instructions of this Ritual must have had recourse to one of the superior spirits. The instructions, however, are not described *ad clerum*, and it is scarcely possible to extract from them an intelligible method of procedure. The name and surname of the operator must apparently be written below the character of the spirit, following a prescribed manner, which is also omitted ; the conjuration of the spirit must be added and incense burnt in his honour.

Conjuration to Lucifer

Lucifer ✠, Ouyar ✠, Chameron ✠, Aliseon ✠, Man-dousin ✠, Premy ✠, Oriet ✠, Naydrus ✠, Esmony ✠, Eparinesont ✠, Estiot ✠, Dumosson ✠, Danochar ✠, Casmiel ✠, Hayras ✠, Fabelleronthon ✠, Sodirno ✠, Peatham ✠, *Come* ✠, Lucifer ✠. Amen.

Conjuration for Beelzebuth

Beelzebuth ✠, Lucifer ✠, Madilon ✠, Solymo ✠, Saroy ✠, Theu ✠, Ameclo ✠, Segrael ✠, Praredun ✠, Adrica-norom ✠, Martiro ✠, Timo ✠, Cameron ✠, Phorsy ✠, Metosite ✠, Prumosy ✠, Dumaso ✠, Elivisa ✠, Alphrois ✠, Fubentronty ✠, *Come*, Beelzebuth ✠. Amen.

The Mystery of the Sanctum Regnum

CONJURATION FOR ASTAROTH

ASTAROTH ✠, ADOR ✠, CAMESO ✠, VALUERITUF ✠, MARESO ✠, LODIR ✠, CADOMIR ✠, ALUIEL ✠, CALNISO ✠, TELY ✠, PLEORIM ✠, VIORDY ✠, CUREVIORBAS ✠, CAMERON ✠, VESTU-RIEL ✠, VULNAVII ✠, BENEZ ✠, MEUS CALMIRON ✠, NOARD ✠, NISA CHENIBRANBO CALEVODIUM ✠, BRAZO ✠, TABRASOL ✠, *Come* ✠, ASTAROTH ✠. AMEN.

Having repeated seven times the conjuration addressed to one of these superior spirits, the same will forthwith manifest to perform whatsoever shall be desired. NOTE.—Such conjuration must have been written on virgin paper or parchment before invoking the spirits. These, having been satisfied, may be dismissed by using the following

DISCHARGE

Go in peace unto your places; may peace be with you, and be ye ready to come whensoever I shall call upon you, In the Name of the Father ✠ *and of the Son* ✠ *and of the Holy Ghost* ✠. *Amen.*

CONJURATION FOR INFERIOR SPIRITS

O SURMY ✠, DELMUSAN ✠, ATALSLOVM ✠, CHARUSIHOA ✠, MELANY ✠, LIAMINTHO ✠, COLEHON ✠, PARON ✠, MADOIN ✠, MERLOY ✠, BULERATOR ✠, DONMEO ✠, HONE ✠, PELOVM ✠, IBASIL ✠, MEON ✠, ALYMDRICTELS ✠, PERSON ✠, CRISOLSAY ✠, LEMON SEFLE NIDAR HORIEL PEUNT ✠, HALMON ✠, ASOPHIEL ✠, ILNOSTREON ✠, BANIEL ✠, VERMIAS ✠, ESLEVOR ✠, NOELMA ✠, DORSAMOT ✠, LHAVALA ✠, OMOT ✠, FRANGAM ✠, BELDOR ✠, DRAGIN ✠, *Come* ✠.

The name of the required spirit must here be added on the parchment, when he will duly appear—the ordinary accidents excepted—and will grant what is desired of him—that is to say, if it so happen—after which he may be dismissed by the previous Discharge.

The characters should be burnt in each case, as they avail once only.

ANOTHER CONJURATION

I conjure thee, N., by the great living God, the Sovereign Creator of all things, to appear under a comely human form, without noise and without terror, to answer truly unto all questions that I shall ask thee. Hereunto I conjure thee by the virtue of these Holy and Sacred Names.

THE IMP STATUE.   LINCOLN.

CHAPTER VI

The Mysteries of Infernal Evocation according to the Grand Grimoire

§ 1. *The Rite of Lucifuge*

THE *Grand Grimoire* divides with the *Grimoire of Honorius* the darksome honour of an intelligible and unmutilated Ritual of Black Magic. Each after its own kind is indeed an exceedingly curious work. In the first is contained what is probably the only printed method of making pacts; the second is remarkable, firstly, on account of its pretended origin and the elaboration with which it is set forth, secondly, for the ecclesiastical complexion of its process, which can scarcely have failed to impose upon some credulous and priestly sorcerers of the illiterate kind, and assuming their willingness to disgrace the vows of ordination. Both require, in a study of the present kind, to be printed almost *in extenso*, and, setting aside their preliminary portions, already adequately dealt with, they are given practically verbatim in the chapters which here follow.

It will be remembered that the operator, or Karcist, as he is termed in the *Grand Grimoire*, is recommended continence, fasting and similar privations for an entire quarter of the moon, such quarter coinciding with that of the luminary. On the morning which succeeds the first night of the quarter, he must repair to a druggist's, and purchase a blood-stone, called *Ematille* (*id est, Hæmatites*), which must be carried continually about him for fear of accident, and in expectation that the spirit whom it is proposed to compel and bind will henceforth do all in his power to overwhelm the operator with terror, so as to incite him to abandon the enterprise, hoping in this manner to escape from the wiles which are beginning to be woven about him.

The next operation is the purchase of a virgin kid, which must be decapitated on the third day of the moon. Previously to the sacrifice, a garland of vervain must be wound about the neck of the animal, immediately below the head, and secured by means of a green ribbon. The sacrifice must be offered on the scene of the coming evocation, a forlorn and isolated spot free from all interruption. There, with the right arm bared to the shoulder, having armed himself with a blade of fine steel, and having kindled a fire of white wood, the Karcist shall recite the following words in a hopeful and animated manner :—

INITIAL OFFERING

I immolate this victim to Thee, O grand ADONAY, ELOIM, ARIEL *and* JEHOVAM, *to the honour, glory and power of Thy Name, which is superior to all Spirits. O grand* ADONAY ! *Vouchsafe to receive it as an acceptable offering. Amen.*

Here he must cut the throat of the kid, skin it, set the body on the fire and reduce it to ashes, which must be collected and cast towards the rising of the sun, at the same time repeating the following words :—*It is to the honour, glory and dominion of Thy Name, O grand* ADONAY, ELOIM, ARIEL, JEHOVAM, *that I spill the blood of this victim! Vouchsafe, O Thou grand* ADONAY, *to receive its ashes as an acceptable sacrifice.*

While the victim is being consumed by the flames, the

operator shall rejoice in the honour and glory of the grand ADONAY, ELOIM, ARIEL and JEHOVAM, taking care to preserve the skin of the virgin kid to form the round or grand Kabalistic circle, in which he must himself stand on the day of the supreme enterprise.

The sacrifice of the victim is followed by the selection and composition of the Blasting Rod, of which a description has been given. From the purpose for which it is intended, and from the silence of the Grimoire, it may be inferred that the preparation of the goatskin is exceedingly simple and does not involve the removal of the hair.

When the night of action has arrived, the operator shall gather up his rod, goatskin, the stone called *Ematille*, and shall further provide himself with two vervain crowns, two candlesticks and two candles of virgin wax, made by a virgin girl and duly blessed. Let him take also a new steel and two new flints, with sufficient tinder to kindle a fire, likewise half a bottle of brandy, some blessed incense and camphor, and four nails from the coffin of a dead child. All these must be carried to the place chosen for the great work, where everything hereinafter laid down must be scrupulously performed and the dread Kabalistic circle must be described in an accurate manner. Lastly, it must be carefully borne in mind that there should be either one or three taking part in the ceremony, the Karcist included, who is the person appointed to address the spirit, holding the Destroying Rod in his hand. The evoking process may be given in the actual words of the Grimoire.

CONCERNING A TRUE REPRESENTATION OF THE GRAND KABALISTIC CIRCLE

You must begin by forming a circle with strips of kid's skin, fastened to the ground by means of your four nails. Then with the stone called *Ematille* you must trace the triangle within the circle, beginning at the eastern point. A large A, a small E, a small A, and a small J, must be drawn in like manner, as also the sacred name of Jesus between two crosses. By this means the spirits will have no power to harm you from behind The Karcist and his assistants may then fearlessly proceed to

THE GRAND KABALISTIC CIRCLE

their places within the triangle, and, regardless of any noises, may set the two candlesticks and the two vervain crowns on the right and left sides of the triangle within the circle. This being done, the two candles may be lighted, taking care that there is a new brazier in front of the Karcist, piled with newly consecrated charcoal. This must be kindled by the Karcist casting a small quantity of the brandy therein and a part of the camphor, the rest being reserved to feed the fire periodically, in proportion to the length of the business. Having punctually performed all that is mentioned above, the chief operator may repeat the following prayer:—*I present Thee, O great* ADONAY, *this incense as the purest I can obtain; in like manner, I present Thee this charcoal prepared from the most ethereal of woods. I offer them, O grand and omnipotent* ADONAY, ELOIM, ARIEL *and* JEHOVAM, *with my whole soul and my*

THE CIRCLE OF WHITE MAGIC

whole heart. Vouchsafe, O great ADONAY, *to receive them as an acceptable holocaust. Amen.*

You should also be careful, says the Grimoire, to have no alloyed metal about your person, except a gold or silver coin wrapped in paper, which you must fling to the spirit when he appears outside the circle, so as to prevent him from harming you. While he is picking up the coin, begin promptly the following prayer, fortifying yourself with courage, energy and prudence. Be, also, especially careful that the Karcist is the sole speaker; the assistants must preserve a determined silence, even if they are questioned or menaced by the spirit.

FIRST PRAYER

O great and living God, subsisting in one and the same person, the Father, the Son and the Holy Ghost ; I adore Thee with the deepest veneration, and I submit with the liveliest confidence to Thy holy and sufficient protection. I believe with the most sincere faith that Thou art my Creator, my Benefactor, my Preserver and my Lord, and I testify to Thy sovereign Majesty that my sole desire is to belong to Thee through the whole of eternity. So be it. Amen.

SECOND PRAYER

O great and living God, Who hast created man to enjoy felicity in this life, Who hast adapted all things for his necessities, and didst declare that everything should be made subject to his will, be favourable to this my design, and permit not the rebellious spirits to be in possession of those treasures which were formed by Thine own hands for our temporal requirements. Grant me, O great God, the power to dispose of them by the potent and terrific names in Thy Clavicle : ADONAY, ELOIM, ARIEL, JEHOVAM, TAGLA, MATHON, *be ye propitious unto me. So be it. Amen.*

OFFERTORY

I offer Thee this incense as the purest which I have been able to obtain, O sublime ADONAY, ELOIM, ARIEL *and* JEHOVAM *; vouchsafe to receive it as an acceptable holocaust. Incline to me in Thy power, and enable me to succeed in this great enterprise. So be it. Amen.*

246

The Mysteries of Infernal Evocation

FIRST CONJURATION

Addressed to the Emperor Lucifer

*Emperor Lucifer, Master and Prince of Rebellious Spirits,
I adjure thee to leave thine abode, in whatsoever quarter of the
world it may be situated, and come hither to communicate with
me. I command and I conjure thee in the Name of the Mighty
living God, Father, Son and Holy Ghost, to appear without
noise and without any evil smell, to respond in a clear and
intelligible voice, point by point, to all that I shall ask thee,
failing which, thou shalt be most surely compelled to obedience
by the power of the divine* ADONAY, ELOIM, ARIEL, JEHOVAM,
TAGLA, MATHON, *and by the whole hierarchy of superior intelligences, who shall constrain thee against thy will.* Venité,
Venité! Submiritillor Lucifuge, *or eternal torment shall overwhelm thee, by the great power of this Blasting Rod.* In subito.

SECOND CONJURATION

*I command and I adjure thee, Emperor Lucifer, as the
representative of the mighty living God, and by the power of
Emanuel, His only Son, Who is thy master and mine, and by the
virtue of His precious blood, which He shed to redeem mankind from thy chains, I command thee to quit thine abode, where
soever it may be, swearing that I will give thee one quarter of an
hour alone, if thou dost not straightway come hither and communicate with me in an audible and intelligible voice, or, if thy
personal presence be impossible, despatch me thy Messenger
Astarôt in a human form, without either noise or evil smell,
failing which I will smite thee and thy whole race with the terrible
Blasting Rod into the depth of the bottomless abysses, and that by
the power of those great words in the Clavicle—By* ADONAY,

247

ELOIM, ARIEL, JEHOVAM, TAGLA, MATHON, ALMOUZIN, ARIOS, PITHONA, MAGOTS, SYLPHÆ, TABOTS, SALAMANDRÆ, GNOMUS, TERRÆ, CŒLIS, GODENS, AQUA. *In subito.*

Notice.—Before uttering the third Conjuration, should the spirit refuse to comply, read what follows in the Clavicle, and smite all the spirits by plunging both the forked extremities of your rod into the flames. Be not alarmed in so doing at the frightful howls which you may hear, for at this extreme moment all the spirits will manifest. Then, before reading the Clavicle, and in the midst of the commotion, recite the third Conjuration.

THIRD CONJURATION

I adjure thee, Emperor Lucifer, as the agent of the strong living God, of His beloved Son and of the Holy Ghost, and by the power of the Great ADONAY, ELOIM, ARIEL *and* JEHOVAM, *to appear instantly, or to send thy Messenger Astarôt, forcing thee to forsake thy hiding-place, wheresoever it may be, and warning thee that if thou dost not manifest this moment, I will straightway smite thee and all thy race with the Blasting Rod of the great* ADONAY, ELOIM, ARIEL *and* JEHOVAM, *&c.*

At this point, should the spirit still fail to appear, plunge the two ends of your rod a second time into the flames, and recite the following potent words from the grand Clavicle of olomon :—

GRAND CONJURATION

Extracted from the Veritable Clavicle

I adjure thee, O Spirit! by the power of the grand ADONAY, *to appear instanter, and by* ELOIM, *by* ARIEL, *by* JEHOVAM, *by* AQUA, TAGLA, MATHON, OARIOS, ALMOAZIN, ARIOS, MEMBROT,

The Mysteries of Infernal Evocation

VARIOS, PITHONA, MAJODS, SULPHÆ, GABOTS, SALAMANDRÆ, TABOTS, GINGUA, JANNA, ETITNAMUS, ZARIATNATMIX, &c. A. E. A. J. A. T. M. O. A. A. M. V. P. M. S. C. S. J. C. G. A. J. F. Z. &c.

LUCIFUGE ROFOCALE

After a second repetition of these sublime and powerful words, you may be sure—as the deposition affirms—that the spirit will respond after the ensuing manner.

Of the Manifestation of the Spirit

Lo, I am here! What dost thou seek of me? Why dost thou disturb my repose? Smite me no more with that dread rod!

LUCIFUGE ROFOCALE

Reply to the Spirit

Hadst thou appeared when I first invoked thee, I had by no means smitten thee; remember, if the request which I make thee be refused, I am determined to torment thee eternally.

SOLOMON

The Spirit's Answer

Torment me no further. Say, rather, what thou dost require at my hands.
LUCIFUGE ROFOCALE

The Requisition

I require that thou shalt communicate two several times on each night of the week, either with myself or with those who are entrusted with my present Book, the which thou shalt approve and sign; I permit thee the choice of those hours which may suit thee, if thou approvest not those which I now enumerate. To wit:

On Monday at nine o'clock and at midnight.

On Tuesday at ten o'clock and at one in the morning.

On Wednesday at eleven o'clock and at two in the morning.

On Thursday at eight and ten o'clock.

On Friday at seven in the evening and at midnight.

On Saturday at nine in the evening and at eleven at night.

Further, I command thee to surrender me the nearest treasure, and I promise thee as a reward the first piece of gold or silver which I touch with my hands on the first day of every month. Such is my demand.
SOLOMON

The Spirit's Reply

I cannot comply with thy request on such terms, nor on any

others, unless thou shalt give thyself over to me in fifty years, to do with thy body and soul as I please.

LUCIFUGE ROFOCALE

Rejoinder to the Spirit

Lo, will I smite thee and thy whole race, by the might of great Adonay, if, on the contrary, thou dost not comply with my request.

Notice.—Here plunge the points of the Blasting Rod into the fire and repeat the Grand Conjuration of the Clavicle till the spirit surrenders himself to your will.

Answer and Compliance of the Spirit

Smite me no further; I pledge myself to do what thou desirest two several times on every night of the week. To wit:
On Monday at ten o'clock and at midnight.
On Tuesday at eleven o'clock and at one in the morning.
On Wednesday at midnight and at two in the morning.
On Thursday at eight and at eleven o'clock.
On Friday at nine o'clock and at midnight.
On Saturday at ten o'clock and at one in the morning.
I also approve thy Book, and I give thee my true signature on parchment, which thou shalt affix at its end, to make use of at thy need. Further, I place myself at thy disposition, to appear before thee at thy call when, being purified, and holding the dreadful Blasting Rod, thou shalt open the Book, having described the Kabalistic circle and pronounced the word Rofocale. *I promise thee to have friendly commerce with those who are fortified by the possession of the said Book, where my true signature stands, provided that they invoke me according to rule, on the first occasion that they require me. I also engage to*

251

deliver thee the treasure which thou seekest, on condition that thou keepest the secret for ever inviolable, art charitable to the poor and dost give me a gold or silver coin on the first day of every month. If thou failest, thou art mine everlastingly.

LUCIFUGE ROFOCALE

IMPRIMATUR

Reply to the Spirit
I agree to thy conditions.

SOLOMON

INVITATION OF THE SPIRIT

Follow me, and come lay thy hands on the treasure.

Thereupon the Karcist, armed with the Blasting Rod and the stone called *Ematille*, shall issue from the circle at that point where the door of mighty Adonay is figured, and shall follow the spirit ; the assistants, however, shall not stir one step from the circle, but shall remain firm and immovable within it, whatever reports they hear, whatever visions they behold. The spirit shall then conduct the Karcist to the vicinity of the treasure, when it may befall that the Karcist shall behold the apparition of a large and fierce dog, with a collar as resplendent as the sun. This will be a Gnome, which he can drive off by the point of his rod, when the apparition will make off towards the treasure. The Karcist must follow, and, on reaching the treasure, will be astonished to discover the person who has hidden it, who also will endeavour to grapple with him, but will be unable so much as to approach him. The Karcist must be provided with a sheet of virgin parchment inscribed with the grand conjuration of the Clavicle. This he must cast upon the treasure, grasping one of its coins at the same moment as a pledge and a surety, and previously flinging down a piece of his own money bitten by his own teeth, after which he may retire, walking backwards and carrying away what he can of the treasure. The rest cannot escape him after the above precautions. He must, however, take heed not to turn round, whatever noise he may hear, for at this critical moment it will truly seem as if all the mountains in the world were being precipitated upon him. He must for this cause be fortified with special intrepidity, must take fright at nothing but keep perfectly firm. So acting, he will be led back by the Spirit to the entrance of the circle. Then shall the Karcist recite the following discharge of the Spirit.

CONJURATION AND DISCHARGE OF THE SPIRIT

O Prince Lucifer, I am, for the time, contented with thee. I now leave thee in peace, and permit thee to retire wheresoever it may seem good to thee, so it be without noise and without leaving any evil smell behind thee. Be mindful, however, of our engagement, for shouldst thou fail in it, even for a moment, be assured that I shall eternally smite thee with the Blasting Rod of the great ADONAY, ELOIM, ARIEL *and* JEHOVAM. *Amen.*

ACT OF THANKSGIVING

O Omnipotent God, Who hast created all things for the service and convenience of men, we return Thee most humble thanks for the benefits which, in Thy great bounty, Thou hast poured out on us during this night of Thine inestimable favours, wherein Thou hast granted us according to our desires. Now, O Almighty God, have we realised all the scope of Thy great promises, when Thou didst say to us : Seek and ye shall find, knock and it shall be opened unto you. And as Thou hast commanded and warned us to succour the poor, we promise Thee, in the presence of the great ADONAY, ELOIM, ARIEL *and* JEHOVAM, *to be charitable and to pour out on them the beneficent beams of the Sun with which those four potent divinities have enriched us. So be it. Amen.* VALE

§ 2. *Concerning the Genuine Sanctum Regnum, or the True Method of Making Pacts*

There are two kinds of pacts, says the *Grimorium Verum*, the tacit and the manifest ; but know at the same time that among the several kinds of spirits there are some which bind and some which do not bind, save only in a very light manner. As to the first, they are those which require something personally belonging to you whensoever a pact is agreed. Against these you must be on your guard, because the guileful friend becometh an open enemy.[1] The *Grimorium Verum* does not,

[1] Catholic theologians who have concerned themselves with the question of the pact have so extended the sphere of its operation that it includes the mere process of communicating with spirits. In his *Theological Dictionary* Bergier defines the pact as an express or tacit agreement made with the demon in the hope of accomplishing things which transcend the powers of Nature. It is express and formal when the operator himself invokes and demands the help of the demon, whether that personage really appears in response, or the sorcerer believes that he beholds him, that is to say, is hallucinated. It is also express and formal when the demon is invoked by the mediation of some one supposed to be in relation with him ; in other words, the consultation of a sorcerer is equivalent to a compact with Satan. The performance of any act with the expectation of a result from the demon is another compact of this kind. The pact is tacit or equivalent when an act is performed with a view to some effect which cannot naturally follow, while the intervention of God is not to be expected. There remains only the fiend. For example, should any one cure a disease by uttering certain words, this could only take place by the operation of the Infernal Spirit, because the words do not themselves possess the required virtue, and God is not likely to infuse it. Hence all theologians conclude that not only every species of Magic, but every kind of superstition involves at least a tacit and equivalent compact with the demon. St. Augustine and St. Thomas are said to have taken this view. It is by precisely such judgments as these that the theology of the Middle Ages brought itself to a by-word, and it is also for this reason that sorcery most flourished when such doctrines ruled, because a power which condemns everything to the same penalty condemns nothing effectually, and that which is over-judged is always vindicated in the eyes of the people. We have come to see that horse-stealing is not murder, and we no longer avenge it by the gallows ; so also, with due respect to the masters of Theology, the follies of a village maiden who believes in a sooth-

however, entertain more largely the question of a compact with Satan or his ministers, though it may perhaps be inferred from its pages that all commerce with evil spirits is founded on a law of exchange.[1] They can be bent to the intention of the operator, but it is on the express understanding that they are satisfied for their part, because, as we have seen, these kinds of creatures give nothing for nothing.

With the author of the *Grand Grimoire*, the pact is a concession to the poverty of the operator's resources. In Black Magic, as in some other processes, the necessitous must be ready to sacrifice, and the sorcerer who is insufficiently equipped must pay a higher price in the end. The genuine *Sanctum Regnum* of the Grand Clavicle, otherwise termed the *Pacta Conventa Dæmonum*, is explained by the *Grand Grimoire* for the information of those who are desirous to bind spirits, but are devoid of the requisite resources for composing the Blasting Rod and Kabalistic circle. Such persons, it is affirmed, will never succeed in evoking spirits unless they perform, point by point, all that is detailed hereinafter concerning the manner of making pacts with any spirit whatsoever, whether the object in view may be the possession of treasures concealed in the earth, the enjoyment of women or girls, and for obtaining any desired favour at their hands, whether for the discovery of the most hidden secrets in all Courts and Cabinets of the world, whether for the revelation of the most impenetrable mysteries, whether for engaging a spirit to perform one's work in the

---

saying gipsy, and the trickeries of a quack-doctor who is absurd enough to take *Abracadabra* seriously, are not the crime of Faust. But the learned Bishop of Hippo and the Angel of the Schools produced Goethe as their ultimate antithesis; when the girl who draws lots for her lover is given over to Satan, the apotheosis of Faust is certain. Behind the manifest exaggerations of such definitions there lies, however, a hidden pearl of truth, which concerns the temerity of opening the door to evil, and in this sense even the heedless act or the act of folly carries all its consequences and all to which it may lead like an implicit within it.

[1] But Lucifer, in ordinary cases, is contented with a cat, though it may be suggested that it is held only as a kind of hostage.

night, whether to cause a fall of hail or a storm in any appointed place, whether to open seals, to behold what is passing in private houses and learn all the skill of the shepherds, whether to obtain the Hand of Glory and discern all the qualities and virtues of metals, minerals and vegetables, of animals both pure and impure, and "to perform things so astounding that no person in existence can fail to be in a condition of utter bewilderment on seeing that by means of a pact with certain spirits one can discover the grandest secrets of Nature, which are hidden from the eyes of all other men."

It is to the Clavicle of the great King Solomon, says the Grimoire, that we owe the discovery of the genuine method of making pacts, which he also made use of himself for the acquisition of his immense riches, for the pleasure of such innumerable women and for the revelation of the most impenetrable arcana of Nature, whereby every species of good and evil may be accomplished.

With the highest potentates of Infernus, with Lucifer, Beelzebuth and Astaroth, it does not seem possible to enter into a binding compact. The sorcerer must be content with some one among the six governors,[1] who will generally work by their agents. An invariable covenant of the pact should bargain for service by one of the three superiors among such special subordinates.

Having determined to make a pact, continues the *Grand Grimoire*, you must begin on the previous evening by cutting with a new and unused knife a rod of wild hazel, which has never borne fruit and shall be similar to the Blasting Rod, as it has been previously described.

This must be done precisely at the moment when the sun appears upon our horizon. The same being accomplished, arm

---

[1] See c. iii. sec. 1.

yourself with the stone called *Ematille* and with two blessed candles, and proceed to select a place for the coming operation where you will be wholly undisturbed ; you may even make the pact in some isolated room, or in some subterranean part of an old ruinous castle, for the spirit has the power to transport the treasure—or, presumably, one of its alternatives—to any required place.

This having been duly fulfilled, describe a triangle with the stone called *Ematille*—which is exclusively needed on the first occasion of making a pact.

Then set the two blessed candles in a parallel position on either side of the Triangle of Pacts, inscribing the Holy Name of Jesus below, so that no spirits can injure you after any manner. You may now take up your position in the middle of the triangle, holding the mysterious rod, together with the grand Conjuration of the Spirit, the Clavicle, the written Requisition which you mean to make and the Discharge of the Spirit.

Having exactly fulfilled what things soever have been above described, begin by reciting the following Conjuration with decision and hopefulness :—

GRAND CONJURATION OF SPIRITS WITH WHOM IT IS SOUGHT TO MAKE A PACT

Taken from the Grand Clavicle

Emperor Lucifer, Master of all the revolted Spirits, I entreat thee to favour me in the adjuration which I address to thy mighty minister, LUCIFUGE ROFOCALE, being desirous to make a pact with him. I beg thee also, O Prince Beelzebuth, to protect me in my undertaking. O Count Astarôt ! be propitious to me, and grant that to-night the great LUCIFUGE may appear to me under a human form, free from evil smell, and that he may accord me, in virtue of the pact which I propose to enter into, all the riches that I need. O grand LUCIFUGE, I pray thee to quit thy dwelling, wheresoever it may be, and come hither to speak with me; otherwise will I compel thee by the power of the strong living God, His beloved Son and the Holy Spirit. Obey promptly, or thou shalt be eternally tormented by the power of the potent words in the grand Clavicle of Solomon, wherewith he was accustomed to compel the rebellious spirits to receive his compact. Then straightway appear, or I will persistently torture thee by the virtue of these great words in the Clavicle.

AGLON, TETRAGRAM, VAYCHEON STIMULAMATON EZPHARES RETRAGRAMMATON OLYARAM IRION ESYTION EXISTION ERYONA ONERA ORASYM MOZM MESSIAS SOTER EMANUEL SABAOTH ADONAY, *te adoro, et te invoco.* AMEN.

You may rest assured that the recitation of these potent words will be followed by the appearance of the spirit, who will say :—

Manifestation of the Spirit

Lo, I am here! What dost thou seek of me? Why dost thou disturb my repose? Answer me.
                    LUCIFUGE ROFOCALE

Reply to the Spirit

It is my wish to make a pact with thee, so as to obtain wealth at thy hands immediately, failing which I will torment thee by the potent words of the Clavicle.

The Spirit's Reply

I cannot comply with thy request except thou dost give thy-

PLATE IX

THE GOËTIC CIRCLE OF PACTS.

self over to me in twenty years, to do with thy body and soul as I please.   LUCIFUGE ROFOCALE

Thereupon throw him your pact, which must be written with your own hand on a sheet of virgin parchment; it should be worded as follows, and signed with your own blood :—*I promise the grand* LUCIFUGE *to reward him in twenty years' time for all treasures that he may give me. In witness whereof I have signed myself*   N.N.

Reply of the Spirit

I cannot grant thy request.

LUCIFUGE ROFOCALE

In order to enforce his obedience, again recite the Supreme Appellation, with the terrible words of the Clavicle, till the spirit reappears, and thus addresses you :—

Of the Spirit's Second Manifestation

Why dost thou torment me further ?   Leave me to rest, and I will confer upon thee the nearest treasure, on condition that thou dost set apart for me one coin on the first Monday of each month, and dost not call me oftener than once a week, to wit, between ten at night and two in the morning. Take up thy pact ; I have signed it.   Fail in thy promise, and thou shalt be mine at the end of twenty years.

LUCIFUGE ROFOCALE

Reply to the Spirit

I agree to thy request, subject to the delivery of the nearest treasure which I can at once carry away.

Follow the spirit without fear, cast your pact upon the hoard, touch it with your rod, remove as much as you can, return into the triangle, walking backwards, place the treasure in front of you, and recite the Discharge of the Spirit, as given in the preceding Rite.

It will be seen from the wording of the compact that it is designedly evasive and the final response of the supposed spirit seems to recognise that it can obtain only by neglect on the part of the sorcerer.   But if there are Courts of Judgment in the nethermost world, the sorcerer might find a certain difficulty in arguing such a case with the *advocatus diaboli*.   Lucifer and his deputies are accredited with an awkward skill in getting possession of the defendant when the time of the pact expires. There were apparently more binding contracts, and better ways of over-riding them, for in the year 1678 the Abbé Eynatton published a *Manual of Exorcisms* which contains the following formal process for forcing the Demon to return any writing which constitutes an agreement with him :—

EXORCISM

O most merciful God, Whose power hath no limit, Whose dominion is supreme over all beings, so that nothing can possibly be estreated from Thy rule by apostasy ; behold, we have sinned against Thee, we have provoked Thy most just wrath, when we have failed to obey Thy commands, above all when, forsaking Thy rule and Thy friendship, we have abjured Thee and have consorted with the impious demons, nor yet contented with Thy denial, have bound ourselves in writing to those demons, surrendering the document of our voluntary obligation against Thee into their custody.   But Thy mercies are without number, O Lord of loving-kindness, and it is Thine to spare and to pardon ; look, therefore, with compassion upon this Thy creature, who, having formerly denied Thee and given himself in writing to the demons, but now, having returned to himself by the help of Thine infinite goodness, doth abhor his impiety, doth desire to be restored unto Thee his true Lord, and to be received with contrite heart into Thy favour. We know, O Lord, that a contrite and humble heart Thou wilt not despise, nor can any writing be an impediment in the way of Thy mercy; we beseech Thee, therefore, that, by the abundance of Thy clemency, not only may the heinousness of this sin be blotted out with the Blood of Thy Son our Lord Jesus Christ, but that the demon, by the word of Thy power, may be compelled to restore the deed and obligation and delivery, lest he glory in his tyranny and pretend to any right over the man whom we pray to be delivered through Thy Son from his bonds. Through the same Jesus Christ, Thy Son, our Lord, &c.

The propitiation of offended Deity is followed by a citation of the demon who is required to disgorge his prey.

EXORCISM

I exorcise thee, O impious Satan, who, when thy power has passed away, dost still pretend to impose a tyrant yoke on man. I exorcise thee by Jesus Christ, Who came into this world for the salvation of sinners; I conjure thee to remove thy yoke immediately from this creature, who, deceived by thy wiles, formerly delivered himself unto thee. Abandoning thee henceforth, he commits himself to the Divine mercy, seeking His service unto Whom he alone is owing, Who also promises the reward of eternal life to those who follow Him. I exorcise thee by the precious Blood of Jesus Christ, by which the deed of judgment against us hath been blotted out, so that when Jesus receiveth the sinner into His favour, thou shalt dare not to advance anything against him, and shalt not fail to restore the deed by which this creature bound himself unto thee, the same being now cancelled by the Blood of Jesus Christ.

Hear, therefore, accursed Satan, who art powerless over a servant of God, when, encouraged by his true Lord, he turneth unto another service ; in vain dost thou boast of this deed ; I command thee to restore it in the name of the Lord, as a proof before the whole world that when God receiveth a sinner, thou hast no longer any rule over his soul. I abjure thee, by Him who expelled thee from thy stronghold, bereft thee of the arms which thou didst trust in and distributed thy spoils. Return therefore this deed, whereby this creature of God foolishly bound himself to thy service ; return it, I say, in His name by Whom thou art overcome ; when thy power has come to nothing, presume not longer to retain this useless document. By penitence already hath this creature of God restored himself to his true Lord, spurning thy yoke, hoping in the Divine mercy for defence against thine assaults, and assisted by the Most Holy and Glorious Virgin Mary, Mother of God, through whose intercession he shall obtain from Jesus Christ, His Son, that which he himself is not worthy to expect. Through the same Christ our Lord.

Whether this process was supposed to insure the visible and material return of the incriminating document, or, failing this, was held to cancel it formally, does not certainly appear and will matter little ; for what with the subtleties of the sorcerer and the assistance of the Church in the revocation of such acts and deeds, there was little chance for Infernus,[1] and the reluctance of Lucifuge Rofocale to enter into the tricky contract is, on the whole, exceedingly intelligible.

[1] But contracts with Infernus could apparently be repudiated with even greater facility. "If you are disposed to renounce the devil after having entered into a compact with him," says the *Vocabulaire Infernal*, "spit three times on the ground, and he will have no further power over you,"—in which case Black Magic with all its grim theatricals is the Art of exploiting lost Angels with impunity. But the lost angel within the operator would not be exploited with impunity like this at the end.

CHAPTER VII

The Method of Honorius

THE *Grimoire of Honorius* is perhaps the most frankly diabolical of all the Rituals connected with Black Magic, and yet, as we have already seen, its enormities have been much exaggerated. It suffers comparison, for example, with the *Key of Solomon*, and it is preferable to the *Lemegeton* because it is less disguised. Its most evident objections are : 1. Profanation of the mysteries of religion. 2. A bloody sacrifice, characterised by details of a monstrous kind. A less manifest objection is the superstitious nature of some of its ordinances. It must be confessed that such a charge seems fantastic, having regard to the innumerable offices of vain observance with which I have been dealing. But a vain observance, it should be remembered, is not necessarily superstitious. To assume that a virtue is resident in parchment prepared from the skin of an animal which has not engendered, and that such virtue is wanting in the skin of one which has reproduced its species,

MYSTIC FIGURES FROM THE TITLE-PAGE OF THE "GRIMOIRE OF HONORIUS"

265

may have no foundation in fact, and may be eminently foolish, but it is not a superstitious assumption. It has been well pointed out by Éliphas Lévi that the term superstition signifies survival; that is to say, it is the sign surviving the idea. Thus, the Catholic doctrine of Transubstantiation, in its open theological sense, may or may not be true doctrine, but in neither case can the worship of the consecrated elements be superstitious, because such worship draws directly from the idea which has created the outward sign. If a time could be supposed when the Elements should continue to be worshipped after the doctrine itself had passed away, that would be a superstitious observance. But the etymological conception of superstition connects also with the idea of redundance. Thus, a double consecration of the Eucharistic elements would be a superstitious observance, as well as blasphemously absurd, because the first consecration is effectual by the theological hypothesis. But the repetition of the Angelical Salutation in the devotion of the Holy Rosary is not superstitious, because the first recitation is not necessarily effectual by the devotional hypothesis. So also the magical practice which consists with the magical hypothesis will not be superstitious, though it may not consist with reason. The slaughter of a kid with a view to securing a virgin parchment is not a superstitious but a precautionary or assumptive measure. The conversion of this slaughter into a sacrifice is not superstitious, because it has a purpose which consists with the magical hypothesis, namely, the increase of virtue by the consecration of the religious motive. The importation into such sacrifice of ceremonies which are not precautionary, and do not, by the hypothesis, increase the virtue, are redundant and so far superstitious. Such offices do not occur in the Grimoires, with the exception of that of Honorius, in which Ritual they are further characterised by brutal features. The slaughter of a black cock and the extraction of the eyes, tongue and heart, which must be reduced into powder, and that powder subsequently sprinkled on the lambskin, is a redundant and monstrous observance. Were I therefore an occultist, with a belief in the efficacy of magical rituals, I should say that the *Grimoire of Honorius* must be avoided, but it should be unnecessary at the present day to warn any one against practices to which no one is likely to resort, which belong to the foolish mysteries of old exploded doctrines, and are interesting assuredly, but only as curiosities of the past. It should be added that the profanations of the mysteries of religion prescribed by the *Grimoire of Honorius* are not intentional profanations, and may be condoned to that extent. Their purpose is not outrage, but increase of efficacy.

Having made these initial provisions, the substance of this exceedingly curious Ritual may now be offered to the student in the words of its writer. It will be remembered that the person who desires to invoke the perverse "Spirits of Darkness" according to the method of Honorius must observe a three days' fast ; he must further confess and approach the Holy Altar. He should also, by the hypothesis, be a priest of the Latin Church. After these three days, upon the morrow, and at the hour of sunrise, he shall recite the Seven Gradual Psalms, with the accompanying Litanies and Prayers,[1] the whole on his knees ; further, he must drink no wine and eat no meat on that day. Next, he shall rise at midnight on the first Monday of the month,[2] and, seeing that he is apparently a priest, shall say a Mass of the Holy Ghost.[3]

[1] The reference is probably to the Litany of the Saints and the various orations which follow it.

[2] The three days' fast must therefore have been regulated so that it expired on the previous Saturday.

[3] The Mass of Pentecost, except the Epistle, which should be that of the Tuesday after Pentecost, and the Gradual, for which there are special versicles.

After the consecration, taking the Host in his left hand, he shall recite the following prayer on his knees :—

PRAYER

My Sovereign Saviour Jesus Christ, Son of the living God! Thou Who for the Salvation of all mankind didst suffer the death of the Cross; Thou Who, before being abandoned to Thine enemies, by an impulse of ineffable love, didst institute the Sacrament of Thy Body; Thou Who hast vouchsafed to us miserable creatures the privilege of making daily commemoration thereof; do Thou deign unto Thine unworthy servant, thus holding Thy Living Body in his hands, all strength and ability for the profitable application of that power with which he has been entrusted against the horde of rebellious spirits. Thou art their true God, and if they tremble at the utterance of Thy Name, upon that Holy Name will I call, crying Jesus Christ! Jesus, be Thou my help, now and for ever! Amen.

After sunrise, a black cock must be killed, the first feather of its left wing being plucked and preserved for use at the required time. The eyes must be torn out, and so also the tongue and heart; these must be dried in the sun and afterwards reduced to powder. The remains must be interred at sunset in a secret place, a cross of a palm in height being set upon the mound, while at each of the four corners the signs which here follow must be drawn with the thumb :—

The Method of Honorius

A later edition substitutes the following signs :—

On this day also the operator should drink no wine and abstain from eating meat.

On Tuesday, at break of day, let him say a Mass of the Angels,[1] placing the feather taken from the bird upon the altar, together with a new penknife. The signs hereinafter represented must be inscribed on a sheet of clean paper with the consecrated wine which is the Blood of Jesus Christ :—

In an edition *circa* 1800 the following signs are substituted :—

They should be written upon the altar, and at the end of the Mass the paper should be folded in a new veil of violet silk, to be concealed on the morrow, together with the oblation of the Mass and a part of the consecrated Host.[2]

---

[1] The Mass for the Apparition of St. Michael, May 8, with a special Epistle, Gospel, Commemoration, &c.

[2] I give this direction as I find it : the oblation is the bread and wine, and the sacrilegious reservation is the root-matter out of which the theory and practice of modern French Satanism has obviously arisen.

On the evening of Thursday the operator must rise at midnight and, having sprinkled holy water about the chamber, he must light a taper of yellow wax, which shall have been prepared on the Wednesday and pierced in the form of a cross. When it is lighted he shall recite Psalm lxxvii.[1]—*Attendite, popule meus, legem meam,* &c.—without the *Gloria Patri.* He shall then begin the *Office of the Dead* with *Venite exultemus Domino,* &c. He shall recite Matins and Lauds, but in place of the versicle of the ninth Lesson[2] he shall say : *Deliver us, O Lord, from the fear of hell. Let not the demons destroy my soul when I shall raise them from the deep pit, when I shall command them to do my will. May the day be bright, may the sun and moon shine forth, when I shall call upon them. Terrible of aspect are they, deformed and horrible to sight ; but do Thou restore unto them their angelic shapes when I shall impose my will upon them. O Lord, deliver me from those of the dread visage, and grant that they shall be obedient when I shall raise them up from hell, when I shall impose my will upon them.*

After the *Office of the Dead* the operator shall extinguish the taper, and at sunrise shall cut the throat of a male lamb of nine days, taking care that the blood does not gush forth upon the earth. He shall skin the lamb, and shall cast its tongue and heart into the fire. The fire must be freshly kindled, and the ashes shall be preserved for use at the proper time. The skin of the lamb shall be spread in the middle of a field and for the space of nine days shall be sprinkled four times every day with holy water. On the tenth day, before the rising of the sun, the lambskin shall be covered with the

[1] This Psalm is numbered lxxviii. in the Authorised Version.

[2] This is extremely confused'; the Office of the Dead does not begin with the *Venite exultemus.* The ninth Lesson belongs to the third Nocturne of the Matins. The prayer given in the Grimoire is based on the verses which it replaces.

ashes of the heart and tongue, and with the ashes also of the cock. On Thursday,[1] after sunset, the flesh of the lamb shall be interred in a secret place where no bird can come, and the priest with his right thumb shall inscribe on the grave the characters here indicated :—

In the edition already cited the signs are varied thus :—

Moreover, for the space of three days he shall sprinkle the four corners with holy water, saying : *Sprinkle me, O Lord, with hyssop, and I shall be cleansed! Wash me, and I shall be made whiter than snow!*

After the aspersion let him recite the following prayer, kneeling with his face towards the east :—

PRAYER

Christ Jesus, Redeemer of men, Who, being the Lamb without spot, wast immolated for the salvation of the human

---

[1] The days on which the various operations should be performed have been confused, after the prevailing manner of the Grimoires.

race, Who alone wast found worthy to open the Book of Life, impart such virtue to this lambskin that it may receive the signs which we shall trace thereon, written with Thy blood, so that the figures, signs and words may become efficacious ; and grant that this skin may preserve us against the wiles of the demons ; that they may be terrified at the sight of these figures and may only approach them trembling. Through Thee, Jesus Christ, Who livest and reignest through all ages. So be it.

The Litanies of the Holy Name of Jesus must then be repeated, but instead of the *Agnus Dei*, substitute : *Immolated Lamb, be Thou a pillar of strength against the demons ! Slain Lamb, give power over the Powers of Darkness ! Immolated Lamb, grant favour and strength unto the binding of the Rebellious Spirits. So be it.*

The lambskin shall be stretched for eighteen days, and on the nineteenth day the fleece shall be removed, reduced into powder and interred in the same place. The word *vellus* shall be written above it with the finger, together with the following character and the words :—*May this which hath been reduced into ashes preserve against the demons through the name of Jesus.*

Or, according to the later edition :—

Add also these signs :—

Or, according to the later edition :—

Lastly, on the eastern side, the said skin must be set to dry in the sun for three days, the ensuing characters being cut with a new knife :—

This being accomplished, recite Psalm lxxi., *Deus, judicium tuum regi da*, &c., and cut the following characters :—

The figure being thus far completed, recite the verses *Afferte Domino, patriæ gentium*, occurring in Psalm xcv. : *Cantate Domino Canticum novum*, of which the seventh versicle is : *Offerte Domino, Filii Dei*, &c., and cut subsequently these characters :—

Next recite Psalm lxxvii. : *Attendite, popule meus, legem meam*, and compose the following figure :—

This being accomplished, recite Psalm ii. : *Quare fremuerunt gentes et populi meditati sunt inania ?* Then make another figure as follows :—

Or, alternatively :—

And recite Psalm cxv. : *Credidi propter quod locutus sum.* Finally, on the last day of the month a Mass for the Dead shall be offered ; the prose shall be omitted and also the Gospel of St. John, but at the end of the Mass the priest shall recite the Psalm *Confitemini Domino quoniam bonus,* &c.[1]

---

[1] At this point the process of the Grimoire becomes almost unintelligible. The recitation of the seventy-two names apparently succeeds the Psalm and is followed by the Second Gospel, which is not omitted after all. There is then an extension of the *Deo Gratias ;* this concluded the Mass, which seems immediately followed by the evocation. But the use of the Pentacles of Solomon and St. John does not appear, in the one case, till the close of the Conjurations and not at all in the other.

The Method of Honorius

In Honour of the Most Holy and August Trinity, the Father, the Son, and the Holy Ghost. Amen.

The Seventy-two Sacred Names of God.—TRINITAS, SOTHER, MESSIAS, EMMANUEL, SABAHOT, ADONAY, ATHANATOS, JESU, PENTAGNA, AGRAGON, ISCHIROS, ELEYSON, OTHEOS, TETRAGRAMMATON, ELY, SADAY, AQUILA, MAGNUS HOMO, VISIO, FLOS, ORIGO, SALVATOR, ALPHA AND OMEGA, PRIMUS, NOVISSIMUS, PRINCIPIUM ET FINIS, PRIMOGENITUS, SAPIENTIA, VIRTUS, PARACLITUS, VERITAS, VIA, MEDIATOR, MEDICUS, SALUS, AGNUS, OVIS, VITULUS, SPES, ARIES, LEO, LUX, IMAGO, PANIS, JANUA, PETRA, SPONSA, PASTOR, PROPHETA, SACERDOS, SANCTUS, IMMORTALITAS, JESUS, CHRISTUS, PATER, FILIUS HOMINIS, SANCTUS, PATER OMNIPOTENS, DEUS, AGIOS, RESURRECTIO, MISCHIROS, CHARITAS, ÆTERNAS, CREATOR, REDEMPTOR, UNITAS, SUMMUM BONUM, INFINITAS. AMEN.

Hereinafter follow the three small pentacles of Solomon, and that of the Gospel of St. John.

275

The Beginning of the Holy Gospel according to John. Glory be to Thee, O Lord.

IN THE BEGINNING WAS THE WORD, &c., *in extenso, so far as the end of the fourteenth versicle.*

Thanks be to God. Hosanna to the Son of David! Blessed is He Who cometh in the Name of the Lord. Hosanna in the Highest. We invoke Thee. We adore Thee. We praise Thee. We glorify Thee, O blessed and glorious Trinity! May the Name of the Lord be blessed, now and henceforth for ever! Amen. In the Name of the Father, of the Son and of the Holy Ghost, Jesus of Nazareth, King of the Jews. May Christ conquer ✠, reign ✠, command ✠ and defend me from all evil. Amen.

UNIVERSAL CONJURATION

I, N., do conjure thee, O Spirit N., by the living God, by the true God, by the holy and all-ruling God, Who created from nothingness the heaven, the earth, the sea and all things that are therein, in virtue of the Most Holy Sacrament of the Eucharist, in the name of Jesus Christ, and by the power of this same Almighty Son of God, Who for us and for our redemption was crucified, suffered death and was buried; Who rose again on the third day and is now seated on the right hand of the Creator of the whole world, from whence He will come to judge the living and the dead; as also by the precious love of the Holy Spirit, perfect Trinity. I conjure thee within the circle, accursed one, by thy judgment, who didst dare to tempt God: I exorcise thee, Serpent, and I command thee to appear forthwith under a beautiful and well-favoured human form of soul and body, and to fulfil my behests without any deceit whatso-

ever, as also without mental reservation of any kind, by the great Names of the God of gods and Lord of lords, ADONAY, TETRAGRAMMATON, JEHOVA, TETRAGRAMMATON, ADONAY, JEHOVA, OTHEOS, ATHANATOS, ISCHYROS, AGLA, PENTAGRAMMATON, SADAY, SADAY, SADAY, JEHOVA, OTHEOS, ATHANATOS, *à Liciat* TETRAGRAMMATON, ADONAY, ISCHYROS, ATHANATOS, SADY, SADY, SADY, CADOS, CADOS, CADOS, ELOY, AGLA, AGLA, AGLA, ADONAY, ADONAY. *I conjure thee, Evil and Accursed Serpent, N., to appear at my will and pleasure, in this place, before this circle, without tarrying, without companions, without grievance, without noise, deformity or murmuring. I exorcise thee by the ineffable Names of God, to wit, Gog and Magog, which I am unworthy to pronounce : Come hither, Come hither, Come hither. Accomplish my will and desire, without wile or falsehood. Otherwise St. Michael, the invisible Archangel, shall presently blast thee in the utmost depths of hell. Come, then, N., to do my will.*

THE GRAND PENTACLE OF SOLOMON

The Book of Ceremonial Magic

A. P.

Why tarriest thou, and why delayest? What doest thou? Make ready, obey thy master, in the name of the Lord, BATHAT *or* RACHAT *flowing over* ABRACMENS, ALCHOR *over* ABERER.

L. Q. L. F. A. P.

Behold the Pentacle of Solomon which I have brought into thy presence! I command thee, by order of the great God, ADONAY, TETRAGRAMMATON *and* JESUS! *Hasten, fulfil my behests, without wile or falsehood, but in all truth, in the name of the Saviour and Redeemer, Jesus Christ.*

DISCHARGE

Go in peace unto your places. May there be peace between us and you, and be ye ready to come when ye are called. In the Name of the Father, and of the Son, and of the Holy Ghost. Amen.

ACT OF THANKSGIVING

Praise, honour, glory and blessing be unto Him Who sitteth upon the throne, Who liveth for ever and ever. Amen.

CONJURATION OF THE BOOK [1]

I conjure thee, O Book, to be useful and profitable unto all who shall have recourse to thee for the success of their affairs. I conjure thee anew, by the virtue of the Blood of Jesus Christ, contained daily in the chalice, to be serviceable unto all those who shall read thee. I exorcise thee, in the Name

---

[1] This is the *Liber Spirituum* of Pseudo-Agrippa, sufficiently described in Part I. The introduction of it in this Grimoire presupposes either an acquaintance in the reader or information which is omitted.

The Method of Honorius

of the Most Holy Trinity, in the Name of the Most Holy Trinity, in the Name of the Most Holy Trinity!

What follows must be said before the sealing of the Book

I conjure and command you, O Spirits, all and so many as ye are, to accept this Book with good grace, so that whensoever we may read it, the same being approved and recognised as in proper form and valid, you shall be constrained to appear in comely human form when you are called, accordingly as the reader shall judge. In no circumstances shall you make any attempt upon the body, soul or spirit of the reader, nor inflict any harm on those who may accompany him, either by mutterings, tempests, noise, scandals, nor yet by lesion or by hindrance in the execution of the commands of this Book. I conjure you to appear immediately when the conjuration is made, to execute without dallying all that is written and enumerated in its proper place in the said book. You shall obey, serve, instruct, impart and perform all in your power for the benefit of those who command you, and the whole without illusion. If perchance some of the invoked spirits be unable to come or appear when required, they shall be bound over to send others vested with their power, who also shall swear solemnly to execute all that the reader may demand, and ye are all hereby enjoined by the Most Holy Names of the Omnipotent Living God, ELOYM, JAH, EL, ELOY, TETRAGRAMMATON, to fulfil everything as it is set forth above. If ye obey me not, I will force you to abide in torments for a thousand years, as also if any one of you receive not this Book with entire resignation to the will of the reader.

CONJURATION OF THE DEMONS

In the Name of the Father, and of the Son, and of the Holy Ghost. Take heed! Come, all Spirits! By the virtue and power of your King, by the seven crowns and chains of your Kings, all Spirits of the Hells are forced to appear in my presence before this pentacle or circle of Solomon, whensoever I shall call them. Come, then, all at my orders, to fulfil that which is in your power, as commanded. Come, therefore, from the East, South, West and North! I conjure and command you, by the virtue and power of Him Who is three, eternal, equal, Who is God invisible, consubstantial, in a word, Who has created the heavens, the sea and all which is under heaven.

After these Conjurations you shall command them to affix the Seal

Concerning the Figure of the Circle

Circles should be described with charcoal or holy water, sprinkled with the wood of the blessed Cross.[1] When they have been duly made, and the words have been written about the circle, the holy water which has served to bless the same may also be used to prevent the spirits from inflicting any hurt. Standing in the middle of the circle, you shall command them in a lively manner, as one who is their master.

WHAT MUST BE SAID IN COMPOSING THE CIRCLE

O Lord, we fly to Thy virtue! O Lord, confirm this work! What is operated in us becomes like dust driven before the wind, and the Angel of the Lord pausing (sic), let the darkness disappear, and the Angel of the Lord ever pursuing, ALPHA, OMEGA, ELY, ELOHE, ELOHIM, ZABAHOT, ELION, SADY.

---

[1] On the hypothesis that the *Method of Honorius* is dealing in efficacious Rites provided that its conditions are fulfilled, the operation must fail because this requirement is unattainable, if not indeed impossible. I mention this point for the benefit of those occultists who may possibly believe in the efficacy. I do not think that they exist, but seeing that there is no end to occult foolishness, it is within the compass of a dream.

The Method of Honorius

Behold the Lion Who is the conqueror of the Tribe of Judah, the Root of David! I will open the Book, and the seven seals thereof. I have beheld Satan as a bolt falling from heaven. It is Thou Who hast given us power to crush dragons, scorpions and all Thine enemies beneath Thy feet. Nothing shall harm us, not even ELOY, ELOHIM, ELOHE, ZABAHOT, ELION, ESARCHIE,

THE MAGIC CIRCLE OF HONORIUS

ADONAY, JAH, TETRAGRAMMATON, SADY. *The earth is the Lord's and all those who dwell therein, because He established it upon the seas and prepared it in the midst of the waves. Who shall ascend unto the mountain of the Lord? Who shall be received in his Holy Place? The innocent of hands and clean of heart. Who hath not received his soul in vain and hath not sworn false witness against his neighbour. The same shall be blessed of God and shall obtain mercy of God to his salvation. He is of the generation of those who seek Him.*

The Book of Ceremonial Magic

*Open your gates, ye princes, open the eternal gates, and the
King of Glory shall enter! Who is this King of Glory? The
Lord Almighty, the Lord, mighty in battle. Open your gates,
ye princes! Lift up the eternal gates. Who is this King of*

A LESSER PENTACLE OF SOLOMON

*Glory? The Lord Almighty. This Lord is the King of Glory.
Glory be to the Father, &c.*

*To dismiss them, the Pentacle of Solomon must be exhibited,
at the same time saying as follows :—*

*Behold your sentence! Behold that which forbids rebellion
to our wills and doth ordain you to return unto your abodes.
May peace be between us and you, and be ye ready to come,
each and all, as ye are called to do my will.*

282

The Method of Honorius

CONJURATION OF THE KING OF THE EAST

I conjure and invoke thee, O powerful King of the East, MAGOA, *by my holy labour, by all the names of Divinity, by the name of the All-Powerful : I command thee to obey, and to come to me, or that failing, forthwith and immediately to send unto me* MASSAYEL, ARIEL, SATIEL, ARDUEL, ACORIB, *to respond concerning all that I would know and to fulfil all that I shall command. Else thou shalt come verily in thine own person, to satisfy my will ; which refusing, I shall compel thee by all the virtue and power of God.*

The Grand Pentacle or Circle of Solomon will answer for the above and following Conjurations, which can be said on all days and at all hours. If it be desired to speak only with one spirit, one only need be named, at the choice of the reader.

CONJURATION OF THE KING OF THE SOUTH

O EGYM, *great King of the South, I conjure and invoke thee by the most high and holy Names of God, do thou here manifest, clothed with all thy power ; come before this circle, or at least send me forthwith* Fadal, Nastrache, *to make answer unto me, and to execute all my wishes. If thou failest, I shall force thee by God Himself.*

CONJURATION OF THE KING OF THE WEST

O BAYMON, *most potent King, who reignest in the Western quarter, I call and I invoke thee in the name of the Deity ! I command thee by virtue of the Most High, to send me immediately before this circle the Spirit* Passiel Rosus, *with all other Spirits who are subject unto thee, that the same may answer in everything, even as I shall require them. If thou failest, I*

283

will torment thee with the sword of fire divine ; I will multiply thy sufferings and will burn thee.

CONJURATION OF THE KING OF THE NORTH

O thou, AMAYMON, *King and Emperor of the Northern parts, I call, invoke, exorcise and conjure thee, by the virtue and power of the Creator, and by the virtue of virtues, to send me presently, and without delay,* Madael, Laaval, Bamlahe, Belem *and* Ramath, *with all other Spirits of thine obedience, in comely and human form ! In whatsoever place thou now art, come hither and render that honour which thou owest to the true living God, Who is thy Creator. In the name of the Father, of the Son and of the Holy Ghost, come therefore, and be obedient, in front of this circle, without peril to my body or soul. Appear in comely human form, with no terror encompassing thee. I conjure thee, make haste, come straightway, and at once. By all the Divine names—*SECHIEL, BARACHIEL—*if thou dost not obey promptly,* BALANDIER, suspensus, iracundus, Origratiumgu, Partus, Olemdemis, *and* Bautratis, N. *I exorcise thee, do invoke and do impose most high commandment upon thee, by the omnipotence of the living God, and of the true God ; by the virtue of the holy God, and by the power of Him Who spake and all things were made, even by His holy commandment the heaven and earth were made, with all that is in them ! I adjure thee by the Father, by the Son and by the Holy Ghost, even by the Holy Trinity, by that God Whom thou canst not resist, under Whose empire I will compel thee ; I conjure thee by God the Father, by God the Son, by God the Holy Ghost, by the Mother of Jesus Christ, Holy Mother and perpetual Virgin, by her sacred heart, by her blessed milk, which the Son of the Father sucked, by her most holy body and soul, by all the parts and members of this Virgin, by all the sufferings,*

284

afflictions, labours, agonies which she endured during the whole course of her life, by all the sighs she uttered, by all the holy tears which she shed whilst her dear Son wept before the time of His dolorous passion and on the tree of the Cross, by all the sacred holy things which are offered and done, and also by all others, as in heaven so on earth, in honour of our Saviour Jesus Christ, and of the Blessed Mary, His Mother, by whatsoever is celestial, by the Church Militant, in honour of the Virgin and of all the Saints. In like manner, I conjure thee by the Holy Trinity, by all other mysteries, by the sign of the Cross, by the most precious blood and water which flowed from the side of Jesus Christ, by the sweat which issued from His whole body, when He said in the Garden of Olives: My Father, if it be possible, let this chalice pass from me. I conjure thee by His death and passion, by His burial and glorious resurrection, by His ascension, by the coming of the Holy Ghost. I adjure thee, furthermore, by the crown of thorns which was set upon His head, by the blood which flowed from His feet and hands, by the nails with which He was nailed to the tree of the Cross, by the holy tears which He shed, by all which He suffered willingly through great love of us: by the lungs, the heart, the hair, the inward parts, and all the members of our Saviour Jesus Christ. I conjure thee by the judgment of the living and the dead, by the Gospel words of our Saviour Jesus Christ, by His preachings, by His sayings, by His miracles, by the child in swaddling-clothes, by the crying child, borne by the mother in her most pure and virginal womb; by the glorious intercession of the Virgin Mother of our Saviour Jesus Christ; by all which is of God and of His Most Holy Mother, as in heaven so on earth. I conjure thee by the holy Angels and Archangels, by all the blessed orders of Spirits, by the holy patriarchs and prophets, by all the holy martyrs and confessors, by all the

holy virgins and innocent widows, by all the saints of God,
both men and women. I conjure thee by the head of St. John
the Baptist, by the milk of St. Catherine, and by all the Saints.

Conjurations for each Day of the Week
For Monday, to Lucifer

This experience is commonly performed in the circle
between eleven and twelve o'clock, or between three and four.

Requisites : coal, and consecrated chalk to compose the circle,
about which these words must be written : *I forbid thee, Lucifer,*
in the name of the Most Holy Trinity, to enter within this
circle. A mouse must be provided to give him ; the master
must have a stole and holy water, an alb also and a surplice.
He must recite the Conjuration in a lively manner, commanding
sharply and shortly, as a lord should address his servant,[1] with
all kinds of menaces : Satan, Rantam, Pallantre, Lutais,

---

[1] This is in opposition to the higher counsels of the averse art, which enjoins a certain
reverence in addressing the lost angels, presumably on account of what they were.

CORICACOEM, SCIRCIGREUR, *I require thee to give me very humbly*, &c.

CONJURATION

I conjure thee, Lucifer, by the living God, by the true God, by the holy God, Who spake and all was made, Who commanded and all things were created and made! I conjure thee by the Ineffable Names of God, ON, ALPHA and OMEGA, ELOY, ELOYM, YA, SADAY, LUX, MUGIENS, REX, SALUS, ADONAY, EMMANUEL, MESSIAS ; *and I adjure, conjure, and exorcise thee by the Names which are declared under the letters V, C, X, as also by the Names* JEHOVAH, SOL, AGLA, RIFFASORIS, ORISTON, ORPHITNE, PHATON IPRETU, OGIA, SPERATON, IMAGON, AMUL, PENATON, SOTER, TETRAGRAMMATON, ELOY, PREMOTON, SITMON, PERIGARON, IRATATON, PLEGATON, ON, PERCHIRAM, TIROS, RUBIPHATON, SIMULATON, PERPI, KLARIMUM, TREMENDUM, MERAY, *and by the most high Ineffable Names of God*, GALI, ENGA, EL, HABDANUM, INGODUM, OBU ENGLABIS, *do thou make haste to come, or send me N., having a comely and human form, in no wise repulsive, that he may answer in real truth whatsoever I shall ask him, being also powerless to hurt me, or any person whomsoever, either in body or soul.*

For Tuesday, to Frimost[1]

This experience is performed in its proper circle at night from nine to ten o'clock, and the first stone found is given to him. He is to be received with dignity and honour. Proceed as on Monday ; compose the circle, and write about it : *Obey me,* FRIMOST! *Obey me,* FRIMOST! *Obey me,* FRIMOST!

CONJURATION

I conjure and command thee, FRIMOST, *by all the names wherewith thou canst be constrained and bound! I exorcise*

---

[1] Otherwise, *Nambroth.*

thee, NAMBROTH, by thy name, by the virtue of all spirits, by all characters, by the Jewish, Greek and Chaldean conjurations, by thy confusion and malediction, and I will redouble thy pains and torments from day to day for ever, if thou come not now to accomplish my will and submit to all that I shall com-

mand, being powerless to harm me, or those who accompany me, either in body or soul.

For Wednesday, to Astaroth

This experience is performed in its circle at night, from ten to eleven o'clock; it is designed to obtain the good graces of the King and others. Write in the circle as follows: *Come,* ASTAROTH! *Come,* ASTAROTH! *Come,* ASTAROTH!

CONJURATION

I conjure thee, ASTAROTH, wicked spirit, by the words and virtues of God, by the powerful God, Jesus Christ of Nazareth, unto Whom all demons are submitted, Who was conceived of the Virgin Mary; by the mystery of the Angel Gabriel, I conjure thee; and again in the name of the Father, and of the Son, and of the Holy Ghost; in the name of the glorious Virgin Mary and of the Most Holy Trinity, in Whose honour do all the Archangels, Thrones, Dominations, Powers, Patriarchs,

Prophets, Apostles and Evangelists sing without end; Hosannah, Hosannah, Hosannah, Lord God of Hosts, Who art, Who wast, Who art to come, as a river of burning fire! Neglect not my commands, refuse not to come. I command thee by Him Who shall appear with flames to judge the living and the dead, unto Whom is all honour, praise and glory. Come, therefore, promptly, obey my will; appear and give praise to the true God, unto the living God, yea, unto all His works; fail not to obey me, and give honour to the Holy Ghost, in Whose name I command thee.

289   T

For Thursday, to Silcharde

This experience is made at night, from three to four o'clock, at which hour he is called, and appears in the form of a King. A little bread must be given him when he is required to depart; he renders man happy and also discovers treasures.

Write about the circle as follows: *Holy God! Holy God! Holy God!*

CONJURATION

I conjure thee, SILCHARDE, *by the image and likeness of Jesus Christ our Saviour, Whose death and passion redeemed the entire human race, Who also wills that, by His providence, thou appear forthwith in this place. I command thee by all the Kingdoms of God. I adjure and constrain thee by His Holy Name, by Him Who walked upon the asp, Who crushed the lion and the dragon. Do thou obey me and fulfil my commands,*

The Method of Honorius

being powerless to do harm unto me or any person whomsoever, either in body or soul.

For Friday, to Bechard

This experience is performed at night from eleven to twelve

o'clock, and a nut must be given to him. Write within the circle: *Come*, BECHARD! *Come*, BECHARD! *Come*, BECHARD!

CONJURATION

I conjure thee, BECHARD, *and constrain thee, in like manner, by the Most Holy Names of God*, ELOY, ADONAY, ELOY, AGLA, SAMALABACTAY, *which are written in Hebrew, Greek and Latin; by all the sacraments, by all the names written in this book; and by him who drove thee from the height of Heaven. I conjure and command thee by the virtue of the Most Holy Eucharist, which hath redeemed men from their sins; I conjure thee to come without any delay, to do and perform all my biddings, without any prejudice to my body or soul, without harming my book or doing injury to those that accompany me.*

For Saturday, to Guland[1]

This experience is performed at night from eleven to twelve o'clock, and so soon as he appears burnt bread must be given him. Ask him anything that you will, and he will obey you

on the spot. Write in his circle: *Enter not*, GULAND! *Enter not*, GULAND! *Enter not*, GULAND!

CONJURATION

I conjure thee, O GULAND, *in the name of Satan, in the name of Beelzebub, in the name of Astaroth, and in the name of all other spirits, to make haste and appear before me. Come, then, in the name of Satan and in the names of all other demons. Come to me, I command thee, in the Name of the Most Holy*

---

[1] Otherwise, *Nabam.*

The Method of Honorius

Trinity. Come without inflicting any harm upon me, without injury to my body or soul, without maltreating my books or anything which I use. I command thee to appear without delay, or, that failing, to send me forthwith another Spirit having the same power as thou hast, who shall accomplish my commands and be submitted to my will, wanting which, he whom thou shalt send me, if indeed thou comest not thyself, shall in no wise depart, nor until he hath in all things fulfilled my desire.

For Sunday, to Surgat [1]

This experience is performed at night from eleven to one

o'clock. He will demand a hair of your head, but give him one of a fox, and see that he takes it. His office is to discover and transport all treasures and perform anything that you may will. Write in his circle: TETRAGRAMMATON, TETRAGRAM-

---

[1] Otherwise, *Aquiel.*

293

MATON, TETRAGRAMMATON. ISMAEL, ADONAY, IHUA. And in a second circle : *Come*, SURGAT ! *Come*, SURGAT ! *Come*, SURGAT !

CONJURATION

I conjure thee, O SURGAT, *by all the names which are written in this book, to present thyself here before me, promptly and without delay, being ready to obey me in all things, or, failing this, to despatch me a Spirit with a stone which shall make me invisible to every one whensoever I carry it ! And I conjure thee to be submitted in thine own person, or in the person of him or of those whom thou shalt send me, to do and accomplish my will and all that I shall command, without harm to me or to any one, so soon as I make known my intent.*

Very Powerful Conjuration for all days and hours of the Day or Night, being for Treasures hidden by men or Spirits, that the same may be possessed and transported

I command you, O all ye demons dwelling in these parts, or in what part of the world soever ye may be, by whatsoever power may have been given you by God and our holy Angels over this place, by the powerful Principality of the infernal abysses, as also by all your brethren, both general and special demons, whether dwelling in the East, West, South or North, or in any side of the earth, and, in like manner, by the power of God the Father, by the wisdom of God the Son, by the virtue of the Holy Ghost, by the authority I derive from our Saviour Jesus Christ, the only Son of the Almighty and the Creator, Who made us and all creatures from nothing, Who also ordains that you do hereby abdicate all power to guard, habit and abide in this place ; by Whom further I constrain and command you, nolens volens, *without guile or deception, to declare me your names and to leave me in peaceable possession and rule over this place, of whatsoever legion you be and of whatsoever part of the world ; by order of the Most Holy Trinity and by the merits of the Most Holy and Blessed Virgin, as also of all the saints, I unbind you all, spirits who abide in this place, and I drive you to the deepest infernal abysses. Thus : Go, all Spirits accursed, who are condemned to the flame eternal which is prepared for you and your companions, if ye be rebellious and disobedient. I conjure you by the same authority, I exhort and call you, I constrain and command you, by all the powers of your superior demons, to come, obey and reply positively to what I direct you, in the Name of Jesus Christ. Whence, if you or they do not obey promptly and without tarrying, I will shortly increase your torments for a thousand years in hell. I constrain you therefore to appear here in comely human shape, by the Most High Names of God,* Hain, Lon, Hilay, Sabaoth, Helim, Radisha, Ledieha, Adonay, Jehova, Yah, Tetragrammaton, Sadai, Messias, Agios, Ischyros, Emmanuel, Agla, *Jesus Who is* Alpha *and* Omega, *the beginning and the end, that you be justly established in the fire, having no power to reside, habit or abide in this place henceforth ; and I require your doom by the virtue of the said Names, to wit, that St. Michael drive you to the uttermost of the infernal abyss, in the Name of the Father, and of the Son, and of the Holy Ghost. So be it.*

I conjure thee, Acham, *or whomsoever thou mayest be, by the Most Holy Names of God, by* Malhame, Jae, May, Mabron, Jacob, Dasmedias, Eloy, Aterestin, Janastardy, Finis, Agios, Ischyros, Otheos, Athanatos, Agla, Jehova, Homosion, Aga, Messias, Sother, Christus vincit, Christus imperat, Increatus Spiritus Sanctus.

I conjure thee, Cassiel, *or whomsoever thou mayest be, by all the said names, with power and with exorcism ! I warn thee*

*by the other Sacred Names of the most great Creator, which are
or shall hereafter be communicated to thee ; hearken forthwith
and immediately to my words ; observe them inviolably, as
sentences of the last dreadful day of judgment, which thou
must obey inviolately, nor think to repulse me because I am a
sinner, for therein shalt thou repulse the commands of the Most
High God. Knowest thou not that thou art bereft of thy powers
before thy Creator and ours ? Think therefore what thou re-
fusest, and pledge therefore thine obedience, swearing by the
said last dreadful day of judgment and by Him Who hath
created all things by His word, Whom all creatures obey.* P. per
sedem Baldarey et per gratiam et diligentiam tuam habuisti
ab eo hanc nalatimanamilam, *as I command thee.*[1]

---

[1] It is impossible to restore the Latin so that it shall possess an intelligible and constructive
sense.

HORUS-RA, WEARING THE SOLAR
DISC AND URÆUS.

CHAPTER VIII

𝔐𝔦𝔰𝔠𝔢𝔩𝔩𝔞𝔫𝔢𝔬𝔲𝔰 𝔞𝔫𝔡 𝔐𝔦𝔫𝔬𝔯 𝔓𝔯𝔬𝔠𝔢𝔰𝔰𝔢𝔰

§ 1. *Concerning Works of Hatred and Destruction*

THE following process appears in several manuscript copies of the *Key of Solomon*, but has been omitted by the English editor of that work, as others are also omitted, presumably as a Goëtic interpolation. But we have seen that a Goëtic process in a book like the *Key of Solomon* is not necessarily an interpolation, while as regards this particular instance it is very nearly evident that it is an integral portion of that dubious collection. In the second chapter of the first book we are told that the days and hours of Mars are suitable for overthrowing enemies, while the hours of Saturn and Mars, and also the days on which the Moon is in conjunction with those planets, are excellent for experiments of hatred, enmity, quarrel and discord. In the first chapter of the second book it is said :—As for operations of destruction and desolation, we should put them into execution on the day of Saturn at the first hour, or rather at the eighth or fifteenth of the day, and from the first until the eighth hour of the night. . . . From these statements it seems fair to infer that there must have been a section containing directions as to the performance of such works. In this case, the *Key of Solomon* is neither better nor worse than any other Grimoire of Black Magic—as indeed we have reason to know by its admitted sections. The apologists of the Clavicle—if there are any apart from its English editor—will probably cite in defence of it a passage which occurs in Book i. c. 8, in which the author proffers his secrets on the express condition that they shall not be used to ruin and destroy one's neighbour. But when every allowance has been made for this stipulation, we shall do well to remember that similar warnings are not wanting in purely Goëtic rituals. There is further another test by which the authenticity of the following process may be largely determined, and that is the manner of its wording, which corresponds closely with the prevailing manner of the Clavicle. It is a loose and general wording, covering several classes of experiment, and—if any one is sufficiently ridiculous or sufficiently ultra-serious to desire that the question be tested—it may be compared with Book I. c. xv., xvi., xvii., in which the same characteristics will be found.

The process itself is as follows :—Experiments upon enemies may be performed in several ways, but, whether with waxen images or some other instrument, the particulars of each must be diligently and faithfully observed. Should the day and hour fail thee, proceed as already laid down, and prepare the image or instrument proper to this effect in the order and manner thereof. Fumigate with the proper perfumes, and if writing be required on the image, let it be done with the needle or stylet of the art, as aforesaid. Next recite the following words once over the said image :—Vsor, DILAPIDATORE, TENTATORE, SOIGNATORE, DEVORATORE, CONCITORE, ET SEDUCTORE. *O all ye ministers and companions, I direct, conjure, constrain and command you to fulfil this behest willingly, namely, straightway to consecrate this image, which is to be done in the name of . . . . , that as the face of the one is contrary to the other, so the same may never more look one upon another.*

Miscellaneous and Minor Processes

Deposit the image in some place perfumed with evil odours, especially those of Mars, such as sulphur and *assafœtida*. Let it remain there for one night, having duly asperged it, observing the proper hour and time. Do likewise when the experiment is performed with characters and names, by touching the lovers [1] with words, or by whatsoever other manner. But when the experiment is made by giving something to be eaten, the same must be performed on the day and hour proper to this work. All things being prepared, place them before you, and say: Where are ye, SOIGNATORE, USORE, DILAPIDATORE, and DENTORE; CONCISORE, DIVORATORE, SEDUCTORE, and SEMINATORE? *Ye who sow discord, where are you? Ye who infuse hatred and propagate enmities, I conjure you by Him who hath created you for this ministry, to fulfil this work, in order that whensoever N. [naming the person] shall eat of like things, or shall touch them, in whatsoever manner, never shall he go in peace.*

Give then whatsoever you please to the person designated, but let it be in the hour of Saturn or that of Mars, observing all things needful for such experiments.

§ 2. *Concerning Venereal Experiments*

We have seen that the sorcerer of the Middle Ages was usually squalid and necessitous; hence he coveted treasures: he was usually despised, and hence he longed for mastery, for the prestige of mystery and the power of strange arts: he was usually lonely and libidinous, and hence he sought, by means of spells and philtres, to compel the desire of women. To be rich in worldly goods, to trample on one's enemies and to gratify the desires of the flesh—such are the ends, variously qualified and variously attained, of most Ceremonial Magic; hence also the Rituals abound in Venereal Experiments.

---

[1] This means that the experiment is for the occult consolation of a rival. It will be seen, however, that there is a certain confusion, as the adjuration which follows will exhibit.

In such as the *Grimorium Verum* there is no attempt to hide their illicit nature; in the *Key of Solomon* it is disguised, but the process for obtaining favour and love which occurs in that work is not really a more lawful experiment than that *Pour faire venir une Fille vous trouver, si sage qu'elle soit*. The *Key of Solomon* is reticent and the Grimoires are frank; the one promises the fulfilment of the operator's desire without defining it; the others are explicit and particular. It is true also that the one has recourse to Adonai and implores his assistance, while the others invoke the powers of Hell.

The *Book of True Black Magic* for once ignores the experience of the Clavicle and substitutes the following :—

Concerning the Experiment of Love

Whatsoever person be the object of this experiment, whether man or woman, it is needful in making it to observe the proper day and hour. Note further that it is performed by means of an image of wax or other suitable matter. Before composing it, say the following words over the wax : NOGA, JES, ASTROPOLIM, ASMO, COCCAV, BERMONA, TENTATOR, SOIGNATOR—*I conjure you, ministers of love and incontinence, by Him who hath condemned you to hell! Do ye consecrate this wax in a regular manner, that it may acquire the desired virtue, by the power of the Most Holy Adonay, Who liveth and reigneth for ever and ever. Amen.*

The image must then be composed and suitable characters inscribed thereon with the male goose-quill of the Art, after which it must be fumigated while reciting the following words : —*O thou most powerful King* PAYMON, *whose absolute rule and reign is in the western quarter! O thou,* EGIM, *most strong King, whose empire is in the cold region! O thou,* ASMODEUS, *who governest in the South! O thou,* AYMAMON, *most noble*

Miscellaneous and Minor Processes

King, monarch of the Eastern world, whose reign began from of old and will endure to the end of time! I invoke and beseech you by Him Who spake and it was, Whose sole word hath created all, Whom all creatures obey; by the seat of His Majesty; by His Will and His Name; by Him Who was before the ages and hath created the ages; Whose Name is written with the four letters JOD, HE, VAU, HE; *by the enchantments and power thereof; and by all the signal Names of the Creator; I conjure you to consecrate this image and grant that it may acquire virtue according to our desire, by the Most Holy Name Adonay, the power of which is without beginning or end.*

This being done, conjure with the Conjuration of the image, and if the woman or man should not appear, place the said image beneath the pillow of your bed, and before three days you shall behold admirable things, while chains or earth shall not stay the desired person from coming to you, for the fulfilment of your purpose, nothing being excepted.

But if the experience be to find the beloved person, place the image under the door which he or she must pass. In either case a powder must be made and cast upon the person, or given them with their meat or drink. The solemnities of the hours, matters and instruments must be faithfully observed, and the Spirits conjured by name, saying also: *I conjure and constrain you, ye Devils, who have the power to disturb the hearts of men and women! By Him Who hath created you from nothing and by this image, I conjure you this night into my presence, that I may have the power to compel whomsoever I will to love me, whether male or female.*

When the characters and images have been prepared, say over them: *I conjure you, O* ANAËL, DONQUEL, THELIEL, *princes of love, and all your ministers, who have power to fill with fervour the hearts of men and women, and to kindle the fire of love! I conjure you by Him Who is seated upon the Cherubim and guardeth the abysses, by Him Who maketh the world to tremble, Whom all creatures obey! Grant that these characters and figures may possess this virtue, that such man or woman may love me, may desire me and thirst for my love, and that it shall be impossible for him or her to love any person save me.*

Place the image in a vessel for one night, operate on the day and in the hour appropriate thereto, and you shall behold a wonder.

The compiler of the *Grimorium Verum*, who seems to have selected almost invariably the most bizarre processes, instructs his pupils

How to Cause the Appearance of Three Ladies or Three Gentlemen in One's Room after Supper

§ 1. *Preparation*

Abstain for three days from the hidden offices, and then shall your spirit be fortified. On the fourth day, you shall cleanse and prepare your chamber as soon as it is morning, immediately after dressing, the whole fasting. But see you do it in such a way that it will not be liable to disarrangement during the remainder of the day. Note that there must be no hangings, nor anything set crosswise, no tapestries, no hanging clothes, hats, bird-cages, bed curtains, &c. Above all, let the appointments be clean in every respect.

§ 2. *Ceremony*

After supper pass in secret to your chamber, made ready as above; kindle a good fire; place a white cloth on the table, round which set three chairs, and before each chair, upon the

Miscellaneous and Minor Processes

table, let there be a wheaten roll and a glass full of fresh clear water. Lastly, draw up a chair and settee to the side of the bed and retire to rest, uttering the following

CONJURATION

Besticitum consolatio veni ad me vertat Creon, Creon, Creon, cantor laudem omnipotentis et non commentur. Stat superior carta bient laudem omviestra principiem da montem et inimicos meos ô prostantis vobis et mihi dantes que passium fieri sincisibus.

The three persons, having arrived, will rest themselves near the fire, drinking, eating and finally thanking him or her who has entertained them; for if it be a young lady who performs this ceremony, three gentlemen will come; but if it be a man, three young ladies will appear. The said three persons will draw lots among each other to know which of them shall remain with you. If a man be the operator, she who wins will place herself in the arm-chair which you have set by the bed, and she will remain and commune with you until midnight, at which hour she will depart with her companions, without any need of dismissal. As regards the two others, they will keep themselves by the fire, while the other entertains you. So long as she remains you may question her upon any art or science, or upon what subject soever, and she will immediately give you a positive answer. You may also inquire of her whether she is aware of any hidden treasure, and she will instruct you as to its locality and the precise time suited to its removal. She will even appear there with her companions to defend you against the assaults of the Infernal Spirits who may have it in their possession. At parting, she will present you with a ring, which, worn on the finger, will render you lucky at play, while if it be placed upon the finger of any woman or girl, you shall there and then have your will with them. Observe, however, that you must leave your window open in order that they may enter.

This ceremony may be repeated frequently at the will of the operator.

It must be acknowledged that the above experiment offers a large return for very small pains in the preparation, and hence it is very popular with the makers of Grimoires. The same observation applies to the following process, which is common to the supplementary portions of the *Grand Grimoire*, the *Grimorium Verum*, the *Grimoire of Honorius* and most of the minor collections. It is described as an experience of the wonderful power of the Superior Intelligences. The nature of the superiority may, however, be inferred from the title.

To Cause a Girl to Seek you out, however Prudent she may be

Whether in the increase or wane of the Moon, a star must be observed between eleven o'clock and midnight. But before

beginning do as follows. Take a virgin parchment. Write thereon her name whose presence you desire. The parchment must be shaped as represented in the following figure. On the other side inscribe these words: *Melchiael, Bareschas*. Then place your parchment on the earth, with the person's name against the ground. Set your right foot above it, while your left knee is bent to the earth. In this position observe the brightest star in the firmament, holding in the right hand a taper of white wax, large enough to last for an hour, and recite the following

Miscellaneous and Minor Processes

CONJURATION

I salute and conjure you, O beautiful Moon, O beautiful Star, O bright light which I hold in my hand! By the air which I breathe, by the breath which is within me, by the earth which I touch, I conjure you, and by all the names of the spirits who are princes residing in you; by the ineffable Name ON, *which hath created all; by thee, O Resplendent Angel Gabriel, together with the Prince Mercury,* Michiael *and* Melchidael! *I conjure you again by all the Divine Names of God, that you send down to obsess, torment and harass the body, spirit, soul and five senses of the nature of N., whose name is written here below, in such a way that she shall come unto me and accomplish my will, having no friendship for any one in the world, but especially for N., so long as she shall be indifferent to me. So shall she endure not, so shall she be obsessed, so suffer, so be tormented. Go then, promptly; go,* Melchidael, Baresches, Zazel, Firiel, Malcha, *and all those who are without you* (sic). *I conjure you by the great living God to accomplish my will, and I, N., do promise to satisfy you duly.*

Having thrice pronounced this conjuration, place the taper on the parchment and let it burn. Take the parchment on the morrow, put it in your left shoe and there leave it until the person for whom you have operated shall have come to seek you out. You must specify in the Conjuration the day that you desire her to come, and she will not fail.

This process has its disadvantages, and even its difficulties. It seems absurd to suppose that there are Spirit Princes inhabiting the flame of a taper, and the treatment invoked upon the lady is of a turbulent kind, nor is there any colourable pretence on which the position of the rival lover can be justified;

305   U

but it has the touch of the picturesque, and, making all allowance for the potencies which may inhere in *Sator, Arepo, Tenet, Opera, Rotas*, it does not suffer seriously by comparison with the method of the Clavicle.

§ 3. *Concerning the Experiment of Invisibility*

We shall see later on that there are certain processes found in the Grimoires which do not connect with Black Magic otherwise than by their place in the Grimoires. There are also other processes which are not in themselves Goëtic, but are objectionable on account of the abuse to which they are liable. It is curious to observe how experiments of this kind will in one Ritual appear under a harmless guise but will in another bear all the marks of diabolism. The experience of Invisibility, with which we are here concerned, illustrates all these points.

Here Ceremonial Magic pretends to place its adepts in possession of the ring of Gyges. Presuming that the *Key of Solomon* is the most ancient of all the Rituals, it is there that the formal process first occurs. It is accomplished, however, without the intervention of a ring, by means of a simple preliminary invocation, and an address to *Almiras*, Master and Chief of Invisibility, whatsoever may be necessary for the particular occasion, such as characters and circles, being left to the discretion of the operator. There is also a complementary process by means of a waxen image; it occurs in one manuscript copy and is given by the English editor. The person who has duly made and consecrated this image is supposed to become invisible when he carries it. If we now turn to the *Book of True Black Magic*, we shall find the first experiment adapted as follows:—Before making the experiment of invisibility these words must be committed to memory: SCABOLES, HABRION,

Miscellaneous and Minor Processes

ELÆ, ELIMIGIT, GABOLII, SEMITRION, MENTINOBOL, SABANITEUT, HEREMOBOL, CANE, METHÉ, BALUTI, CATEA, TIMEGUEL, BORA, *by the empire which ye exert over us, fulfil this work, so that I may become invisible.*[1] The said words must be written with the blood before mentioned,[2] and the following Conjuration recited : *O ye Spirits of Invisibility, I conjure and constrain you incontinently and forthwith to consecrate this experiment, so that, surely and without trickery, I may go invisible. Furthermore, I conjure you by Lucifer, your prince, by the obedience which you owe to him and by the power of God, incontinently to aid me by consecrating this experiment, without loss of my body or my soul. So be it, so be it, so be it.*

Prepare all things required for this experiment with due solemnity and diligence, as it is laid down in the chapter proper thereto : so shalt thou operate with certainty and so find the truth ; but failing any of the things needful, thou shalt not attain thy desire, for not by the walls but the gate may any man enter a town.

This is merely a shorter recension of the process contained in the Clavicle, with the reference to Lucifer interpolated.

In place of these bald and somewhat unmeaning directions, the *Grimorium Verum* supplies an excessively curious process, at once monstrous and fantastic, recalling the sorceries of Thessaly and having direct connections with folk-lore.

To become Invisible

Begin this operation on a Wednesday before the sun rises, being furnished with seven black beans. Take next the head

---

[1] These names are given as follows by the English editor: *Sceaboles, Arbaron, Elohi, Elimigith, Herenobulcule, Methe, Baluth, Timayal, Villaquiel, Teveni, Yevie, Ferete, Bacuhaba, Guvarin.*

[2] Possibly that of a mole, used in the consecration of the instruments.

of a dead man ; place one of the beans in his mouth, two in his eyes and two in his ears. Then make upon this head the character of the figure which here follows. (*Omitted in all the Grimoires.*) This done, inter the head with the face towards heaven, and every day before sunrise, for the space of nine days, water it with excellent brandy. On the eighth day you will find the cited spirit, who will say unto you : *What doest thou?* You shall reply : *I am watering my plant.* He will then say : *Give me that bottle ; I will water it myself.* You will answer by refusing, and he will again ask you, but you will persist in declining, until he shall stretch forth his hand and shew you the same figure which you have traced upon the head suspended from the tips of his fingers. In this case you may be assured that it is really the spirit of the head, because another might take you unawares, which would bring you evil, and further, your operation would be unfruitful. When you have given him your phial, he will water the head and depart. On the morrow, which is the ninth day, you shall return and will find your beans ripe. Take them, place one in your mouth, and then look at yourself in a glass. If you cannot see yourself, it is good. Do the same with the rest, or they may be tested in the mouth of a child. All those which do not answer must be interred with the head.

The advantage of occasional invisibility in the pursuits of illicit affection seems to have fascinated the compiler of the *Little Albert*, and he refers to the adultery of Gyges with evident relish in prefacing his process for

Invisibility by means of a Ring

This important operation must be performed on a Wednesday in spring-time, under the auspices of Mercury, when it is known to be conjoined with other favourable planets, such as the Moon, Jupiter, Venus or the Sun. Taking good mercury, fixed and well purified, compose a large ring thereof, so that the same will pass easily over the middle finger of the hand. Let the collet be enriched by a small stone which is found in the pewit's nest, and about the ring let the following words be enchased : *Jesus passing* ✠ *through the midst of them* ✠ *disappeared.* ✠ [1]

Next, having placed the ring on a palette-shaped plate of fixed mercury, compose the perfume of mercury, and thrice expose the ring to the odour thereof; wrap it in a small piece of taffeta corresponding to the colour of the planet, carry it to the pewit's nest from which the stone was obtained, let it remain there for nine days, and when removed, fumigate it precisely as before. Then preserve it most carefully in a small box, made also of fixed mercury, and use it when required. The method of use is to place the ring upon the finger with the stone outwards ; it will so fascinate the spectators by its virtue that one may be present without being beheld. When the wearer no longer desires to be invisible, he has merely to turn the ring, so that the stone shall be inward, and close the hand over it,

But Éliphas Lévi affirms that the only authors who have written seriously concerning the ring of Gyges or its equivalents are Porphyry, Iamblichus and Peter of Apono ; that their discourse is allegorical and that they are referring to the Great Magical Arcanum. However this may be, the *Little Albert* supplies an alternative process which it pretends to derive from these authorities and also from Cornelius Agrippa, sometimes termed the master of Peter of Apono in defiance of chronology

---

[1] Compare the Magic Circle of Honorius.

and the centuries. The first requisite is a tuft of hair taken from the head of a hyena, and from the upper part thereof. These hairs must be plaited into a ring, which must be carried, like the other, to a pewit's nest and deposited therein, also for the space of nine days. The perfumes of mercury must be used in like manner. The person who wears this ring will be invisible and he will reappear by removing it from his finger.

Éliphas Lévi observes that the directions recall the history of the bell of Rodilard, but the criticism is scarcely commensurate, for the material is certainly obtainable, nor would it be necessary to catch one's own hyena. The point which was missed by the occultist may be evident to the ordinary reader ; the head of the hyena is short-coated, and the hairs could not be braided. It is not, however, unreasonable that impossible conditions should attach to an impossible object.[1]

§ 4. *Concerning the Hand of Glory*

No person who is familiar with the humours of Ingoldsby will have forgotten the wondrous legend of the Hand of Glory, which includes a transcript from the Grimoires. It is less generally known that there are two processes, serving distinct uses, and there can be little doubt that they should both be in the possession of every well-equipped operator who is anxious to test the virtues of White and Black Magic in this particular form. The possession of the first alone might be a source of temptation, as it is designed primarily for the protection of burglars. The second renders housebreaking unnecessary, as

[1] A process was also provided against fascination and deception by means of the ring of invisibility. It consists in the composition of a ring similarly shaped, made of refined lead, and enchased with the eye of a female ferret which has had only one litter. The words *Apparuit Dominus Simoni* should be engraved about the circumference. It should be composed on a Saturday when Saturn is in opposition with Mercury, perfumed three times with the perfume of Saturday, wrapped in a piece of a winding-sheet, next buried for nine days in a churchyard, perfumed, when disinterred, as before, and it is then ready for use.

it ensures a decent competence, but is at the same time without prejudice to its companion, which might be serviceable in a number of emergencies not, at least technically, illegal.

According to the *Albertus Parvus Lucii Libellus*, the Hand of Glory is indifferently the right or left hand of a criminal who has been gibbeted. The sorcerer obtains it as he can, and in the days of Tyburn Tree such requisites might have cost nothing beyond the personal risk of the adventure ; it is indispensable, however, that it should be wrapped in a piece of winding-sheet, and this suggests that the criminal must have been previously cut down with a view to interment. Thus enclosed, the hand must be well squeezed so as to force out any blood which may possibly remain in the member, after which it must be placed in an earthen vessel, together with some zimort, saltpetre, common salt and pepper-corns—all pounded. It should remain in this vessel for fifteen days and when extracted should be exposed to the heat of the sun during the time of the dog-star until it is extremely desiccated. If solar warmth be insufficient, it may be placed in a furnace, heated with bracken and vervain. The object is to extract all the grease from the member, and therefrom, in combination with virgin wax and sesame from Lapland, to compose a species of candle. Wheresoever this frightful object is lighted, the spectators will be deprived of all motion and the sorcerer can do what he will. It is possible to destroy its influence by anointing the threshold of the door, or other places through which entrance may be gained to a house, with an unguent composed of the gall of a black cat, grease from a white fowl and the blood of a screech-owl. This should also be confected in the dog-days.

It is to be regretted that this signal process does not rest upon the personal testimony of its historian, but he was present, as report tells us, at the trial of several who confessed, under torture, that they had applied it with complete success. It is to be regretted also that the alternative experiment must remain, as regards its materials, in the language of its inventor. It will be seen, however, that the Hand of Glory is not a hand, but a serpent; the process has, in fact, no connection whatever with its name, but this is wholly in accordance with the genius of Black Magic, its variants and its substitutes.

Arrachez le poil avec sa racine d'une jument en chaleur, le plus près de la nature, saying: DRAGNE, DRAGNE, DRAGNE. Tie the same in a knot, and go forthwith to purchase, without haggling, a new earthen pot, fitted with a lid. Return home at full speed; fill the said pot with spring water within two inches of the brim. Place your material therein, cover the vessel, and set it where neither you nor any one can perceive it, for the same is danger, saith the Grimoire. At the end of nine days, and at the hour of concealment, bring it forth, open it, and you will discover a small animal in the form of a serpent, which will at once spring up. Say then: I accept the pact. Touch not the creature with your hand, but transfer it into a new box, purchased expressly, without bargaining; for the food of the monster give husks of wheat only, and those daily. When you are in want of gold or silver, place as much as you need in the box ; retire to rest with the box at your bedside ; sleep, if you wish, for the space of three or four hours ; then rise, and you will find double the amount of money which you have entrusted to the serpent. What you originally placed in the box must, however, be left therein ; and it becomes therefore a sort of transcendental savings-bank which doubles its capital daily. Should the reptile be of ordinary appearance, you must not try for more than one hundred francs at a time ; but if your planet give you the ascendant in things supernatural, the serpent will have a human face, and you may deposit a thousand francs. In either case, should the operator part with his possession, two conditions must be observed : the recipient must be a consenting party to the gift, and a figure, to be drawn on virgin parchment, but omitted by the Grimoire, must be placed in the box. If, however, you prefer to destroy it, let the serpent be provided, not with his usual bran, but with some of the flour used for consecration in the first Mass of a priest, after eating which he will die. On the whole, it will be simpler to retain the enchanted animal, more especially as the vague responsibilities of the pact are not apparently transferred in the one or annulled in the other case. No jest is intended, says the dry author of the *Grimorium Verum*, but the process of the Gold-Finding Hen is on the whole simpler, as it is also more cleanly.

§ 5. *Concerning the Vision of Spirits in the Air*

For the Masters of Black Magic, as for the author of the *Comte de Gabalis*, the air is the abode of far other beings than the bird and fly, but the process by which they are rendered visible is complicated through the exceptional nature of the required materials. It is, of course, quite possible to secure the brain of a cock, and dissection with that object may perhaps be performed by deputy; the kitchen-maid or the poulterer's assistant would be easily secured. The dust from the grave of a dead man is the second ingredient of the process; but a visit to the nearest cemetery will not be sufficient, because it is useless to collect it on the surface; that which is next to the coffin will alone serve the purpose. In addition to these substances there are only oil of almonds and virgin wax. A compost must be made of the four, and it must be wrapped in a sheet of virgin parchment inscribed previously with the words GOMERT, KAILOETH, and with the character of *Khil*.

The materials being thus prepared, it remains to set them alight, whereupon the operator will behold that which the Grimoire characterises as prodigious, but does not specify except by the indication of the title. This experiment, it adds, should be performed only by those who fear nothing.

It is easy to deride the process, but reflective persons will see that it is the quintessence and summary of the whole art. This is Black Magic—and most of the white kind—in the proverbial nutshell—a combination in equal proportions of the disgusting and the imbecile. There are many more elaborate experiments, but few of such a representative kind. It is not necessary to add that it has been exceedingly popular and is to be found in most of the Grimoires.

§ 6. *Concerning Divination by the Word of Uriel*

As there are many practices passing under the name of White Magic which are doubtful in character on the surface, while they are more than doubtful within, so there are experiences described in the Grimoires, or in the treasuries of secrets which accompany them, having nothing in their nature which can be termed especially repulsive; they belong, however, to the Grimoires; their connections in occult literature are those of Black Magic, and they deserve a place here. Moreover, a process which in one Ritual will be merely curious or diverting, hypnotic or clairvoyant, may in another bear all the outward marks of diabolism. The mode of divination termed the Word or Speech of Uriel—signifying answers or oracles obtained from that spirit ceremonially invoked—appears in the *Grimorium Verum* as an experiment in lucidity induced by means of Hydromancy, but in the *Verus Jesuitarum Libellus* the Conjuration of Uriel appears as an infernal conjuration, and it is a process of Black Magic undisguised.

The experiment in the *Grimorium Verum* is worded as follows :—

THE INVOCATION OF URIEL

To succeed in this operation, it is needful that whosoever makes the experiment shall do in all things as hereinafter enjoined. Let him choose a small chamber or cabinet which has not been frequented by impure women for at least nine days. Let such place be well cleansed and consecrated by aspersions and fumigations. In the middle of the said chamber let there be a table covered with a white cloth ; set as follows thereon— to wit, a new glass phial filled with spring water, drawn shortly before the operation ; three small tapers of virgin wax mixed with human fat ; a sheet of virgin parchment six inches square ; a raven's quill cut ready for writing ; a china ink-well filled with fresh ink ; a small pan furnished with the materials for a fire. Let there be also a young boy of nine or ten years, cleanly and modestly dressed and of good behaviour, who must be placed near the table. One of the three tapers should be fixed upon a great new needle at a distance of six inches behind the phial,

*and the two others, erected after the same manner, should stand
on the right and left at the same distance. While arranging
these matters, recite the following words :—*Gabamiah, Adonay,
Agla, *O Lord God of Powers, do Thou assist us !*

The virgin parchment should be on the right and the pen
with the ink on the left side of the phial. The windows and
door must be closed before beginning the operation. The fire
should then be stirred, the tapers lighted, and the boy placed
on his knees so that he can look into the phial ; observe that he
should be bareheaded and his hands joined. The Master of
the operation shall thereupon command him to gaze fixedly into
the phial, when, approaching his right ear, and in a moderate
tone of voice, but as distinctly as possible, let him make the
following

CONJURATION

Uriel, Seraph, Josata, Ablati, Agla, Caila, *I pray and
conjure thee by the Four Words which God uttered with His
mouth unto His servant Moses,* Josata, Ablati, Agla, Caila,
*and by the Nine Heavens wherein thou dwellest, as also by
the virginity of this child who is before thee, that thou appearest,
and without any delay, visibly in this phial, to discover, without
disguising, the truth which I desire to know ; which done, I
will discharge thee in peace and goodwill, in the Name of the
Most Holy Adonay.*

After this conjuration the child must be asked whether he
beholds anything in the phial ; and if he should reply that he
beholds an Angel or another apparition, the Master of the
operation shall say in an affable tone of voice : *Blessed Spirit,
be thou welcome ! I conjure thee once more, in the Name of
the Most Holy Adonay, to give me prompt enlightenment*

upon, &c. [Here name the subject upon which information is desired.] *And if for reasons unknown to us, thou art unwilling to proceed in an audible tone of voice,*[1] *I conjure thee in the Most Holy Name of Adonay to write upon the virgin parchment here present, between now and to-morrow morning, or at least reveal unto me that which I desire this coming night in my sleep.*

If the Spirit make answer to what is said, he shall be heard respectfully ; should he fail to speak after thrice making the same supplication, let the tapers be extinguished and withdraw from the chamber, closing the door until the morrow, when the operator may return in the morning, and that which was required will be found within, on the virgin parchment, unless indeed it shall have been made known in the night.

In the *Verum Jesuitarum Libellus* this experiment in the induction of clairvoyance by means of a seering cup and a fantastic ceremonial, having only one monstrous condition, is replaced by a fierce conjuration of many pages, commanding the Spirit Uriel by all the words which have ever proceeded out of the mouth of the Creator of Heaven and Earth against the Evil Angels, and on pain of compulsion and torture, to appear before the operator, an unworthy servant of God, wherever the said Spirit may be, even in the abyss of Hell. He is directed to appear visibly and modestly in a human form, and to bring whatsoever is desired in all tranquillity and patience, without tumult, without detriment, without blinding, without dumbness, without whispering, without thunder, without hail, without explosion, without puffing up, without trembling. It is unnecessary to quote the entire citation, as the

---

[1] That is, in a voice audible to the clairvoyant boy, the process being obviously intended for those who are not themselves seers. It recalls the vast seering experiments of Dr. Dee.

process is not complete; but it is evident that the Conjuration of Uriel in the forged treatise on the Magic of the Jesuits is intended for the compulsion of a devil and not for the solicitation of favours from the Blessed Spirit of the *Grimorium Verum*.

§ 7. *Concerning the Mirror of Solomon, suitable for all Kinds of Divination*

The following process is found in the *Grimorium Verum* and in some other compilations. It is a mode of divination akin to that given in the preceding section. It does not connect with Black Magic except by the use of blood and is really an auto-hypnotic experiment fortified by conventional ceremonies.

To Compose the Mirror of Solomon

In the Name of the Lord, Amen. Ye shall behold in this mirror all things whatsoever that ye may desire. In the Name of the Lord Who is blessed, in the Name of the Lord, Amen.

In the first place, ye shall do no fleshly actions, nor sin in thought or deed, during the period hereinafter prescribed. In the second place, ye shall perform many good works of piety and mercy. In the third place, take a shining and well-polished plate of fine steel, slightly concave, and with the blood of a white pigeon inscribe thereon—to wit, at the four corners—the names JEHOVA, ELOYM, METATRON, ADONAY. Place the said steel in a clean and white cloth. Now, when ye shall behold the new moon during the first hour after sunset, draw nigh unto a window, look up to Heaven with devotion, and say: *O Eternal! O King Eternal! God ineffable! Thou Who hast created all things for love of men, and by a secret*

Miscellaneous and Minor Processes

judgment for the health of man, do Thou deign to look upon me, N., Thy most unworthy servant, and upon this my intention. Vouchsafe to send unto me Thine Angel ANAËL, even upon this mirror, who doth order, command and ordain his companions and Thy subjects, whom Thou hast made, O Thou Almighty

Lord, Who hast been, Who art, Who shalt remain eternally, that in Thy Name they may judge and act justly, instructing me in all that I shall require of them.

Lastly, cast upon burning coals a suitable perfume, and while casting it say : *In this, by this, and with this, which I pour out before Thy face, O God, my God, Who art blessed,*

Three and One, and in the most sublime exaltation, Who sittest above the Cherubim and above the Seraphim, Who wilt judge the world by fire, hear Thou me !

Repeat this three times, and having done so, breathe also thrice upon the mirror, and say : *Come,* ANAËL, *come, and may it be thy good pleasure to be with me by thy will, in the Name* ✠ *of the Father most mighty, in the Name* ✠ *of the Son most wise, in the Name of the Holy Spirit most living! Come,* ANAËL, *in the Name of the terrible Jehovah! Come,* ANAËL, *by the virtue of the immortal Elohim! Come,* ANAËL, *by the right arm of the almighty* METATRON ! *Do thou come unto me, N.* (here repeat your name over the mirror), *and so command thy subjects that in love, joy and peace, they may make manifest unto my eyes the things which are hidden from me. So be it. Amen.*

Having said and done as above, lift your eyes to heaven and say : *O Lord Almighty, Who dost cause all things to move according to Thy good pleasure, hear Thou my prayer, and may my desire be agreeable unto Thee! Lord, O Lord, if Thou wilt, condescend to look upon this mirror and bless it, that so* ANAËL, *one of Thy servants, may pause thereon with his companions, to satisfy me, N., Thy poor and humble servant, O God, blessed and exalted above all the heavenly Spirits, Who livest and reignest for ever and ever. Amen.*

When you shall have accomplished these things, make the sign of the Cross upon yourself and upon the mirror on the first and following days for forty-five days in succession, at the end of which time *Anaël* will appear to you under the form of a beautiful child, will salute you, and will command his companions to obey you. Observe—says the process in its benignity—that it does not invariably require forty-five days to compose the mirror. The Angel will frequently appear on the fourteenth day, according to the intention, devotion and fervour of the operator. When he shall appear, ask of him that which you desire, and pray him to come at all times, whensoever you shall invoke him, to grant your demands. On subsequent occasions, when you desire to see in this mirror, it is not necessary to recite all the prayers as above provided, but having perfumed it, say only : *Come* ANAËL, *come, according to thy good pleasure,* &c.

To dismiss him, say : *I thank thee,* ANAËL, *because thou hast appeared and hast satisfied my demands. Do thou therefore depart in peace, and return when I shall call thee.*

The perfume of *Anaël* is saffron.

§ 8. *Concerning the Three Rings of Solomon, Son of David*

One more experiment, which is only incidentally connected with Black Magic, may be cited here, as the complement of those given in the preceding sections. It is scarcely a complete process and is not intelligible as it stands in the *Grimorium Verum*, where the characters on which it depends are omitted. The scheme presupposes that the operator is in possession of a talisman inscribed with the Pentacles of Solomon,[1] when it is open to him to proceed in accordance with the following directions :—

Compose your circle, but before entering therein, perfume it with musk, amber, aloes-wood and incense. When invoking, the perfume should be incense only. Take care also that

---

[1] The grand pentacle, as given by the *Grimoire of Honorius*, will be found on p. 277.

you have fire whensoever you make invocation, and fumigate only in the name of the Spirit whom you would call. When placing perfume on the fire, say : *I burn this* N. *in the name and to the honour of* N. When invoking, see that you hold the invocation in the left hand, having the rod of elder [1] in your right, while the ladle [2] and knife should be at your feet. These things being arranged, place yourself within the circle ; if accompanied, your companions should hold each other by one hand. When within, trace the circle with the Knife of the Art, and take up the rods one after the other, saying the Fiftieth Psalm, namely, *Miserere mei.* The circle being composed, perfume and sprinkle the same with holy water. Then write the characters at the four corners ; let the Spirit be forbidden in formal terms to enter, after which begin the invocations, which must be repeated seven successive times. When the Spirit shall have appeared, cause him to sign the character which you hold in your hands, promising to come always at your call. Ask for whatsoever you deem suitable, and you shall be satisfied. Dismiss him with these words : *Go in peace unto your places, and peace be with you until you return at my call. In the name, &c. Amen.*

[1] See the method for the composition of the Magic Rod according to the *Grimorium Verum* in the second chapter of this part.
[2] Not previously mentioned under this name.

THE ASP OR CERASTES.

CHAPTER IX

Concerning Infernal Necromancy

IT is only within recent times that the attempt to communicate with the dead has been elevated to the dignity of White Magic. Here it is necessary to affirm that the phenomena of Modern Spiritualism are to be distinguished clearly from those of old Necromancy. The identity of purpose is apt to connect the methods, but the latter differ generically. To compare them would be almost equivalent to saying that the art of physical Alchemy is similar to mercantile pursuits because the acquisition of wealth is the end in either case. To appreciate the claim of Modern Spiritualism would be to exceed the limits of this inquiry ; it is mentioned only with the object of setting it quite apart. It should, however, be added that occult writers—with the indiscrimination which is common to their kind—have sometimes sought ambitiously to represent the communication with departed souls by means of Ceremonial Magic as something much more exalted than mere Spiritualism, whereas the very opposite is nearer the truth. Ancient Necromancy was barbarous and horrible in its rites ; it is only under the auspices of Éliphas Lévi and Pierre Christian that it has been purged and civilised, but in the hands of these elegant magicians it has become simply a process of auto-hallucination, having no scientific consequence whatever. The secret of true evocation belongs to the occult sanctuaries, by the hypothesis of those who are their spokesmen ; it is not the process of Spiritualism, and still less, so far as may be gleaned, is it that of the magical Rituals, nor would the secret at best seem respected by those who possess it, because the higher soul of man transcends evocation, and that which does respond ought to be beneath the initiate. The claim, however, is naturally one of delusion complicated by imposture.

In any case, the Necromancy of the Rituals is, properly speaking, a department of Black Magic, and for this reason no doubt it was excluded from the theurgic scheme of the *Arbatel;* nor do even such composite works as the two Keys of Solomon and the *Magical Elements* contain any account of a process which was always held in execration. It was lawful apparently for the Magus to conjure and compel the devils, to rack the hierarchy of Infernus by the agony of Divine Names, but he must leave the dead to their rest.

Where the process is given, as in the Fourth Book of Cornelius Agrippa, it is confined to the evocation of those souls who might be reasonably supposed to be damned, and it involves revolting rites. It assumes that the evil liver carries with him into the next world the desires which have depraved him here, and it allures him by his persistent affinities with the relinquished body.[1] In this way the use of blood came to be regarded as indispensable, because blood was held to be the medium of physical life; so also a portion of the body itself, whether flesh or bone, was prescribed in the rite. There is not any need to say that evocations involving the use of such materials belong to Black Magic, but they would not in any case offer a redeeming feature to the consideration of the informed student.

" It is also to be understood," says pseudo-Agrippa, " that

---

[1] The more intimate the knowledge possessed by the operator concerning the deceased person, the more easily he was supposed to call him up.

those who are proposing to raise up the souls of any deceased persons must do so in places with which it is known that they were familiar, in which some special alliance between soul and body may be assumed, or some species of attracting affection, still leading the soul to such places. . . . Therefore the localities most suited for the purpose are churchyards, and, better still, those which have been the scene of the execution of criminal judgments "—in plain words, the immediate neighbourhood of a gibbet. A battlefield or other place of public slaughter is still more favourable, but best of all is the scene of a murder before the removal of the carcase.

The ritual of Necromantic Evocation is indicated but not given by the authority just cited ; we must seek it in Ebenezer Sibley and in the supplementary portions of the *Grand Grimoire* and the *Red Dragon*. The astrologer Sibley does not give account of his sources, but they were evidently not in printed books. The Sloane MS. numbered 3884 in the Library of the British Museum would appear to have been one. It is, in any case, not an invented process ; it develops the principles laid down in pseudo-Agrippa and is quite in harmony with the baleful genius of Black Magic. It is here given verbatim.

But if, instead of infernal or familiar spirits, the ghost or apparition of a departed person is to be exorcised, the Magician, with his assistant, must repair to the churchyard or tomb where the deceased was buried, exactly at midnight, as the ceremony can only be performed in the night between the hours of twelve and one. The grave is first to be opened, or an aperture made by which access may be had to the naked body. The magician having described the circle, and holding a magic wand in his right hand, while his companion or assistant beareth a conse-crated torch, he turns himself to all the four winds, and, touching the dead body three times with the magical wand, repeats as follows :—*By the virtue of the Holy Resurrection, and the torments of the damned, I conjure and exorcise thee, Spirit of N. deceased, to answer my liege demands, being obedient unto these sacred ceremonies, on pain of everlasting torment and distress.* . . . BERALD, BEROALD, BALBIN, GAB, GABOR, AGABA. *Arise, arise, I charge and command thee.*[1]

After these forms and ceremonies, the ghost or apparition will become visible, and will answer any questions put to it by the exorcist. But if it be desired to put interrogatories to the spirit of any corpse that has hanged, drowned or otherwise made away with itself, the conjuration must be performed while the body lies on the spot where it is first found after the suicide hath been committed, and before it is touched or removed. The ceremony is as follows. The exorcist binds upon the top of his wand a bundle of St. John's wort or *Millies perforatum*, with the head of an owl ; and having repaired to the spot where the corpse lies, at twelve o'clock at night, he draws the circle and solemnly repeats these words :—*By the mysteries of the deep, by the flames of Banal, by the power of the East and the silence of the night, by the Holy Rites of Hecate, I conjure and exorcise thee, thou distressed spirit, to present thyself here and reveal unto me the cause of thy calamity, why thou didst offer violence to thy own liege life, where thou art now in being, and where thou wilt hereafter be.*

Then gently smiting the carcase nine times with the rod, he adds :—*I conjure thee, thou Spirit of this N. deceased, to answer my demands that I propound unto thee, as thou ever hopest for the rest of the holy ones and ease of all thy misery ; by the*

---

[1] The process by which the soul was called back into the dead body prior to its interment constituted necromancy proper. The calling up of the shadow was sometimes termed sciomancy.

Concerning Infernal Necromancy

Blood of Jesus which He shed for thy soul, I conjure and bind thee to utter unto me what I shall ask thee.

Then, cutting down the carcase from the tree, they shall lay its head towards the east; in the space that this following conjuration is repeating, they shall set a chafing-dish of fire at its right hand, into which they shall pour a little wine, some mastic and some gum-aromatic, and lastly [the contents of] a vial full of the sweetest oil. They shall have also a pair of bellows and some unkindled charcoal to make the fire burn bright when the carcase rises. The conjuration is this :—

I conjure thee, thou Spirit of N., that thou do immediately enter into thy ancient body again and answer to my demands; by the virtue of the Holy Resurrection, and by the posture of the body of the Saviour of the world, I charge thee, I conjure thee, I command thee, on pain of the torments and wandering of thrice seven years, which I, by the force of sacred magic rites, have power to inflict upon thee; by thy sighs and groans I conjure thee to utter thy voice. So help thee God and the prayers of the Holy Church. Amen.

This ceremony being thrice repeated, while the fire is burning with mastic and gum-aromatic, the body will begin to rise, and at last will stand upright before the exorcist, answering with a faint and hollow voice the questions propounded unto it : why it destroyed itself, where its dwelling is, what its food and life are, how long it will be ere it enter into rest, and by what means the magician may assist it to come to rest; also of the treasures of this world, where they are hid. Moreover, it can answer very punctually concerning the places where ghosts reside, and of the manner of communicating with them, teaching the nature of Astral Spirits and hellish beings so far as its capacity alloweth.

All this when the ghost hath fully answered, the magician ought out of commiseration and reverence to the deceased, to use what means can possibly be used for procuring rest unto the spirit, to which effect he must dig a grave, and, filling the same half full of quick-lime, with a little salt and common sulphur, must put the carcase naked into it. Next to the burning of the body into ashes, this is of great force to quiet and end the disturbance of the Astral Spirit. But in this and in all cases where the ghosts or apparitions of deceased persons are raised up and consulted, great caution is to be observed by the Magician to keep close within the circle; for if, by the constellation and position of the stars at his nativity, he be in the predicament of those who follow the Black Art for iniquitous purposes, it is very dangerous to conjure any spirits without describing the form of the circle, and wearing upon the heart, or holding in the hand, the Pentacle of Solomon. For the ghosts of men deceased can easily effect sudden death to the magician born under such a constellation of the planets, even whilst in the act of being exorcised.

It must be confessed that this process is grim and depressing, and the occult student will not envy the sorcerer at the first palpitation of the corpse. Yet the rite is methodical, and even sober, when compared with the monstrous alternative of the *Grand Grimoire*, which must be given on the authority of Lévi; for no available editions of the work which is in question, nor yet of the *Red Dragon*, nor indeed any ritual of my acquaintance, contains it. There is reasonable probability that he invented it to make out his case at the moment.

"There are also necromantic processes, comprising the tearing up of earth from graves with the nails, dragging out some of the bones, setting them crosswise on the breast, then assisting at midnight mass on Christmas Eve, and flying out of the church at the moment of consecration, crying : ' Let the dead rise from their tombs ! '—then returning to the graveyard, taking a handful of earth nearest to the coffin, running back to the door of the church, which has been alarmed by the clamour, depositing the two bones crosswise, again shouting : ' Let the dead rise from their tombs ! '—then, if we escape being seized and shut up in a madhouse, retiring at a slow pace, and counting four thousand five hundred steps in a straight line, which means following a broad road or scaling walls ; finally, having traversed this space, lying flat upon the earth as if in a coffin, repeating in doleful tones : ' Let the dead rise from their tombs ! '—and calling thrice on the person whose apparition is desired."

The object of Necromantic evocations was much the same as the other operations of the Grimoires. If the sorcerer of old, like the modern magician, had ever dispossessed the shade of Apollonius of its eternal rest, it would have been upon a question of finance. The remaining process in Necromancy will be therefore an appropriate conclusion to our whole inquiry, as it is designed to raise up and expel a human spirit who is supposed to stand guard over a hidden treasure. It is from the *Verus Jesuitarum Libellus*, and is the *ne plus ultra* of Ceremonial Magic, however distributed according to the colours of the spectrum. The end of all things is money, says the sorcerer, and if asked to define Occult Science, he would answer that it was the method of obtaining concealed money. The testimony of the entire literature coincides with this definition.

A CONJURATION FOR THE SPIRIT GUARDIANS OF HIDDEN TREASURE

I cite, require and command thee, Human Spirit, who frequentest this place, and in thy life hast interred thy treasure

herein, who also of recent time, to wit, in the day or night of
. . . ., about the hour of . . . ., hast shewn thyself in the form
of a fire at this spot : I conjure thee by God the Father ✠, by
God the Son ✠, by God the Holy Spirit ✠, by the most glorious
and Holy Mother ✠ of God ✠, by the most holy wounds of our
Saviour, by all miracles performed through His Divine sorrows,
passion and tears, by His material death, by His descent into
Hell, by His triumphant Resurrection, by His most glorious
ascension into Heaven, by His sitting on the right hand of God
the Father, giving rule to His angels from thence over the whole
earth ✠. I conjure thee by the terrible Day of Judgment ✠,
by the power and virtue of St. John the Baptist ✠, by all the
martyrs, apostles and prophets. Come to me. I adjure and
beseech thee by the terrible, ineffable and Divine Names inscribed on this sheet, and in reverence and confession of their
power, to come before me, and to make thy sign visible, without
lightning, without thunder, without noise of dread tempests,
without causing fear or trembling, harm to body or soul, or
annoyance of any kind. But do thou perform my will in all
things, even as I shall command thee, by the virtue of the one
stupendous and holy Name, which even the adverse and inferior
powers of the Abyss do venerate and adore, ever confessing the
Almighty, Whose creatures we all are. Be this done by the
virtue of God the Father ✠, by His blessed Son ✠ and by the
union of the Holy Spirit ✠, even by the Trinity in unity, Which
liveth and reigneth for ever and ever. Amen ✠. Incessantly
do I call, adjure, conjure, ordain and require thee, Human Spirit,
by the Most Holy and Undivided Trinity, by the immortality
which cometh after death, by the power and victory of Hell,
by the bearer of the Seven Swords, by the Most Holy and
Secret Seal, by the sacred love of Jesus, by all the Ministers and
Archangels of God, Ophanim ✠, Aralim ✠, Hasmalim ✠,

Concerning Infernal Necromancy

Cherubim ✠, Seraphim ✠, and Malachim ✠, and by the terrible torments of the demons. I conjure thee also by the good angels Maluzim ✠, Penpalabim ✠, and Calizantin ✠, by all the powers of Heaven ✠, by the earth ✠ and by the torments of Hell; I adjure thee by all mysteries, by the Crucifixion, by the dolorous scourging, by the crowning with thorns, by the bitterness of the Divine death, by the Most Holy and Ineffable Name of Jesus ✠, which is sacred unto all Christians, but terror and anguish to the evil, for they have refused the salvation which has been offered them by the great living God. I conjure thee to come before me immediately, in thy proper human form, even as when thy treasure was buried. Come before this circle, answer me faithfully, without falsehood and without enigmas. This I command thee, in the Name and by the power of the Triune God, Father, Son and Holy Ghost. Amen.

A CONJURATION COMPELLING OBEDIENCE

I adjure and command thee, Human Spirit, to appear before me under the similitude of fire. By the ineffable Name JEHOVAH, *by the ineffable and incomprehensible* Fiat, *by the power which created all things and sustains all things, I conjure and adjure thee to come visibly before this circle. By the goodness of God when He created man in His own likeness, by the power of His justice, which expelled the demons, enchaining them in the Infernal Abyss; by His infinite mercy when He sent His Son to redeem us; by all Divine Names and Attributes; by the omnipotence of our Saviour Jesus Christ, destroying the works of hell, blessing the seed of the woman and empowering it to crush the serpent's head—do thou answer me and obey faithfully. By the ineffable Name* TETRAGRAMMATON, *inscribed on this rod, answer me without deception or equivocation. By the power of our Saviour, Who shall judge both thee and me, the quick and the dead, I conjure thee. Come.*

IF THE SPIRIT BE OBSTINATE

I conjure thee, Human Spirit, by the Ineffable Name of God, written on this sheet, but not to be pronounced; by my blood, most excellently redeemed by the Lord of the Prophets, Jesus Christ; by His most Glorious Mother; by the insignia of His humility; by the great book of the judgments of God; by the angels, archangels and all the host of heaven. Be thou obedient unto me, a Christian baptized in the holy waters of Jordan. Answer me exactly, without enigma or pretence. Make known the power which aids thee. I command thee by the most holy Name of God, Who hath condemned thee to frequent this place wherein thou hast buried thy treasure. Amen. Amen. Amen.

Citation

COLPRIZIANA, OFFINA, ALTA, NESTERA, FUARO, MENUET.

Charge

ALIM, JEHOH, JEHOVAH, AGLA, ON, TETRAGRAMMATON.

When the Spirit makes visible appearance, say :—

ADON, SCHADAI, ELIGON, AMANAI, ELION, PNEUMATON, ELII, ALNOAL, MESSIAS, JA, HEYNAAN, TETRAGRAMMATON.

Add the following Conjuration :—

ADONAI, ZEBOTH, ADON, SCHADAI, ELION, TETRAGRAMMATON, ELOI, ELOHIM, MESSIAS, JA, HAGIOS, HO THEOS. Amen.

Say inwardly :—

ALLEY, FORTISSIAN, FORTISSIO, ALLINSON, ROA.

Concerning Infernal Necromancy

The Discharge

OMGROMA, EPYN, SEYOK, SATANY, DEGONY, EPARYGON, GALLIGANON, ZOGOGEN, FERSTIGON.

The most barbarous and unintelligible words are said by Picus de Mirandola to be the most powerful in Black Magic, and the affirmation applies everywhere, for the whole art is one of illiterate delight in unintelligible images. As those here cited from the *Verus Jesuitarum Libellus* seem in most cases fortuitous assemblages of letters, they are doubtless all that can be desired, but additional constraints and conjurations, should the spirit of the deceased miser refuse to appear, will readily occur to the reader.

Here ends the Complete Grimoire of
Black Magic

APOPHIS.

CONCLUSION

THE ceremonial literature of White and Black Magic has now spoken for itself in the catholic sense of the words. We see exactly what the Rituals had to offer, by the hypothesis of their own claim, to those who followed in their putative practical courses. I presume once more that it is unnecessary to debate whether the Olympic Spirits will make gold in a moment by Magic, transport precious stones, prolong life to several hundred years, teach all arts and provide the operator with ministering spirits in visible and corporal form. These claims merely externalise the cupidity and other desires of the artist. Hereof at least is the domain of the occult working where it happens to suffer the title of transcendental; its entire term and horizon are within the limits of low material gain and pleasure; and the ambition of the Magus was to secure these advantages—firstly—by the trickery and artifice of the occult world, instead of by his proper activity, and—secondly—on a very much larger scale than was normally likely or possible.

When we turn, however, to the Rituals which I have classed as composite, we shall find that we are dealing with a much more valued and popular series of handbooks, and the head or crown of all is held in the polite opinion of occult circles to be white by its essential nature and only Goëtic in its accretions. As a matter of fact, it is Goëtic by intention and essence, and white only in the sense that some of its distracted processes might, apart from their sanguinary nature, be termed

Conclusion

harmless. It is obvious, however, from the text that the Intelligences who are the subjects of conjuration are fallen spirits, and that one of the anxieties in respect of their apparition is the hideousness of their native form. The main purposes of experiment are (1) the recovery of stolen goods; (2) the power to go invisible, for reasons which are not less certain because they pass unsaid; (3) the possession of a buried treasure; (4) the seeking of love and favour. Those that remain are more expressly and literally of the order of Fairyland. This is so far concerning what is accepted as the prototype and fountain of the Art. The Infernal Hierarchy of the *Lemegeton* seems from time to time a promise of things more important, but the diabolism of practical Magic was essentially of a popular kind in the bulk of its documents, and those which aimed too high—as, for example, at logic and philosophy, the liberal sciences, eloquence and good understanding—had comparatively few votaries. To give riches, to kindle love and lust, to discover treasures—as these were the sum of ambition, so they were the qualifications in chief demand from the spirits. The class of people to whom such considerations would appeal were those obviously—and as I have otherwise indicated—who could not obtain their satisfaction through the normal channels —the outcasts, the incompetent, the ignorant, the lonely, the deformed, the hideous, the impotent and those whom Nature and Grace alike denied.

This is the category into which the modern psychic mind would enter unwittingly, could I suppose for a moment that, outside such purlieus as Paris, there has been any revival of Ceremonial Magic in the nineteenth or twentieth century. The typical occult student is preposterous enough in his preoccupations, but when he takes the Grimoires seriously he has usually some assumption as to a meaning behind them—not that they are allegorical writings, but rather that they are the final issue in abuse and travesty of something that looms to his intelligence like real knowledge. The tendency in this direction has been promoted by that knavish hypothesis concerning occult sanctuaries to which I alluded far back in this work, and to which I must refer again for a moment in these final words.

As part of the root-matter out of which comes the lying art of spirits there stands forth the hypothetical efficacy of adjuration, prayer and ceremonial acts of worship in connection therewith. But in Magic that efficacy can be manifested only over things trivial or abominable, because it is obvious that for any higher purpose we should have recourse thereto through the ordinary channels of religion. If the hypothesis of prayer is true, Magic is out of court on the side of holy things because there is a more excellent way of obtaining the great gifts, the good gifts and the gifts that do not pass away. But if it is not true, Magic is out of court also because it depends from and comes down to the earth with that false assumption which is at its basis. As a matter of fact, Magic, White or Black, is the attempt to direct the admitted efficacy into evil channels—to compel the infernal cohorts with the assistance of the blessed hierarchies, and to enlist the sympathies of the latter on the warrant of their appeasing invocation in foolish or discreditable transactions. I should add that I characterise as of the essence of evil the desire after power which puts the owner at an advantage over those about him by interventions of an occult nature, against which it would be generally impossible to guard. I characterise the acquisition of knowledge without learning in the same way and for the same reasons. The other ambitions, desires, greeds do not need express condemnation on my part, for they speak too plainly on their own. Out of the

Conclusion

mouth of their proper hypotheses, the pseudo-art or science is that of the abyss. It remains, however, in most cases the abyss of evil intention, as the operator is left with his base, sordid, sorry or fatuous ambition and not with the fruition thereof.

It may seem at first sight that I have been breaking laidly worms on larger wheels than would have been required for Gargantua, Behemoth or Leviathan ; but I am concerned first of all with the preservation of the Secret Tradition inviolate and with the separation of fungoids and diseased and monstrous growths which have come to overlay it. The magic of the Ceremonial Rituals is no part of the real tradition ; it is not in any form that we know it of the veils thereof, nor are they even its debasement. At the same time—and as we have sufficiently seen—they do represent at a very far distance a stream of averse tradition, and it is that of Jewry in the prescription and suspension of the greater and age-long exile. There is no question that the mind of Israel which produced on the one hand the signal mystic testimony of the Zoharic literature did on the other betray the kind of preoccupations which have given us Ceremonial Magic as their last evolution in the pit and pools of thought. And this is their side of importance. It is this only which has justified the present consideration and the length to which it has extended.

THE CORNERS OF PARADISE, GUARDED
BY FIRE-BREATHING URÆI.

Y

DISTRIBUTORS
for the Wordsworth Reference Series

AUSTRALIA

Reed Editions
22 Salmon Street
Port Melbourne
Vic 3207
Australia

Tel: (03) 646 6716
Fax: (03) 646 6925

GERMANY, AUSTRIA & SWITZERLAND

Swan Buch-Marketing GmbH
Goldscheuerstraße 16
D-7640 Kehl am Rhein
Germany

GREAT BRITAIN & IRELAND

Wordsworth Editions Ltd
Cumberland House
Crib Street
Ware
Hertfordshire SG12 9ET

ITALY

Magis Books SRL
Via Raffaello 31/C
Zona Ind Mancasale
42100 Reggio Emilia

Tel: 0522-920999
Fax: 0522-920666

SINGAPORE, MALAYSIA & BRUNEI

Paul & Elizabeth Book Services
 Pte Ltd
163 Tanglin Road No 03-15/16
Tanglin Mall
Singapore 1024

Tel: (65) 735-7308
Fax: (65) 735-9747

SPAIN

Ribera Libros S.L.
Poligono Martiartu, Calle 1-no 6
48480 Arrigorriaga, Vizcaya

Tel: 34-4-6713607 (Almacen)
 34-4-4418787 (Libreria)
Fax: 34-4-6713608 (Almacen)
 34-4-4418029 (Libreria)

PORTUGAL

International Publishing Services Ltd
Rua da Cruz da Carreira, 4B
1100 Lisboa

Tel: 01-570051
Fax: 01-3522066

SOUTHERN AFRICA

Struik Book Distributors (Pty) Ltd
Graph Avenue
Montague Gardens
7441
P O Box 193
Maitland
7405
South Africa

Tel: (021) 551-5900
Fax: (021) 551-1124

USA, CANADA & MEXICO

Universal Sales & Marketing
230 Fifth Avenue
Suite 1212
New York, NY 10001 USA

Tel: 212-481-3500
Fax: 212-481-3534